4055 E

Y0-DNM-637

The Romantic Spirit

A Romance
Bibliography of
Authors and Titles,

by **MARY JUNE KAY**

THE ROMANTIC SPIRIT
1983-1984 UPDATE

Copyright @ 1984
by MJK ENTERPRISES

All rights reserved
Printed in the United States of America
No part of this publication may
be reproduced, stored in a retrieval
system, or transmitted,
in any form or by any means,
electronic, mechanical, photocopying,
recording or otherwise, without the prior
written permission of the publisher.

First Printing, May 1984

ISBN 0-9610996-1-5

"The ROMANTIC SPIRIT...One word - Marvelous!"
PARRIS AFTON BONDS
Author of "LAVENDER BLUE"

"What a perfectly splendid book! I have been dipping into it with interest and curiosity--not to mention the most profound respect for the amount of research and work which must have gone into it."

MARY BURCHELL
Harlequin Author, London England

"THE ROMANTIC SPIRIT is an extraordinary piece of work full of information you've always wanted to know, such as all the pen names of your favorite authors and all the titles by each author. It is the book the romance lover has been hoping someone would write."

JUDE DEVERAUX
Author of "THE MONTGOMERY ANNALS"

"I dreamed that one day some patient and ambitious souls would undertake the awesome task of tracking down the book titles and pseudonyms of many Romance authors...and the miracle has occurred. The result: THE ROMANTIC SPIRIT."

KATHRYN FALK
Publisher, Romantic Times

"Thank you for publishing THE ROMANTIC SPIRIT! I can't begin to tell you how many frustrated hours I've spent at the local library doing research in the Contemporary Authors series."

LYNN E. FISH, Romance Reader
Portland, Oregon

"I've seen so many excellent comments and reviews of THE ROMANTIC SPIRIT that I'd like my own copy..."

JULIA FITZGERALD
Author of "ROYAL SLAVE"
Hough Green Chester England

"I must say how splended your compilation is. The amount of research must have been prodigious and I have found the information of immense interest. It is absolutely fascinating finding out how many different names authors use and very surprising to discover perhaps that two authors whose books you have enjoyed suddenly turn out to be the same person."

CONSTANCE HEAVEN
Author of "LORD OF RAVENSLEY"
Teddington, Middlesex England

"THE ROMANTIC SPIRIT will make a wonderful and useful addition to my library."

CATHERINE LINDEN
Author of "THE BARRON'S WOMAN"

"I echo the words of appreciation of your timely but exacting task expressed by Mary Burchell and others."

WILLIAM STUART LONG
Author of "THE AUSTRALIAN SERIES"
York, Yorkshire, England

"THE ROMANTIC SPIRIT is simply great! I spent several hours pouring over it. It's the reference book every romance reader, writer, and editor should have on her desk."

SUZANNE SIMMS
Author of "DREAM WITHIN A DREAM"

"...As to THE ROMANTIC SPIRIT, I simply love it. All bookstores should have one for reference and should stock them for readers and writers. Thanks for this contribution to the romance field."

JANELLE TAYLOR
Author of "THE ECSTASY SERIES"

"You have compiled THE definitive reference book for readers of Romantic Fiction...THE ROMANTIC SPIRIT belongs in every reference library. It is a much-needed volume, and it's a treasure trove for all of us."

JENNIFER WILDE
Author of "ONCE MORE, MIRANDA"

TO THE USER

The 1983-1984 Update to The Romantic Spirit is in essence simply an update of the existing information in the original book and contains the following:

1.   Authors and titles that had been published and omitted in the original Romantic Spirit.

2.   Authors and titles that have been published since The Romantic Spirit was released.

3.   Additional titles of books for some authors listed in The Romantic Spirit.

4.   Pseudonyms that have become known to the compilers of The Romantic Spirit since its release, as well as psuedonyms for the newly published authors.

5.   Most titles are through June 1984, though some are through December 1984 (some titles may change).

6.   Additional symbols to help the reader understand what the subject matter consists of. We hope to expand on this in the revision at a later date.

The purpose of the update to The Romantic Spirit is to present a useful and usable tool for the Romance reader, libraries, booksellers (both new and used) and for the collector.   The update is composed of two parts:

1. Authors', Titles.   Each letter of the alphabet (except X) is included.   Each letter section includes author and some multi-author

series, with books written by each in alphabetical order sequence for easy reference.Each name is listed in its respective alphabetical section. Bracketed names are [reported to be] the real name of the author(s). Instead of a complete cross referencing as shown in the original book only the author's real name appears under each pseudonym, and under the author's real name all pseudonyms "also writes as" for that author are listed. This same method applies to the Index.

2 Numbered/Category Romances. Appendices list books in each numbered/category in numerical sequence where applicable, alphatetically otherwise. (For example, Jane Arbor's "Handmaid to Midas" #2545 in the Harlequin Romance numbered series, is found under "Arbor" in Authors',Titles and Appendix E4 in Numbered/Category Romances.) All books here are also included in Authors', Titles under the name of the designated author.

Symbols: The following symbols are used in Authors', Titles to indicate type of subject matter in many of the entries:

An asterisk (*) indicates a change or correction in the data originally presented in The Romantic Spirit.

<CO>	Contemporary
<ED>	Edwardian
<ENG>	Published In England
<GEO>	Georgian
<GOT>	Gothic

<HO>	Historical
<HR>	Historical Romance
<IN>	Intrigue
<INSP>	Inspirational
<M&B>	Mills & Boon
<MED>	Medical
<M-GOT>	Modern Gothic
<MO-N>	Modern Novel
<MY>	Mystery
<NF>	Non-Fiction
<P&E>	Politics and Espionage
<PROM>	Promotional
<RE>	Regency
<RS>	Romantic Suspense
<RW>	Romantic Western
<Saga>	Family Saga
<SN>	Supernatural
<VIC>	Victorian
<DNS>	Release "date not set"
<TMC>	"title may change"

(end)   Indicates the end of a that particular series

If NO symbol is evident adjacent to the author's name, it is assumed that all books listed for the author are pure romance. The majority of titles appearing in these lists have romance as an integral part of the story. The degree of romance is as varied as the stories themselves, and the author's writing style. Some, however, are "supernatural" <SN> and "mystery" <MY> books written by authors whose subject is usually romantic.

<HR> Indicates romances situated in a historical setting or time but not portraying any actual historical happening.

<HO>. Indicates that all or a portion of the books listed portray historical facts.

<ED>, <GEO>, <IN>, <INSP> <MED> <P&E> <RE>, <RW>, and <VIC>. These are also used to indicate publisher's designations on various category and/or numbered/category sequences.

<GOT>. Indicated that all or a portion of the books listed are gothics. Definition of Gothic: (1) a kind of English novel with sensational or horrifying events popular in the 18th-19th centuries, (2) a contemporary romance set in a remote place or time and featuring gloom, mystery etc: (Oxford American Dictionary 1980. Edition).

<CO>, <MO-N>, <M-GOT>. Indicates the book is modern in time, setting, and substance.

<RS>. Indicates that all or a portion of the books listed are romantic suspense: which may be defined as romance combined with generally mysterious and puzzling events and circumstances.

A book title entry followed by a second title in parenthesis indicates that the title in parenthesis was the orignial printed title of the same text, and name changed upon reprint.

A title in Authors',Titles, followed by "w/" denotes co-authorship with the person listed. In some cases it may indicate translation into English by the person listed.

In <u>Authors',Titles</u>, the three enclosed initials, which may or may not be appended by a number, following a book title indicates the title preceding the symbol is an entry in a Series located in the alphabetical index. Book titles are indented below the Series entry name. These books all pertain to the same general subject and it would be beneficial to the reader to read them in the sequence listed. If <u>in sequence</u> is inserted it indicates the books following the first entry are actual sequels and should be read in order to maintain the continuity of the story.

An endeavor has been made to keep this update to The Romantic Spirit as uncomplicated and readable as possible. To learn the status of any book, call your local new or used book dealer. Every effort has been made and every resource available has been utilized to ensure accuracy and completeness. <u>However, we do not purport that ALL information is included, or that descrepancies may not exist.</u> If errors are present herein, forgiveness is asked, and if corrections are in order any information to that end would be welcomed. Perfection is the goal.

Our appreciation and sincere thanks to those who have worked with us and given their support to the 1983-84 update of THE ROMANTIC SPIRIT.

MARY JUNE KAY

Authors and Titles

A

AARON, Anna
Sweet Dreams: <YA>
40 Secrets

ABBOTT, Mary Jeanne
(Elizabeth Hewitt)

ABSALOM, Stacy
Harlequin Romance:
2581 Knave of Hearts

ADAIR, Dennis w/ Janet ROSENSTOCK
Story of Canada: (continued) <HO>
Wildfires
Victoria
(end)

ADAMS, Candice
[Lois A. Walker]
Diamonds Of Desire
Candlelight Ecstasy:
232 When Opposites Attract
Candlelight Ecstasy Supreme:
40 Steal Away
Love & Life:
Heartstrings
To Have And To Hold
6 Legal And Tender

ADAMS, Daniel <HO>
[Christopher Nicole]
Brothers And Enemies <Saga>
Defiant Loves

ADAMS, Kasey
[Valerie Whisenand]
Rapture Romance:
35 Untamed Desire
57 Winter's Promise
74 Purely Physical
82 An Unlikely Trio

ADAMS, Kelly
Second Chance At Love:
113 Restless Tides
221 Wildcatter's Kiss

ADAMS, Melodie
Silhouette Romance:
265 I'll Fly The Flags
Silhouette Special Edition:
152 Gentle Possession

ADAMS, Patricia K.
(Julia Howard)

ADAMS, Tricia
To Have And To Hold:
20 Between The Sheets

ADLER, Warren
Random Hearts

AEBY, Jacquelyn
                    (Jocelyn Carew)
                    (Vanessa Gray)
  Double In Diamonds

_____

_____

AFRICANO, Lillian
  Something Old, Something New

_____

AGHADJIAN, Mollie
                    (Moeth Allison)
                    (Mollie Ashton)

AHEARN, Patricia
                    (Kate Meriwether)

AID, Francis
  Torch:
    Passionate Stranger

_____

_____

AIKEN, Joan   <RS>
  Died On A Rainy Sunday

_____

_____

AKS, Patricia   <YA>
  Dreamboy For Katie, A
  New Kind Of Love, A
  Searching Heart, The
  Two Worlds Of Jill, The
  First Love From Silhouette:
    47 Three Weeks Of Love
  Two By Two Romance:
    3 Change Of Heart

_____

_____

ALEXANDER, Bea
  First Love From Silhouette: <YA>
    44 Someone Like Jeremy Vaughn
    69 Advice And Consent
                        (cont'd)

ALEXANDER, Bea (continued)
    85 In The Long Run
  Silhouette Inspirations:
    10 Inlet Of The Heart

_____

ALEXANDER, Megan
                    [Mildred Fisch]
  SuperRomance:
    95 Blossoms In The Snow

_____

ALEXANDER, Susan
  Harlequin Presents:
    719 Marriage Contract, The

_____

ALEXIE, Angela
                    [Angela Talias]
  Harlequin SuperRomance:
    More Than Yesterday

_____

_____

ALGERMISSEN, Jo Ann
                    (Anna Hudson)
  Harlequin American Romance:
    64 Capture The Sun

_____

_____

ALLEN, Anita   <GOT>
  Spell Of Ghoti, The

_____

_____

ALLEN, Catherine R. w/ Dorothea
  JENSEN
                    (Catherine Moorhouse)

ALLEN, Charlotte Vale
  Intimate Friends   <CO>

_____

_____

2

ALLEN, Sheila R.
                    (Sheila O'Hallion)

ALLISON, Elizabeth
          [Alice Harron Orr]
     Rapture Romance:
        24 Dance Of Desire

ALLISON, Moeth
          [Mollie Aghadjian]
     Silhouette Imtimate Moments:
         8 Love Everlasting
        43 Russian Roulette

ALLISON, Penny
          [Carol Katz]
     Silhouette Desire:
        65 Reckless Venture
       143 North Country Nights
     Silhouette Romance:
       271 Night Train To Paradise

ALLISTER, Barbara   <RE>
          [Barbara Teer]
     Prudent Partnership, The

ALLYN, Jennifer
     Love & Life:
        Forgiveness

ALLYNE, Kerry
     Harlequin Romance:
      2407 Reunion At Pitereeka   *
                          (cont'd)

ALLYNE, Kerry (continued)
      2527 Spring Fever
      2593 Somewhere To Call Home
      2647 Time To Forget

ALLYSON, Kym   <GOT>
          [John M. Kimbro]
     Moon Shadow, The

ALSOBROOK, Rosalyn
     Harlequin American Romance:
        63 Tiny Flaw, A

ALSOBROOK, Rosalyn W/ Jean HAUGHT
                    (Jalynn Friends)

AMERICAN EXPLORERS SERIES <AES><HO>
(continued)
         9 Francis Parkman: Dakota
            Legend
                       Randall King
                    [William Krasner]
        10 Escalante: Wilderness Path
                    Peter T. Blairson
        11 Davy Crockett: Frontier
            Fighter
                         Lee Bishop
        12 Alexander Mackenzie: Lone
            Courage
                         Guy Forve
                    [Guy Cimbalo]
        13 John Bozeman: Mountain
            Journey
                         Greg Hunt
        14 Joseph Walker: Frontier
            Sheriff
                       Fred Lawrence
                    [Fred Feldman]

3

AMERICAN INDIAN SERIES: <AIS><HO>
  (continued)
  9 Sioux Arrows
                    Donald Porter
  10 Nez Perce Legend
                    Mick Clumpner
  11 Kiowa Fires
                    Donald Porter
  12 Shoshone Thunder
                    Bill Hotchkiss w/
                    Judith Shears
  13 Arapaho Spirit
                    Jane Toombs
  14 Pawnee Medicine
                    Bill Hotchkiss w/
                    Judith Shears
  _____

  _____

ANDERSON, Ken
  A Hearth Romance:
    1 Doctor's Return, The
  _____

  _____

ANDERSON, Lee
  Avalon:
    Smile In The Sun
  _____

  _____

ANDERSON, Roberta w/ Mary KUCZKIR
                    (Fern Michaels)

ANDERSON, Virginia
                    (Megan Ashe)

ANDERSSON, C. Dean w/ Nina Romberg
  ANDERSSON
                    (Asa Drake)

ANDERSSON, Nina Romberg
                    (Jane Archer)

ANDREWS, Barbara
  Candlelight Ecstasy:
    127 This Bittersweet Love
    176 Passionate Deceiver
                    (cont'd)

ANDREWS, Barbara (continued)
    215 Midnight Magic
    278 Happily Ever After
  Candlelight Ecstasy Supreme:
    2 Emerald Fire
    23 Shady Business
  _____

  _____

ANDREWS, Felicia   <HO>
             [Charles L. Grant]
  Seacliff
  Silver Huntress
  _____

  _____

ANDREWS, Nicola
             [Orania Papazoglou]
  Second Chance At Love:
    139 Forbidden Melody
    180 Reckless Desire
    200 Head Over Heels
    218 Rules Of The Game
  _____

  _____

ANNE-MARIEL   *
  Embrace My Scarlet Heart
  One Evening I Shall Return
  Rendezvous In Peking
  Tigress Of The Evening
  _____

  _____

ANTHONY, Diana
             [Diane Antonio]
  Once A Lover
  Out Of A Dream
  _____

  _____

ANTHONY, Evelyn   <HO>*
             [Evelyn Bridget Patricia
              Stephens Ward-Thomas]
  Anne Boleyn
  All The Queens Men (Eng:
    Elizabeth)
  Cardinal And The Queen (Eng: Anne
    Of Austria)
                    (cont'd)

4

ANTHONY, Evelyn (continued)
  Charles The King
  French Bride, The
  Legend, The
  Rendezvous, The
  Valentina
  Victor And Albert (Eng: Victoria)
  In sequence:
    Clandara
    Heiress, The
  Trilogy:
    Rebel Princess (Eng: Imperial
      Highness)
    Royal Intrigue (Eng: Curse
      Not The King)
    Far Flies The Eagle
                                        <RS><GOT>*
  Assassin, The
  Grave Of Truth, The
  Janus Imperative, The
  Mission To Malaspiga (Eng: The
    Malaspiga Exit)
  Occupying Power, The
  Persian Price, The (Eng: The
    Persian Ransom)
  Poellenberg Inheritance, The
  Return, The
  Silver Falcon, The
  Stranger At The Gates
  Tamarind Seed, The
  In sequence:
    Defector, The

ANTHONY, Page
        [Page & Anthony Traynor]
  To Love Forever

ANTONIO, Diane
               (Diana Anthony)
               (Diana Lyndon)

ANZELON, Robyn
  Harlequin Romantic Suspense:
    Goblin Tree, The
  SuperRomance:
    49 The Forever Spell
  Harlequin SuperRomance:
                   (cont'd)

ANZELON, Robyn (continued)
  120 Sandcastle Dreams

ARBOR, Jane
  Harlequin Classic:
    115 No Silver Spoon   (832)
    119 Towards The Dawn (474)
    128 Dear Intruder   (919)
  Harlequin Romance:
    2545 Handmaid To Midas

ARCHER, Jane   <HR>
        [Nina Romberg Andersson]
  Spring Dreams
  In sequence: *
    Tender Torment
    Rebellious Rapture

ARGERS, Helen   <RE>
  Lady Of Independence, A

ARMSTRONG, Carolyn T.
  Honeysuckle Love   <L&L:#6>

ARMSTRONG, Charlotte   (deceased)
        [Charlotte Armstrong Lewi]
  Friday's Child

ARMSTRONG, Lindsay
  Harlequin Presents:
    559 Melt A Frozen Heart
    607 Enter My Jungle
  Harlequin Romance:
    2443 Spitfire   *
    2582 Perhaps Love

ARNOLD, Francena
  A Hearth Romance:
    2 Deepening Stream, The
    3 Fruit For Tomorrow
    4 Light In My Window

_____

_____

ARNOLD, Margot   <HO>
  Affairs Of State

_____

_____

ARNOUT, Susan   <HO>
  Frozen Lady, The   <Saga>

_____

_____

ARTHUR, Elaine
  First Love From Silhouette: <YA>
    56 Romance In Store

_____

_____

ASCANI, Sparky
  The Avon Romance:
    Ransomed Heart, The

_____

_____

ASH, Melissa
                    [June E. Casey]
  Dawnstar Romance:
    Promises In The Sand

_____

_____

ASHBY, Juliet
                [Louise Lee Outlaw]
  Silhouette Romance:
    258 Midnight Lover
    279 Dream Of Passion

_____

_____

ASHE, Megan
                  [Virginia Anderson]
  Rapture Romance:
    46 Mountain Man, A
    83 Lightning Touch, The

_____

_____

ASHER, Inez
  Family Sins

_____

_____

ASHFIELD, Helen   <RE>
                  [Pamela Bennetts]
    Emerald
    Michaelmas Tree, The
    Midsummer Morning
    Regency Rogue

_____

_____

ASHFORD, Jane   <RE>
                  [Jane LeCompte]
    First Season
    Headstrong Ward, The
    Impetuous Heiress, The
    Radical Arrangement, A
    Repentant Rebel, The

_____

_____

ASHLEY, Faye
                    (Ashley Summers)
    Blue Wildfire

_____

_____

ASHLEY, Jacqueline
                  [Jacqueline Casto]
  Harlequin American Romance:
    20 Love's Revenge
                          (cont'd)

6

ASHLEY, Jacqueline (continued)
    40   Hunting Season
    78   Other Half Of Love, The

_____

_____

ASHLEY, Sarah
  Second Chance At Love:
    133 Cherished Moments

_____

ASHTON, Ann
                    [John M. Kimbro]
  Starlight Romance:
    Lovely And The Lonely, The
    Star Eyes

_____

_____

ASHTON, Mollie   <RE>
                  [Mollie Aghadjian]
  Noble Imposter, The
  Harlequin Regency Romance:
    Debt Of Honor, A

_____

_____

ASTLEY, Juliet   <RS>
                     [Norah Lofts]
  Copsi Castle   *
  Fall Of Midas, The

_____

_____

AUBERT, Rosemary
                      (Lucy Snow)

AUEL, Jean M.
  In sequence: *
    • Clan Of The Cave Bear, The
    • Valley Of The Horses
    Mammoth Hunters, The

_____

_____

AUFDEM-BRINKE, Eleanor
                    (Nora Roberts)

AUMENTE, Joy
                   (Joy Darlington)
                   (Joy Gardner)

AUSTIN, Stephanie
  Love & Life:
    Only A Housewife

_____

_____

AYRE, Jessica
  Harlequin Romance:
    2599 Hard To Handle
    2641 New Discovery

_____

_____

B

BACON, Nancy
  Love Game, The   <CO>
  Love & Life:
    Candles And Cavier
    Honeysuckle Moon
    Winter Morning

_____

_____

BADGER, Rosemary
  Harlequin Romance:
    2617 Corporate Lady
    2629 Girl Called Andy, A

_____

_____

BADGLEY, Anne   <RS>
  Rembrandt Decision, The

_____

_____

BAKER, Darlene
                    (Heather Lang)

BAKER, Fran
                    (Cathlyn McCoy)

BAKER, Marceil
                    (Marica Miller)

BALDWIN, Cathryn Jo
                    (Cathryn Ladame)
                    (Cathryn Ladd)

BALDWIN, Faith   (deceased)
          [Faith Baldwin Cuthrell]
  Departing Wings

_____

_____

BALDWIN, Rebecca   <RE>
                    [Helen Chappel]
  Lady Scandal
  Matter Of Honor, A

_____

_____

BALE, Karen A.   <HR>
  Distant Thunder
  Sweet Medicine's Prophecy:
   (series continued)
    Winter's Love Song

_____

_____

BALIN, Beverly   <HO>
  King In Hell

_____

_____

BALL, Barbara
  Caprice Romanc: <YA>
    34 Hidden Heart, The

_____

_____

BALL, Donna
                    [Rebecca Flanders]

BALL, Margaret
                    (Kathleen Frasher)
                    (Catherine Lyndell)

BANCROFT, Iris
                        (Iris Brent)
                      (Andrea Layton)
  Passionate Heart, The
  Whispering Hope   <CO>

_____

_____

BANGERT, Ethel   <GOT>
  Clover Hill

_____

_____

BANNISTER, Patricia
                    (Patricia Veryan)

BARBER, Lenora
                      [Janet Wing]
    Silhouette Desire:
     78 Blueprint For Rapture

_____

_____

BARBER, Noel
  Farewell To France, A

_____

_____

BARBIERI, Elaine A.   <HR>
  Love's Fiery Jewel
  Sweet Torment
  In sequence:
    Amber Fire   *
    Amber Treasure
    Amber Splendor

_____

_____

BARKER, Berta LaVan
  Avalon:
    Magic Of Happiness

_____

_____

8

BARLOW, Linda
  Second Chance At Love:
    168 Beguiled
    188 Flights Of Fancy
    224 Bewitched

BARNARD, Judith w/ Michael FAIN
                    (Judith Michael)

BARRETT, Jr., Neal
              (see Rebecca Drury)

BARRETT, William E.
  Red Lacquered Gate

BARRIE, Monica
                    [David Wind]
  Silhouette Intimate Moments:
     6 Island Heritage
    20 Gentle Winds, The (sequel
          to Tapestry #24)
    46 Crystal Blue Desire
    62 Breed Apart, A
  Silhouette Special Edition:
    94 Cry Mercy, Cry Love
  Tapestry: <HR>
    24 Gentle Fury
        Turquoise Sky

BARRIE, Susan
                  (Anita Charles)
                  (Pamela Kent)
  Harlequin Classic:
    123 Moon At The Full   (904)
    147 Castle Thunderbird (997)

BARRY, Andrea
          [Hania 'Annette' Bartle]
  Silhouette Romance:
    194 African Enchantment

BARRY, Jane
  Time In The Sun, A

BARRY, Lucy
  Stagestruck Secretary

BARTHOLOMEW, Barbara
  Silhouette Inspirations:
     4 Something Special

BARTLE, Hania 'Annette'
                    (Andrea Barry)

BARTLETT, Kathleen
  Lovers In Autumn

BASILE, Gloria Vitanza   <RS>
                    (Michaela Morgan)
  Global 2000: Eye Of The Eagle
  Global 2000: Jackal Helix, The

BASTIEN, Dorothy
  Wildfire: <YA>
    I Want To Be Me

BATES, Jenny
                    [Maura Seger]
  Second Chance At Love:
    175 Dazzled
  To Have And To Hold:
      5 Gilded Spring

BATTLE, Lois
  Season Of Change
  Southern Women   <Saga>
  War Brides
  Yesterday's Music

  _____

  _____

BAUGHMAN, Dorothy   <GOT>
  Avalon:
    Icy Terror

  _____

  _____

BAULING, Jayne
  Harlequin Presents:
    663 Valentine's Day

  _____

  _____

BAUMGARDNER, Cathie
                    (Cathie Linz)

BAUMGARTEN, Sylvia
                    (Ena Halliday)

BAWDEN, Nina   <GOT>
  Devil By The Sea
  Solitary Child, The

  _____

  _____

BAXTER, Mary Lynn
  Silhouette Imtimate Moments:
    19 Another Kind Of Love
    52 Memories That Linger
        Everything But Time
  Silhouette Special Edition:
    96 Autumn Awakening

  _____

  _____

BAYNER, Rose
  First Love From Sihouette: <YA>
    80 Endless Summer

  _____

  _____

BEARDSLEY, Charles
  (see Lee Davis Willoughby <MOAS>)

BEATY, Betty w/ David BEATY   <HO>
  Wings Of The Morning   *

  _____

  _____

BEAUMONT, Helen
                    (Jill Anderson)
                    (Jill Eckersley)
                    (Anna Stanton)
  Sapphire Romance: <ENG>
    Whisper To The Waves

  _____

  _____

BECHKO, Peggy
  SuperRomance:
    47 Dark Side Of Love

  _____

  _____

BECKMAN, Patti
    [Charles and/or Patti Boechman]
  Silhouette Inspirations:
    8 With The Dawn
  Silhouette Romance:
    227 Forbidden Affair
    273 Time For Us
  Silhouette Special Edition:
    85 Enchanted Surrender
    109 Thunder At Dawn
    169 Storm Over The Everglades

  _____

  _____

BEEBE, Elswyth
                    (Elswyth Thane)

10

BELL, Anthea   <RE>
  London Season, A

BELL, Betsy
  Avalon:
    Nurse Carrie's Island
    Nurse In The Wilderness

BELL, Josephine   <GOT>
  Stranger On A Cliff (To Let,
  Furnished)   *

BELL, Sallie Lee
  A Hearth Romance:
     5 Barrier, The
     6 By Strange Paths
     7 Last Surrender, The
     8 Long Search, The   <MY>
     9 Romance Along The Bayou
    10 Scar, The
    11 Substitute, The
    12 Through Golden Meadows
    13 Until The Daybreak
    21 Light From The Hill

BELMONT, Kathryn
                    [Mary Jo Territo]
  Silhouette Imtimate Moments:
    40 Time To Sing, A
  Silhouette Special Edition:
    72 Night Music
   112 From The Beginning
   173 From The Flames

BENEDICT, Barbara
  Lovestorm

BENET, Deborah
                  [Deborah Elaine Camp]
  Rapture Romance:
    13 Sweet Passion's Song
    23 Midnight Eyes
    44 Winter Flame
    64 Wrangler's Lady
    76 Riptide
    94 Dream To Share, A

BENJAMIN, Linda
  Ecstasy's Fury

BENNETT, Christine
                [William Arthur Neubauer]
  Sharon Contemporary Teens:
    Girl Of Black Island
    Gloria's Ghost
    Wind In The Sage

BENNETT, Emma
                        [Emma Merritt]
  Candlelight Ecstasy:
   120 That Certain Summer
   135 By Passion Bound
   139 River Enchantment
   167 Beneath The Willow Tree
   228 Loving Brand
   257 With Each Passing Hour
   274 With All My Heart
   285 Passionate Ultimatum
        Pleasurable Conquest

BENNETTS, Pamela
                        (Helen Ashfield)
                        (Margaret James)

BERCKMAN, Evelyn   <RS>
  Stake In The Game, The

11

BERENCSI, Susan
  Starlight Romance:
    Innocent Surrender

_____

_____

BERENSON, Laurie
                    (Laurien Blair)

BERGEN, Fran
    [Frances deTalavera Berger]
  Silhouette Special Edition:
    77   Prelude To Passion
    101 Golden Impulse
    142 Dream Feast

_____

_____

BERGER, Frances deTalavera
                      (Fran Bergen)
                    (Frances Flores)

BERGER, Nomi   *
                    (Alyssa Welles)
  Devotions

_____

_____

BERGSTROM, Kay
                    (Cassie Miles)

BERGSTROM, Louise
  Secret Flower, The
  Avalon:
    Magic Island

_____

_____

BERK, Ariel
                  [Barbara Keiler]
  Silhouette Desire:
    93   Silent Beginnings
    154 Promise To Love

_____

_____

BERNADETTE, Ann
                      [Karen Ray w/
                        D. H. Gazdak]
  Echoes Of The Heart

_____

_____

BERNARD, Dorothy Ann
                    [Dorothy Weller]
  Candlelight Ecstasy:
    190 Destiny's Touch
    275 Just Call My Name

_____

_____

BERNARD, Thelma Rene   <CO>
  Blue Marsh

_____

_____

BEVAN, Gloria
  Harlequin Romance:
    2563 Rouseabout Girl, The
    2618 Greek Island Magic

_____

_____

BEVERLEY, Jane
                    [Dorothy Weller]
  Sapphire Romance: <ENG>
    Journey To Destiny

_____

_____

BIANCHIN, Helen
  Harlequin Presents:
    695 Yesterday's Shadow
    720 Savage Pagan

_____

_____

BIEBER, Janet w/ Joyce THIES
                    (Janet Joyce)

BIERCE, Jane
  Harlequin American Romance:
    15 Building Passion

BINCHY, Maeve
  Light A Penny Candle

BIRD, Beverly
  Silhouette Intimate Moments:
    3 Emeralds In The Dark
    23 Fires Of Winter, The

BIRD, Patricia
  Avalon:
    Blueprint For Love
    Chrystal Heart
    Shipboard Kisses

BIRD, Sarah
                    (Tory Cates)
  Do Evil Cheerfully

BISHOP, Cassandra
  Silhouette Desire:
    129 Madison Avenue Marriage

BISHOP, Claudia
  Second Chance At Love:
    186 Irresistible You
  To Have And To Hold:
    26 That Champagne Feeling
    36 Where The Heart Is

BISHOP, Lee
  Davy Crockett: Frontier Fighter
                        <AES:#11>

BISHOP, Natalie
  Silhouette Special Edition:
    178 Saturday's Child

BISSELL, Elaine   <CO>
                (Whitney Faulkner)
  As Time Goes By

BITTNER, F. Rosanne
  Savage Destiny Saga: In sequence:
    Sweet Prairie Passion
    Ride The Free Wind
    River Of Love

BJORN, Thyra Ferre'
  Papa's Daughter
  Papa's Wife

BLACK, Hermina A.   <RS>
  World Of Love, A (A World of
    Shadows)   *

BLACK, Jackie
                [Jacqueline Casto]
  Candlelight Ecstasy:
    152 Autumn Fires
    170 Promises In The Night
    187 Time For Love, A
  Candlelight Ecstasy Supreme:
    16 Payment In Full
                        (cont'd)

13

BLACK, Jackie (continued)
    28 Fascination

_____

_____

BLACK, Laura   <RS>
 • Strathgallant
    Albany

_____

_____

BLAIR, Christina   <GOT>
  Crystal Destiny

_____

_____

BLAIR, Cynthia
  Just Married
  Love & Life: <CO>
    Battle Scars
    Beautiful Dreamer
    Commitment

_____

_____

BLAIR, Kathryn
                    (Rosalind Brett)
                    (Celine Conway)
  Harlequin Classic:
    121 Mayenga Farm   (941)
    130 Barbary Moon   (972)
    139 Primrose Bride, The (988)

_____

_____

BLAIR, Laurien
              [Laurie Berenson]
  Silhouette Desire:
    105 Sweet Temptation
    130 Between The Covers

_____

_____

BLAIR, Leona
  With This Ring

_____

_____

BLAIR, Rebecca
  Harlequin American Romance:
    92 In Passion's Defense

_____

_____

BLAIRSON, Peter T.
  Escalante: Wilderness Path
                    <AES:#10>

_____

_____

BLAKE, Andrea
                    (Anne Weale)
  Harlequin Classic:
    108 Now And Always   (864)
    126 Whisper Of Doubt   (944)
    134 Night Of The
            Hurricane   (974)

_____

_____

BLAKE, Jennifer   <HR>
              [Patricia Maxwell]
  Midnight Waltz
  Royal Seduction
  Surrender In Moonlight

_____

_____

BLAKE, Jillian
  Silhouette Intimate Moments:
    27 Diana's Folly
            East Side, West Side

_____

_____

BLAKE, Laurel
              [Elaine Fowler Palencia]
  Second Chance At Love:
    154 Stranger In Paradise
    202 Into The Whirlwind

_____

_____

BLAKE, Stephanie   <HR>
                  [Jack Pearl]
  Glorious Passion, A

_____

_____

BLAKE, Susan
  Sweet Dreams: <YA>
    60 Summer Breezes

_____

_____

BLAKE, Vanessa   <GOT>
  Pentallion (The Lady From
    Lisbon)   *

_____

_____

BLANFORD, Virginia
                  (Sarah Crewe)

BLAYNE, Diana
            [Susan Spaeth Kyle]
  Candlelight Ecstasy:
    138 White Sand, White Sea *
    184 Dark Surrender

_____

_____

BLICKLE, Katrinka   <HO>
  Verity (The Vain And The
    Vainglorious)   *

_____

_____

BLOCKLINGER, Betty
              [Peggy O'More]
  Love To Lean On, A (The Rock
    Oak   *

_____

_____

BLOOM, Ursula
                  (Sheila Burns)
                  (Mary Essex)

BLOOM, Ursula w/ Charles EADE
                  (Lozania Prole)

BOCKOVEN, Georgia
  SuperRomance:
    82 Restless Tide
  Harlequin SuperRomance:
    102 After The Lightning
  Harlequin Temptation:
    14 Tracings On A Window

_____

_____

BOECHMAN, Patti and/or Charles
  BOECHMAN
                  (Patti Beckman)

BOLDT, Lana McGraw
  Flower Of The Pacific   <Saga>

_____

_____

BONDS, Parris Afton
  Mood Indigo
  Silhouette Intimate Moments:
    5 Wind Song   *
    41 Widow Woman

_____

_____

BONHAM, Barbara   <HR>
  Bittersweet
  Diagnosis: Love

_____

_____

BONNER, Terry Nelsen   <HO>*
  Australia/New South Wales
    Victoria Series:
      1 Rum Colony
      2 First Families
      3 Free Woman, The
                  [Laura Castoro]
                  (cont'd)

BONNER, Terry Nelsen (continued)
   4 Pioneers, The
                [Mollie Gregory]
   5 Outback, The
   6 Wildings, The
   7 Diggers
                [Steve Krauzer]
   8 Seekers
   9 The Defiant
                [Sheila Raeschild]
  10 Unvanquished
                [Marc Olden]
     (end)

BOOTH, Rosemary
              (Frances Murray)

BOSSE, Malcolm
  Warlord, The   <Saga>

BOSWELL, Barbara
  Loveswept:
    53 Little Consequences

BOURNE, Caroline   <HR>
  On Rapture's Wing

BOURNE, Joanna Watkins   <RE>
  Her Ladyship's Companion

BOWDLER, Lucy
  Avalon:
    Janis Hall Nurse Instructor
    Nurse Sandra's Choice

BOWE, Kate
              [Mary Ann Taylor]
  Harlequin SuperRomance:
   117 Horizons

BOWERS, Mary Curtis
  Avalon:
    Best Nurse In Missouri
    Nurse Becky's New World
    Nurse Carrie's Roses
    Nurse Heather's Choice
    Nurse Jamie's Surprise
    Nurse Jill's Perfect Man
    Nurse Sarah's Confusion

BOWES, Florence
  Starlight Romance:
    Beauchamp
    Macorvan Curse, The   *

BOWMAN, Jeanne
              [Peggy O'More]
  Sharon Contemporary Teens:
    Secret Of The Forest

BOYLE, Ann
              (Audrey Brent)
              (Ann Bryan)
  To Find A Unicorn
  Caprice Romance: <YA>
    33 Never Say Never

BRADER, Norma
  Candlelight Ecstasy:
    244 Settling The Score

BRADFORD, Barbara Taylor   <CO>
  Voice Of The Heart

BRADFORD, Mary Ellen   <YA>
  Make Your Dreams Come True:
    1 Angie's Choice

BRADLEY, Marion Zimmer   <GOT>
  Mists Of Avalon, The   <HO>
  Souvenir Of Monique

BRADLEY, Muriel
  Silhouette Intimate Moments:
    28 Waltz In Scarlet
       Island Man
  In sequence: <HR>*
    Tanya
    Destiny's Star

BRAMSCH, Joan
  Loveswept:
    41 Sophisticated Mountain
       Gal, The
    64 Kiss To Make It Better, A

BRAMWELL, Charlotte
          [John M. Kimbro]
  Stepmother's House

BRAND, Christianna
          [China Thompson]
  Brides Of Aberdar, The

BRAND, Debra
          (Suzanne Rand)

BRAND, Susan   <RS>
  Shadows On The Tor

BRANDEWYNE, Rebecca   <HR>
  Rose Of Rapture

BRANDON, JoAnna
          [Olivia Harper w/
           Ken Harper]
  Candlelight Ecstasy:
    237 Love, Bid Me Welcome

BRANDT, Jane Lewis   <HO>
  Firebrand

BRAUN, Matthew   <HO>
  This Loving Promise (The Stuart
    Women)

BRECK, Vivian
       [Vivian Gurney Breckenfeld]
  Maggie

BREMER, JoAnne w/ Carol I. WAGNER
          (Joellyn Carroll)

BREMER, JoAnne
  Candlelight Ecstasy:
    222 Seductive Illusion
    254 An Expert's Advice

BRENNER, Marie
  Intimate Distance
  _____
  _____

BRENT, Joanna
  Few Days In Weasel Creek, A
  _____

BRENT, Madeleine   <RS>
  Heritage Of Shadows, A
    Stormswift
  _____

BRETT, Brady
  First Love From Silhouette: <YA>
    49 One Of A Kind
  _____
  _____

BRETT, Rosalind
                  [Kathryn Blair]
  Harlequin Classic:
    76 Portrait Of Susan   (783)*
    153 Hotel Mirador   (989)
  _____
  _____

BRETTON, Barbara
  Harlequin American Romance:
    3 Love Changes
    49 Sweetest of Debts, The
    91 No Safe Place
  _____
  _____

BREW, Cathleen   <HR>
  Innocent Revenge
  _____
  _____

BRIAN, Marilyn
                  [Jillian Dagg]
  To Have And To Hold:
    19 Passion's Glow
  _____
  _____

BRICKNER, Richard P.
  Tickets   <CO>
  _____
  _____

BRIDE, Nadja
                  [Josephine Nobisso]
  Torch:
    Hide And Seek
  _____
  _____

BRIGHT, Elizabeth   <HR>
                  [Robert Liston]
  Destiny's Thunder
  _____
  _____

BRIGHT, Laurey
                  [Daphne Clair]
  Silhouette Special Edition:
    143 When Morning Comes
  _____
  _____

BRINDLEY, Louise   <RE>
  In The Shadow Of The Brontes
  _____
  _____

BRINGLE, Mary   <CO>
  Open Heart
  _____
  _____

BRISKIN, Jacqueline
  Onyx, The
  ● Everything And More
  Too Much too Soon

BRISTOWE, Anthony   <RS>
  Tunnel, The

BRITT, Katrina
  Harlequin Premiere III:
      25 Man At Keywest, The

BRITTON, Kate   <GOT>
  Avalon:
    Nightmare At Lilybrook

BROCK, Rose   <GOT>
  Tarn House
      Longleaf

BRONTE, Louisa   <HR>
          [Janet Louise Roberts]
  American Dynasty Series:
    (continued)
      This Shining Splendor
  Greystone Tavern Series:
    In sequence: *
      Greystone Tavern
      Gathering At Greystone
      Freedom Trail To Greystone
      Casino Greystone
      Moonlight At Greystone
      Greystone Heritage

BROOKE, Alice
  Silhouette Romance:
      242 No Gurarantees
                        (cont'd)

BROOKE, Alice (continued)
      Harbor Lights

BROOKES, Beth
                  [Eileen Nauman]
  Second Chance At Love:
      131 On Wings Of Passion
      183 Torrid Nights

BROOKS, Anne Tedlock   <HO>
  Centennial Summer
  Sharon Romance:
    Evergreen Girl

BROOKS, Janice Young   <HO>
  Our Lives, Our Fortunes
  Still The Mighty Waters   *

BROUDE, Craig Howard
              (Melissa Hepburne)
              (Lisa Lenore)

BROUSE, Barbara
              (Araby Scott)
              (Abra Taylor)

BROWN, Diana   <RE>
  Sandalwood Fan, The

BROWN, Sandra
              (Laura Jordan)
              (Rachel Ryan)
              (Erin St. Claire)
  Harlequin American Romance:
      1 Tomorrow's Promise   *
  Loveswept:
      1 Heaven's Price
                        (cont'd)

BROWN, Sandra (continued)
   22 Breakfast In Bed
   51 Send No Flowers
   66 In A Class By Itself
Second Chance At Love:
   106 Relentless Desire (title
        changed from "Shadows
        Of Yesterday")
   137 Temptation's Kiss
   164 Tempest In Eden

_____

_____

BROWNING, Dixie
                        (Zoe Dozier)
Silhouette Desire:
   68 Shadow Of Yesterday
   91 Image Of Love
   111 Hawk And The Honey, The
   121 Late Rising Moon
        Stormwatch
Sihouette Romance:
   191 Loving Rescue   *
   203 Secret Valentine
   221 Practical Dreamer
   275 Visible Heart
   292 Journey To Quiet Waters
   305 Love Thing, The
        First Things Last
Silhouette Special Edition:
   110 Reach Out To Cherish
   181 Just Desserts

_____

_____

BROWNING, Pamela
                        (Pam Ketter)
                        (Melanie Rowe)

BROWNLEIGH, Eleanora   <HO>
                        [Rhoda Cohen]
   Heirloom

_____

_____

BRUCKER, Meredith Babeaux
                    (Meredith Kingston)
                    (Meredith Lindley)

BRUFF, Nancy
                        (Nancy Gardner)
   Desire On The Dunes

_____

_____

BRUNDY, Clyde M.   <HO>
   Call Up The Morning
   Grasslands
   High Empire

_____

_____

BRYAN, Eileen
                        [Ruth Smith]
   Candlelight Ecstasy:
      155 Loving Adversaries
      193 Memory And Desire
   Candlelight Ecstasy Supreme:
      14 Crossfire
      25 Against All Odds
      48 Run For The Roses

_____

_____

BRYSON, Deborah w/ Joyce PORTER
                        (Deborah Joyce)

BUCHEISTER, Patt
                        (Patt Parrish)

BUCK Carol
                        [Carol Buckman]
   Second Chance At Love:
      219 Encore

_____

_____

BUCKHOLDER, Marta
                        (Marta Lloyd)

BUCKHOLTZ, Eileen w/ Ruth GLICK
                        (Amanda Lee)

BUCKHOLTZ, Eileen w/ Ruth GLICK and
   Louise TITCHENOR
                        (Alyssa Howard)

BUCKMAN, Carol
                        (Carol Buck)

BULLARD, Ann Elizabeth
              (Becky Stuart)
              (Casey Stuart)

BURAK, Linda w/ Joan ZEIG
              (Alicia Meadows)

BURCHELL, Mary
              [Ida Cook]
  Harlequin Classic:
    118 Then Come Kiss Me   (422)
    127 For Ever And Ever   (461)
    136 Love Is My Reason   (494)
    145 Stolen Heart   (686)
  Harlequin Romance:
  2528 Masquerade With Music

BURGHLEY, Rose
  Harlequin Classic:
    24 And Be Thy Love   (617)*
  143 Garden Of
        Don Jose, The   (928)

BURMAN, Margaret
  Sweet Dreams: <YA>
    45 Dream Prom

BURNETT, Ruth
  Avalon:
    Beautiful Medic, The
    Love Star
    Nurse Maggie's Dream
    Telltale Kiss, The
    Topaz Promise, The

BURROUGHS, Marjorie   <HR>
  Winter Hearts, The

BUSBEE, Shirlee   <HR>
  Deceive Not My Heart (title was
    changed from "Lover's Duel")

BUSH, Christine
  Avalon:
    Season Of Fear   <GOT>

BUSH, Nancy
  First Love From Silhouette: <YA>
    78 Bittersweet Sixteen

BUTLER, David   <HO>
  Lusitania

BUTLER, Richard
  Against The Wind

BUTLER, Robert Olen
  Alley's Of Eden, The

BUTTERWORTH, Michael
            (Carola Salisbury)

BYERS, Cordia   <HR>
  Calista
  Heather
  Nicole La Belle

BYFIELD, Sue
  Harlequin Romance:
    2529 To Be Or Not To Be
_____

_____

BYINGTON, Kaa
                    (Sybil LeGrand)

BYRNE, Beverly   <HO>
  Griffin Saga: (continued)
    Fiery Splendor
            (end)
_____

_____

C

CABOT, Isobel
  Avalon:
    Nurse Lauren's Challenge
    Nurse Mara's Fear
_____

_____

CADE, Robin
              [Christopher Nicole]
  Fear Dealers, The
_____

_____

CADELL, Elizabeth
  Honey For Tea
  Letter To My Love   <ENG>
  Mixed Marriage   <ENG>
  Remains To Be Seen   <RS>
  Return Match
  Stratton Story, The   <ENG>
_____

_____

CAILLOU, Alan   <HO>
  Prophetess, The
_____

_____

CAIMI, Gina
  Silhouette Desire:
    125 Passionate Awakening
_____

_____

CAINE, Jeffrey   *
  Heathcliff   <HO>
_____

_____

CALDE, Mark   <HO>
  Conquest
_____

_____

CALDWELL, Claire
  First Love From Silhouette: <YA>
    90 Surf's Up For Laney
_____

_____

CALLOWAY, Jo
  Candlelight Ecstasy:
    121 Dawn's Promise
    150 One Of A Kind
    164 Illusive Lover
    188 Windsong
    220 Classic Love, A
    238 Heartbeats
    273 Scattered Roses
    282 To Remember Love
  Candlelight Ecstasy Supreme:
      6 Time Of A Winter Love
     24 Somewhere In The Stars
     41 Touched By Fire
  Finding Mr. Right:
        Mirrors Of Love
_____

_____

CAMERON, Barbara
              [Barbara Cameron Smith]
  Candlelight Ecstasy:
    124 An Affair To Remember
                          (cont'd)

22

CAMERON, Barbara (continued)
    Silhouette Desire:
        Rapture Of The Deep

_____

_____

CAMERON, D. Y.
    Cornish Serenade

_____

_____

CAMERON, Eleanor Elford   <GOT><RS>
    House On The Beach
    Spider Stone, The

_____

_____

CAMERON, Kay
                [Virginia Coffman]
    Scarlett Ribbons: <HR>
        Passion's Rebel

_____

_____

CAMERON, Lou
                (Julie Cameron)
        (see Jonathan Scofield)
    (see Lee Davis Willoughby <MOAS>)

CAMERON, Miranda   <RE>
                    [Mary Kahn]
    Meddlesome Heiress, The
    Reluctant Abigail, The
    Scandalous Bargain, A

_____

_____

CAMP, Candace
                (Lisa Gregory)
                (Kristin James)
                (Sharon Stephens)

CAMP, Debbie
            [Deborah Elaine Camp]
    Gateway To The Heart

_____

_____

CAMP, Debby
            [Deborah Elaine Camp]
    Facade
    Tandem

_____

_____

CAMP, Deborah Elaine
                (Deborah Benet)
                (Debbie Camp)
                (Debby Camp)
                (Elaine Camp)
                (Delaine Tucker)
                (Elaine Tucker)

CAMP, Elaine
            [Deborah Elaine Camp]
    Silhouette Romance:
    270 This Tender Truce
    Silhouette Special Edition:
    113 For Love Or Money
    159 In A Pirate's Arms

_____

_____

CAMPBELL, Caroline   <RE>
                [Leslie A. Safford]
    Love Masque

_____

_____

CAMPBELL, Diana   <RE>
    Counterfeit Countess, The
    Family Affairs
    Reluctant Cyprian, The

_____

_____

CAMPBELL, Drusilla   <HO>
    The Malloys:
        Autumntide

_____

_____

CAMPBELL, Joanna
                          [JoAnn Simon]
  Sweet Dreams: <YA>
    52 Love Notes

_____

_____

CAMPBELL, Wanza J.   <HR>
  Runaway Rapture

_____

CANAVAN, Jean   <GOT>
  Shadow Of The Flame

_____

_____

CANFIELD, Sandra w/ Penny RICHARDS
                     (Sandi Shayne)

CANHAM, Marsha
  The Avon Romance:
    China Rose

_____

_____

CANNON, Helen
  Better Place I Know, A
  Season's Change
  Where The Truth Lies

_____

_____

CANON, Mary   <HR>
  Wild Rose
  O'Hara Dynasty: (continued)
    Exiled, The

_____

_____

CANTOR, Eli
  Love Letters   <CO>

_____

_____

CARD, Orson Scott
  Woman Of Destiny, A

_____

_____

CAREW, Jean
  First Girl
  Sharon Romance:
    Cara's Masquerade
  Sharon Contemporary Teens:
    Stage Struck

_____

_____

CAREW, Jocelyn   <HR>
                    [Jacquelyn Aeby]
  Pavilion Of Passion

_____

_____

CAREY, Suzanne
  Silhouette Desire:
    69 Passion's Portrait
    92 Mountain Memory
   126 Leave Me Never

_____

_____

CARLOW, Joyce
  Emerald's Hope

_____

_____

CARLSON, Nancy
  Loveswept:
    10 Hard Drivin' Man

_____

_____

CARLSON, Nola
  Caprice Romance: <YA>
    41 Spring Dreams

_____

_____

24

CARNEGIE, Sacha
  Guardian, The
  Scarlet Banners Of Love

_____

_____

CARNELL, Lois
  Harlequin American Romance:
    28 Beyond The Flight Of
        Birds

_____

_____

CAROTHERS, Annabel   <HO>
  Kilcaraig

_____

_____

CARPENTER, Amanda
  Harlequin Presents:
    703 Wall, The
  Harlequin Romance:
    2605 Deeper Dimension, A
    2648 Damaged Trust, A

_____

_____

CARPENTER, Cyndy   <HR>
  Rapture's Heaven

_____

_____

CARR, Eleni
                  [Helen Maragakis]
  Silhouette Special Editon:
    130 Play It Again

_____

_____

CARR, John Dickson   <GOT>
  Bride Of Newgate, The

_____

_____

CARR, Nicole
  Make Your Dreams Come True: <YA>
    3 Worthy Opponents

_____

_____

CARR, Philippa
                [Eleanor Burford Hibbert]
  (series corrected)
  • Miracle At St. Brunos, The (is
        the first book of the series)
  (series continued)
    Knave Of Hearts
    Voices In A Haunted Room
    The Return of the Gypsy

_____

CARR, Robyn   <HO>
    Bellerose Bargain, The
    Blue Falcon, The
    Chelynne
    the Braeswood Tapestry
    The Troubadour's Romance
    By Right of Arms

CARR, Sherry
  Second Chance At Love:
    116 Let Passion Soar

_____

_____

CARROL, Shana
                        [Frank Schaefer w/
                         Kerry Newcomb]
  Paxton Women Saga:(continued)
    Live For Love   <4>

_____

_____

CARROLL, Abby
  Two By Two Romance: <YA>
    2 Jed & Jessie

_____

_____

CARROLL, Joellyn
                    [Jo Bremer w/
                     Carol Wagner]
Candlelight Ecstasy:
  131 Run Before The Wind
  159 Flight Of Splendor, A

CARROLL, Malissa
                    [Carol I. Wagner]
Candlelight Ecstasy:
  281 Match Made In Heaven

CARROLL, Mary
                    [Annette Sanford]
Silhouette Romance:
  204 Midnight Sun   *
  222 Two Faces Of Love   *
  246 Where Tomorrow Waits

CARROLL, Rosalyn
                    [Carol Katz]
Rapture Romance:
  67 Enchanted Encore

CARSLEY, Anne   <HR>
  Defiant Desire
  Golden Savage

CARSON, Angela
                    (Sue Peters)
Harlequin Romance:
  2619 Face Of The Stranger, The

CARSON, Nola
  Caprice Romance: <YA>
    26 New Face In The Mirror, A

CARSON, Rosalind
                    [Margaret Chittenden]
SuperRomance:
  91 Such Sweet Magic
Harlequin SuperRomance:
  123 Love Me Tomorrow

CARTER, Alberta Simpson   <GOT>
                    [Alfred Bercovici]
  With Malice Toward All

CARTER, Ann
  His Words Of Love
  Prelude To Summer

CARTER, Ashley
                    [Harry Whittington]
  Falconhurst Series: (continued)
    Rogue Of Falconhurst

CARTER, Helen
                    [Helen Maragakis]
  Second Chance At Love:
    194 Touched By Lightning

CARTER, Rosemary
  Harlequin Presents:
    560 Daredevil
    575 Master Of Tinarua
    615 Lion's Domain
    664 Serpent In Paradise

CARTLAND, Barbara
                    (see APPENDIX D)

CARTWRIGHT, Kate
  To See A Stranger

_____

_____

CASEY, June E.
                         (Melissa Ash)
                      (Casey Douglas)
                 (Constance Ravenlock)
                        (June Trevor)
  Torch:
    Mountain Of Desire

_____

_____

CASEY, Sara
  Two By Two Romance: <YA>
    1 Cassie & Chris

_____

_____

CASSIDY, Becka
            [Beverly Vines-Haines]
  First Love From Silhouette: <YA>
    40 Lucky Star

_____

_____

CASSINI, Igor   <HO>
  Pay The Price   <Saga>

_____

_____

CASSITY, Joan   <HR>
  The Avon Romance:
    Now & Again

_____

_____

CASTLE, Jayne
            [Jayne Ann Krentz]
  Double Dealing
  Candlelight Ecstasy:
    130 Conflict Of Interest

_____

_____

CASTO, Jacqueline
               (Jacqueline Ashley)
                     (Jackie Black)

CASTORO, Laura Parker
                    (Laura Parker)
  (see Terry Nelsen Bonner)

CATES, Tory
            [Sarah McCabe Bird]
  Silhouette Special Edition:
    125 Where Aspens Quake

_____

_____

CATLEY, Melanie
  Candlelight Ecstasy:
    248 Star Attraction

_____

_____

CATO, Nancy   <HO>
  Forefathers

_____

_____

CAVANAGH, Helen
  Wildfire: <YA>
    Place For Me, A
    Second Best

_____

_____

CAVANNA, Betty   <YA>
  Storm In The Heart

_____

_____

CHACE, Isobel
               [Elizabeth Hunter]
  Harlequin Classic:
    144 Flamingoes On The
         Lake   (976)

CHADWICK, Joseph
              (Janet Conroy)
         (JoAnne Creighton)

CHALLONER, Robert   <HO>
  Jamaica Passage

CHAMBERS, Ginger
  Candlelight Ecstasy Supreme:
    18 Heart Divided, A
    43 Harbor Of Dreams
  Harlequin North American:
    32 Game Of Hearts
    71 Passion's Prey

CHANCE, Sara
           [Sydney Ann Clary]
  Silhouette Desire:
    46 Her Golden Eyes
    83 Home At Last
   107 This Wildfire Magic

CHANDLER, Bryn
  Behind The Badge   <CO>
  Love & Life:
    Ambition

CHANDLER, Laurel
        [Nancy L. Jones Holder]
  Rapture Romance:
    15 Treasures Of Love
    30 Heart's Victory
                (cont'd)

CHANDLER, Laurel (continued)
    59 Boundless Love
    85 Shades Of Moonlight

CHANNING, Justin   <HO>
          [Karen Hitzig w/
           Helen Barrett]
  Carolina Woman

CHAPLIN, Patrice
  Unforgotten, The   <M-Got>

CHAPMAN, Renate
  Avalon:
    Dark Moon
    Haunted Heart   <GOT>
    House Of Shadows
    Love's Secret Plan
    Waters Dark/Deep

CHAPPEL, Helen
         (Rebecca Baldwin)

CHARBONNEAU, Louis
  From A Dark Place   <RS>

CHARLES, Esme
  Love Is A Stranger

CHARLES, Iona
       [Carolyn Nichols w/
        Stanlee Miller Coy]
  When Only The Bougainvillea
    Blooms

CHARLES, Maggi
        [Margaret Hudson Koehler]
Silhouette Special Edition:
   158 Mirror Image, The

_____

_____

CHARLES, Marie
        [Marie Rydzynski-Ferrarella]
Second Chance At Love:
   107 Scenes From The Heart
   145 Claimed By Rapture

_____

_____

CHARLES, Theresa
            [Charles Swatridge w/
             Irene Maude Swatridge]
Dark Legacy (Eng: Happy
   Now I Go)   *

_____

_____

CHARLTON, Josephine
Silhouette Desire:
   135 Table For Two

_____

_____

CHASE, Elaine Raco
Candlelight Ecstasy:
   162 Video Vixen
   226 Special Delivery
   272 Dare The Devil
Finding Mr. Right:
   Best-Laid Plans
Silhouette Desire
   104 Calculated Risk
   138 Lady Be Bad

_____

_____

CHASE, Marian
Silhouette Romance:
   267 Share The Dream

_____

_____

CHATER, Elizabeth
                        (Lisa Moore)
   Emerald Love
   Marriage Mart, The   <RE>
   Reformed Rake, The (sequel   <RE>
    to "A Delicate Situation"
    Coventry #191)

_____

_____

CHATFIELD, Susan
        [Susan Chatfield Fasshaurer]
Sapphire Romance: <ENG>
   Love Bargain, The
Torchlite:
   Banyon's Daughter

_____

_____

CHATTERTON, Louise
First Love From Silhouette: <YA>
   92 Just The Right Age

_____

_____

CHEEVER, Susan   <CO>
   Handsome Man, A

_____

_____

CHESNEY, Marion   <RE>
        [Marion Chesney Gibbons]
Duke's Diamonds
French Affair, The
Lady Lucy's Lover
Poor Relation, The
Viscount's Revenge, The
In sequence:
   Westerby Inheritance, The   *
   Westerby Sisters, The
The Six Sisters:
   In sequence:
     Minerva
     Taming Of Annabelle, The

_____

_____

CHESTER, Deborah   \<RE\>
  Heart's Desire

_____

_____

CHRISTMAS, Joyce   \<RS\>
  Dark Tide

_____

_____

CHRISTOPHER, Beth
  Finding Mr. Right:
    Love For The Taking

_____

_____

CHRISTOPHER, Mary
  Dawnstar Romance:
    Budding Rapture, A

_____

_____

CHRISTY, John
                  (see Vera Holding)

CLAGUE, Maryhelen   \<HO\>
  Moment Of The Rose
  In sequence:
    Beyond The Shining River   *
    Beside The Still Waters

_____

_____

CLAIR, Daphne
                        (Laurey Bright)
                        (Claire Lorel)
  Harlequin Presents
    679 Ruling Passion, A
    687 Marriage Under Fire
    711 Take Hold Of Tomorrow

_____

_____

CLAIRE, Eve
                        [Claire DeLong]
  Silhouette Special Edition:
    149 Appalachian Summer

_____

_____

CLAIRE, Evelyn
  Starlight Romance:
    Storm Remembered

_____

_____

CLAPP, Patricia   \<GOT\>
  Jane-Emily

CLARE, Jane
                        [Dinah Shields]
  Silhouette Intimate Moments:
    26 Old Love, New Love
  Silhouette Special Edition:
    70 Traces Of Dreams

_____

_____

CLARE, Shannon
                        [Linda Harrel]
  SuperRomance:
    78 Snow Bride
  Harlequin SuperRomance:
    113 Wake The Moon

_____

_____

CLARK, Eleanor
  Baldur's Gate

_____

_____

CLARK, Marianne
                [Marianne Willman]
  Rapture Romance:
     33 Apache Tears
     38 Here There Be Dragons

CLARK, Norma Lee   <RE>
  Kitty Quinn   <HO>
  Marriage Mart, The
  Perfect Match, The

CLARK, Roberta   <HR>
  Mari's Caress

CLARK, Sandra
  Harlequin Romance:
     2533 Moonlight Enough
     2569 Stormy Weather

CLARKE, Janet K.
                (Jane Christopher)
                (JoAnna Kenyon)
                (Nell Kincaid)

CLARY, Sydney Ann
                (Sara Chance)

CLAY, Rita
                [Rita Clay Estrada]
  Silhouette Desire:
     32 Yesterday's Dreams   *
     45 Experiment In Love
     82 Summer Song
    120 Recapture The Love (is a
          sequel to "Wise Folly"
          Desire #3)

CLIFFORD, Kay
  Harlequin Romance:
     2611 Man Of Gold
     2642 Duke Wore Jeans, The

CLUMPNER, Mick
  Nez Perce Legend   <AES:#10>

COBURN, Jean Ann
  Torch:
     Brief Encounter

COCKCROFT, Ann
  Silhouette Romance:
     294 Beloved Pirate
  Tapestry: <HR>
         Pirate's Promise

COFFARO, Katherine
  Harlequin American Romance:
     44 Logical Passion, A
     70 No Other Love
     81 Sunward Journey

COFFMAN, Virginia
                (Kay Cameron)
                (Victor Cross)
                (Virginia C. Deuvaul)
                (Jeanne Duval)
                (Ann Stanfield)
  Affair At Alkali
  Call Of The Flesh
  Dynasty Of Dreams
  Few Fiends To Tea, A   *
  Master Of The Blue Mire, The   *
  Orchid Tree, The
  Stalking Terror, The (The Small
     Tawny Cat)   *
                (cont'd)

COFFMAN, Virginia (continued)
  Strange Secrets (The Secret
    Of Shower Tree   *
  In sequence: *
    Gaynor Woman, The
    Dinah Faire
  In sequence: *
    Moura
    Beckoning From Moura (The
      Beckoning)
    Dark Beyond Moura (The Dark
      Gondola)
    Vicar Of Moura, The/Devil
      Beyond Moura (The Devil-
      Vicar)
    Vampyre Of Moura, The

_____

_____

COHEN, Rhoda
                (Eleanora Brownleigh)
                (Paige Wolfe)

COHEN, Sharleen Cooper
  Ladies Of Beverly Hills, The <CO>

_____

COHEN, Susan
                (Elizabeth St. Clair)

COLE, Brenda
  First Love From Silhouette: <YA>
    60 Alabama Moon
    79 Larger Than Life

_____

_____

COLE, Dorothy
  Nurse At The Fair

_____

_____

COLE, Hilary
                [Valerie Miller]
  To Have And To Hold:
    34 My Darling Detective

_____

_____

COLE, Hubert   <HO>
  Josephine

_____

_____

COLE, Justine   <HR>
                [Susan Phillips
                 w/ Claire Kiehl]
  Copeland Bride, The

_____

_____

COLE, Marianne
                [Charlotte White]
  Second Chance At Love:
    101 Gentle Awakening
    171 Shining Promise

_____

_____

COLE, Sue Ellen
                [Sue Ellen Gross]
  Silhouette Intimate Moments:
    7   Distant Castle, A
    30 Race Against The Wind

_____

_____

COLETTE
  Claudine And Annie
  Claudine In Paris
  Claudine Married

_____

_____

COLLETT, Dorothy
  Avalon:
    Troubled Kisses

_____

_____

COLLINS, Kathryn
  SuperRomance:
    97 Wings Of Night, The

_____

_____

COLLINS, Marion Smith
                    (Marion Smith)
    Harlequin Temptation:
        5 By Mutual Consent
       20 By Any Other Name

COLLINS, Susanna
                    [Sue Ellen Gross]
    Second Chance At Love:
        94 Breathless Dawn
       134 Parisan Nights
       172 Wrapped In Rainbows
       201 Brief Enchantment

COLLINS, Wilkie   <GOT>
    Lady Of Glenwith Grange, The
    Moonstone, The
    Woman In White, The
    Yellow Mask, The

COMBS, Becky
    Loveswept:
        23 Taking Savannah

COMFORT, Iris
    Starlight Romance:
        Shadow Masque   *

COMPTON, Anne
    Warrior Wives

CONARAIN, Alice 'Nina'
                    (Elizabeth Hoy)

CONAWAY, James   <HO>
                    (Leila Lyons)
                    (Vanessa Valcour)
    World's End

CONKLIN, Barbara
    Sweet Dreams: <YA>
        36 Summer Dreams

CONLEY, Karen
    Passion's Firebird

CONN, Phoebe   <HR>
    Love's Elusive Flame
    Savage Fire

CONNOLLY, Vivian
                    (Susanna Rosse)
    SuperRomance:
        63 Love In Exile
    To Have And To Hold:
        10 I Know My Love
        21 Moonlight And Magnolias
        30 Promises To Keep

CONRAD, Helen
                    [Helen Manak Conrad]
                    (Jena Hunt)
                    (Raye Morgan)
    Dawnstar Romance:
        Heart Of Gold
    Harlequin Temptation:
        3 Everlasting

                    (cont'd)

33

CONRAD, Helen (continued)
  Loveswept:
    8 Temptation's Sting
  _____
  _____

CONROY, Janet   <GOT>
                 [Joseph Chadwick]
  Harlan Legacy, The   *
  _____
  _____

CONVERSE, Jane
                  [Adela Maritano]
  Silhouette Special Edition:
    117 Coral Sea, The
  _____
  _____

CONWAY, Celine
                  [Kathryn Blair]
  Harlequin Classic:
    113 At The Villa Massina (885)
    150 My Dear Cousin   (934)
  Other:
    Ships Surgeon   <M&B>
  _____
  _____

CONWAY, Theresa
  Tapestry: <HR>
    12 Love Chase
  _____
  _____

COOK, Ida
                  (Mary Burchell)

COOKSON, Catherine
              (Catherine Marchant)
               (Katie McMullen)
  Black Velvet Gown, The
  Whip, The
  _____
  _____

COOMBS, Nina
                   [Nina Pykare]
  Rapture Romance:
    1   Love So Fearful
    6   Passion's Domain
    32 Forbidden Joy
    56 Sun Spark
  _____
  _____

COONEY, Caroline B.
  Wildfire: <YA>
    An April Love Story
  Follow Your Heart Romance: <YA>
    3 Stage Set For Love, A
    4 Sun, Sea, And Boys
  _____
  _____

COOPER, Ann
  Harlequin Premiere III:
    26 MacLean's Woman
  Harlequin Romance:
    2630 Maelstrom
  _____
  _____

COPELAND, Frances
                  (Fran Fisher)

COPELAND, Lori
  Candlelight Ecstasy:
    134 Playing For Keeps
    181 Tempting Stranger, A
    217 All Or Nothing
    239 Out Of Control
    267 Winning Combination, The
    294 Rain Bow's End
  Candlelight Ecstasy Supreme:
    39 Two Of A King
  _____
  _____

CORBETT, Paula
  Silhouette Desire:
    156 Maid In Boston
  _____
  _____

CORBY, Jane
  Sharon Romance:
    House Next Door, The

_____

_____

CORCORAN, Dotti w/ Mary Ann
  SLOJKOWSKI
                    (DeAnn Patrick)

CORK, Dorothy
  Silhouette Romance:
    219 Island Spell
    238 Outback Dreaming
    286 Man From The Past, The
    304 Chosen Wife

_____

_____

CORRIE, Jane
  Harlequin Romance:
    2521 Ross's Girl
    2551 Man With Two Faces

_____

_____

CORSON, Martha
                      (Anne Lacey)
                   (Kristin Michaels)

COSCARELLI, Kate
  Fame And Fortune   <CO>

_____

COTT, Christine Hella
  SuperRomance:
    50 Dangerous Delight
    98 Perfume And Lace

_____

_____

COUGHLIN, Pat
                       (Liz Grady)

COULTER, Catherine
           [Jean Coulter Pogany]
  An Intimate Deception   <RE>
                         (cont'd)

COULTER, Catherine (continued)
    Sweet Surrender   <HR>
    Scarlet Ribbons: <HR>
      Chandra

_____

_____

COULTER, Stephen
  Chateau, The

_____

COURTER, Gay
  River Of Dreams

_____

COWAN, Dale
  Sweet Dreams: <YA>
    56 Campfire Nights

_____

COX, Eleanor Anne   <RE>
  Althea Bretleigh

_____

COY, Barbara
  First Love From Silhouette: <YA>
    51 Prairie Girl

_____

COY, Stanlee Miller w/ Carolyn
  NICHOLS
                     (Iona Charles)

CRAIG, Georgia
              [Peggy Gaddis Dern]
  Her Plantation Home
  Sharon Romance:
    Come Home Holly Lowman
  Sharon Contemporary Teens:
    Junior Prom Girl

_____

_____

CRAIG, Jasmine
                    [Jasmine Cresswell]
   Second Chance At Love:
      118 Imprisoned Heart
      170 Refuge In His Arms
      187 Surprised By Love
   To Have And To Hold:
      32 Under Cover Of Night

_____

_____

CRAIG, Mary
                    [Mary Francis Craig]
   Mistress Of Lost River (Ten
      Thousand Doors)   *
   Shadows Of The Past (The Cranes
      Of Ibycus)   *

_____

_____

CRAIG, Mary Francis
                         (Mary Craig)
                    (Mary Shura Craig)
                        (M. S. Craig)
                        (Alexis Hill)
                  (Mary Francis Shura)

CRAIG, Mary Shura   <HR>
                    [Mary Francis Craig]
   Lyon's Pride
   Pirate's Landing

_____

_____

CRAIG, M. S.
                    [Mary Francis Craig]
   Chicagoans: Dust To
      Diamonds   <Saga>

_____

_____

CRAIG, Rianna
                    [Sharron Harrington
                     w/ Rick Harrington]
   Harlequin American Romance:
      56 Love Match

_____

_____

CRANE, Leah
                         [Jean Hager]
   SuperRomance:
      66 Dark Ecstasy

_____

_____

CRANE, Teresa
   Molly

_____

_____

CRANMER, Kathryn
   Harlequin Romance:
      2620 Pas de Deux

_____

_____

CRAVEN, Sara
   Harlequin Presents:
      561 Counterfeit Bride
      599 Sup With The Devil
      616 Pagan Adversary
      647 Bad Enemy, A
      704 Dark Paradise

_____

_____

CRAVENS, Gwyneth
   Love And Work   <CO>

_____

_____

CRAWFORD, Alice Owen
   Sweet Dreams: <YA>
      59 Please Say Yes

_____

_____

CRAWFORD, Diane
                    [Georgette Livingston]
   Second Chance At Love:
      158 Season Of Marriage

_____

_____

CRAWFORD, Matsu
  A Hearth Romance:
    15   Love Is Like An Acorn

———————————————

———————————————

CREEL, Catherine   <HR>
  Breathless Passion

———————————————

———————————————

CRESSWELL, Jasmine
                (Jasmine Craig)
                (Cynthia James)
  Silhouette Desire:
    113 Mixed Doubles

———————————————

———————————————

CREWE, Sarah
                [Virginia Blanford]
  Second Chance At Love:
    135 Golden Illusions
    195 Night Flame

———————————————

———————————————

CRISTY, Ann
                [Helen Mittermeyer]
  Second Chance At Love:
    103 Enthralled
    166 No Gentle Possession
    223 Mystique
  To Have And To Hold:
    3   Tread Softly
    24 Homecoming

———————————————

———————————————

CROCKETT, Christina
  SuperRomance:
    55   To Touch A Dream
                    (cont'd)

CROCKETT, Christina (continued)
  Harlequin SuperRomance:
    103 Moment Of Magic, A

———————————————

———————————————

CROISSANT, Kay w/ Catherine DEES
                (Catherine Kay)

CROMWELL, Elsie
                [Elsie Lee]
  Governess, The (Eng: Guardian
    Of Love)

———————————————

———————————————

CRONE, Alla   <HO>
  North Of The Moon
  Winds Over Manchuria

———————————————

———————————————

CRONIN, A. J.
  Three Loves

———————————————

———————————————

CROSS, Victor   <GOT>
                [Virginia Coffman]
  Blood Sport

———————————————

———————————————

CROWE, Cecily
  Miss Spring

———————————————

———————————————

CROWE, Evelyn A.
  Harlequin SuperRomance:
    112 Summer Ballad

———————————————

———————————————

CUMMINGS, Monette   <RE>
                 [Mona Cummings]
  Lady Sheila's Groom
  See No Love
  _____

  _____

CUNNINGHAM, Jan
                 (Chelsey Forrest)

CURRIE, Katy
              [Susan Spaeth Kyle]
  Silhouette Inspirations:
    5 Blind Promises
  _____

  _____

CURRY, Elissa
                   [Nancy Martin]
  Fair Kate   <HO>
  Second Chance At Love:
    174 Trial By Desire
    178 Winter Wildfire
    193 Lady With A Past
    213 Black Lace And Pearls
  To Have And To Hold:
    18 Playing For Keeps
    23 Kiss Me Cait
  _____

  _____

CURTIS, Richard Hale   <HO>
  Skymasters Series: (continued)
    5 Birds Of War   *
                   [John Toombs]
    6 Wind Nor Rain Nor Dark Of
       Night
                   [Robert Kail]
    7 Aviatrix, The
                   [Dan Streib]
    8 Every Man An Eagle
                   [Len Levinson]
    9 Through Clouds Of Flame
    10 Cry Of The Condor
  _____

  _____

CURTIS, Sharon and Tom
                 [Thomas Dale Curtis
                   w/ Sharon Curtis]
                     (Robin James)
                    (Laura London)
  Loveswept:
    25 Lightning That Lingers
  _____

  _____

CURZON, Lucia
              [Florence Stevenson]
  Second Chance At Love:
    123 Dashing Guardian, The <RE>
  _____

  _____

CUTHRELL, Faith Baldwin
                  (Faith Baldwin)

D

DAGG, Jillian
                  (Marilyn Brian)
                  (Jillian Fayre)
                  (Faye Wildman)

DAHEIM, Mary   <HR>
  Destiny's Pawn
  Love's Pirate
  _____

  _____

DAILEY, Janet
  Silver Wings, Santiago Blue
  Calder Series: (continued)
  Calder Born, Calder Bred
                   (end)
  Silhouette Romance:
    153 Wildcatter's Woman   *
    195 Mistletoe And Holly   *
    213 Separate Cabins
    231 Western Man
  Silhouette Special Editions:
    132 Best Way To Lose, The
    150 Leftover Love
  _____

  _____

DAIR, Christina
                [Louzana Kaku]
  Second Chance At Love:
    217 Winning Ways

DAISH, Elizabeth
  Portrait In Pastel

DALE, Jennifer
              [Charlotte White]
  Rapture Romance:
    7 Tender Rhapsody
   17 Remember My Love
   27 Frostfire

DALEY, Kit
             [Margaret Daley]
  Candlelight Ecstasy:
   205 Dance For Two
   293 And One Makes Five

DALEY, Margaret
          (Kathleen Daley)
              (Kit Daley)
           (Patti Moore)
        (Margaret Ripy)

DALTON, Elyse
  Adventure In Love:
    Mirror Of The Heart

DALTON, Gena
        [Genell Dellin Smith]
  Silhouette Special Edition:
   69 Sorrel Sunset
  147 April Encounter

DALTON, Jenifer   <HR>
               [David Wind]
  Run On The Wind

DALY, Saralyn
  In The Web
  Love's Joy, Love's Pain

DALZELL, Helen
  Harlequin Premiere III:
    27 In Search Of Mary Ann
  Harlequin Romance:
  2570 Not The Marrying Kind

DAMIO, Ward
        (see Rebecca Drury)
  (see Lee Davis Willoughby <MOAS>)

DAMON, Lee
            [Jane H. Look]
  Second Chance At Love:
   120 Laugh With Me, Love With
       Me
  To Have And To Hold:
    16 Lady Laughing Eyes

DANELLA, Utta
      [Franz Schneekluth Verlag]
  Those Von Tallien Women

DANIEL, Megan   <RE>
              [Donna Meyer]
  American Bride, The

DANIELS, Carol   <HR>
                    [Carol Viens]
  Valley Of Dreams

_____

_____

DANIELS, Dorothy
                 (Danielle Dorsett)
                 (Angela Gray)
                 (Cynthia Kavanaugh)
                 (Suzanne Somers)
                 (Geraldine Thayer)
                 (Helen Gray Weston)
  In Sequence: *
    Sisters Of Valcour
    For Love Of Valcour

_____

_____

DANIELS, Laura
  McFadden Romance:
     24 Dream And The Dance, The *

_____

DANIELS, Norman
  Wyndward: In sequence: *
    Wyndward Passion
    Wyndward Fury
    Wyndward Peril
    Wyndward Glory
    Forever Wyndward

_____

_____

DANIELS, Rhett
                    [Judy Pelfrey]
  Silhouette Special Edition:
    184 Overtures Of The Heart

_____

_____

DANIELS, Velma S. w/ Peggy E. KING
  Serenade/Serenata: <INSP>
     6 Fountain Of Love

_____

_____

DANIELSON, Peter   <HO>
  Children Of The Lion: <Saga>
    (continued)
     4 Lion In Egypt, The

_____

_____

DAOUST, Pamela
                 (Katharine Kincaid)

DARCY, Clare   <RE>
  Trilogy: *
    Cecily
    Georgina
    Lydia

_____

_____

DARCY, Emma
  Harlequin Presents:
    648 Twisting Shadows
    680 Tangle Of Torment

_____

_____

DARRELL, Elizabeth   <HO>
  Gathering Wolves, The

_____

_____

DARWIN, Jeanette
                    [Candace Schuler]
  Rapture Romance:
     87 Cherished Account, A

_____

_____

DAVESON, Mons
  Harlequin Romance:
    2534 My Lord Kasseem
    2575 MacKenzie Country

_____

_____

DAVIDS, Marilyn
                    [David Wind]
  Rapture Romance:
    50 Love So Fresh, A

_____

_____

DAVIDSON, Andrea
                [Susan L. Lowe]
  Harlequin American Romance:
    16 Music In The Night
    21 Untamed Possession
    45 Treasures Of The Heart
  Harlequin American Romance
    Premiere Edition:
      Golden Cage, The

_____

_____

DAVIDSON, Vickie
  Velvet Glove:
    Secret Love

_____

_____

DAVIES, Frances
                [Leone Lewensohn]
  Second Chance At Love:
    146 Taste For Loving, A
    192 Love Thy Neighbor

_____

_____

DAVIS, Diane
                    (Delaney Devers)

DAVIS, Gwen   <CO>
  Marriage
  R.O.M.A.N.C.E.   <CO>

_____

_____

DAVIS, John Gordon   <HO>
  Cape Of Storms
  Hold My Hand I'm Dying
  Taller Than Trees
  Years Of The Hungry Tiger, The

_____

_____

DAVIS, Kathryn   <HO>
  The Dakotas Series: In sequence:
    At The Wind's Edge
    Endless Sky, The

_____

_____

DAVIS, Mildred   <GOT>
  Room Upstairs, The

_____

_____

DAVIS, Wendi
            [Nancy L. Jones Holder]
  First Love From Silhouette: <YA>
    46 Sealed With A Kiss

_____

_____

DAY, Jocelyn
                [Lorena McCourtney]
  Second Chance At Love:
    128 Marrying Kind, The
    150 Island Fires
    196 Sometimes A Lady

_____

_____

DEAN, Karen Strickler   <YA>
  Maggie Adams, Dancer
  Mariana

_____

_____

DEAN, Nell Marr
  Trials Of Dr. Carol, The

_____

_____

De ANDREA, William L.
  (see Lee Davis Willoughby <MOAS>)

DEANE, Sonia
  Betrayal Of Doctor Vane, The<M&B>

_____

_____

De BLASIS, Celeste   <HO>
  In sequence:
    Wild Swan

_____

De BOER, Marjorie   <HO>
  Crown Of Desire
  Unwelcome Suitor, The   <RE>

_____

de COVARRUBIAS, Barbara Faith
                    (Barbara Faith)

DEE, D. J.
  Avalon:
    Nurse Mickey's Crisis

_____

DEE, Sherry
            [Sheryl Hines Flournoy]
  Silhouette Desire:
    63 Share Your Tomorrows   *

_____

DEES, Catherine w/ Kay CROISSANT
                    (Catherine Kay)

De GAMEZ, Tana
  Like A River Of Lions
  Yoke And The Star, The

_____

De JAY SCOTT, Marianne   <GOT>
  Van Dyne Collection, The

_____

de JOURLET, Marie
                    [Paul Little]
  Windhaven Series: (continued)
    Windhaven's Destiny
    Windhaven's Hope
            (end)

_____

DELANEY, Laurence
  Blood Red Wine

_____

De LAUER, Marjel
  Where Rivers Run Gold

_____

De LEON, Ana Lisa
                    (Marisa de Zavala)
                    (Rachel Scott)
  Harlequin American Romance:
    61 Kiss Goodnight and Say
            Good-bye

_____

DELINSKY, Barbara
                    (Billie Douglass)
                    (Bonnie Drake)
  Fingerprints
  Harlequin Temptation:
     4 Special Something, A
    17 Bronze Mystique

_____

DELLIN, Genell
            [Genell Dellin Smith]
  First Love From Silhouette: <YA>
    42 Promises To Come

_____

DELMORE, Diana   <RE>
  Anthea
  Leonie
  _____

  _____

DeLONG, Claire
                    (Eve Claire)
                    (Claire Evans)

DeLYONNE, Susan
                [Sue Ellen Gross]
  6 Days, 5 Nights
  _____

  _____

DEMING, Richard
          (see Richard Hale Curtis)
  (see Lee Davis Willoughby <MOAS>)

DENNIS, Roberta
  Silhouette Desire:
    60 Between The Lines
  _____

  _____

DeNORRE, Rochel
                [Roberta Dennore]
  Woman Of New Orleans, A <AWD:#2>
  _____

  _____

DENT, Roxanne   <HO>
                (Melissa Masters)
  Bitter Harvest
  _____

  _____

DENYS, Teresa   <HR>
  Silver Devil, The
  _____

  _____

DERN, Peggy   (deceased)
                  (Peggy Gaddis Dern)
                    (Georgia Craig)
                     (Peggy Gaddis)
                      (Gail Jordan)
                    (Perry Lindsay)
  Harlequin Classic:
    Nora Was A Nurse   <PROM>
  _____

  _____

De ST. JEOR, Owanna
  Judy Sullivan Books:
    Bad Timing   <RS>
  _____

  _____

DEUVAUL, Virginia C.
                [Virginia Coffman]
  Masque By Gaslight   <ENG>
  _____

  _____

DEVERAUX, Jude   <HR>
                [Jude Gilliam White]
  Montgomery Brothers Saga:
    (series continued)
    Velvet Angel   *
      (end)
  Tapestry: <HR>
    15 Sweetbriar   *
  The James River Trilogy:
    Counterfeit Lady
    Lost Lady
    River Lady
  The Twins: <2-Books> <85-86>
    Houston Chandler
    Blair Chandler
  _____

  _____

de VERE, Jane   <ENG><HO>
                    [Julia Watson]
  Scarlet Women, The
  _____

  _____

43

DEVERS, Delaney
                [Diane Davis]
  To Have And To Hold:
    40 Heart Victorious, A

_____

_____

DEVOE, Lily   <CO>
  For Love Of A Stranger

_____

_____

DEVON, Anne
          [Marian Pope Rettke]
  Second Chance At Love:
    105 Defiant Mistress   <RE>

_____

DeWEESE, Jean   <GOT>
          [Eugene DeWeese]
  Starlight Romance:
    Backhoe Gothic, The

_____

_____

DIAMOND, Jacqueline   <RE>
          [Jacqueline Hyman]
  Forgetful Lady, The
  Lady In Disguise
  Lady Of Letters, A
  Song For A Lady
  Harlequin American Romance:
    79 Dream Never Dies, The

_____

_____

DIAMOND, Petra
            [Judith Sacks]
  To Have And To Hold:
    31 Confidentially Yours

_____

_____

DIAMOND, Suzanne
  All She Wants

_____

DICKENS, Monica
  Room Upstairs, The

_____

_____

DIDION, Joan
  Democracy

_____

_____

DI DONATO, Georgia   <HO>
  Woman Of Justice

_____

_____

DINGWELL, Joyce
             (Kate Starr)
  Harlequin Classic:
    112 Third In The House, The
                    (894)
  Harlequin Premiere III:
    28 Man Like Brady, A
  Harlequin Romance:
  2600 Brother Wolf

_____

_____

DIONNE, Leah
  Caprice Romance: <YA>
    32 Love Notes

_____

_____

DIXON, Diana
  Silhouette Special Edition:
    87 Jessica: Take Two
    99 Quest For Paradise
    120 Lia's Daughter
    174 No Strings

_____

_____

DIXON, Dorothy
  Cimarron Rose   <L&L:#5>
  Diamond Queen   <L&L:#7>
  Yellowstone Jewel   <L&L:#9>

_____

DIXON, Rhonda
  Judy Sullivan Books:
    Man Around The House   <CO>
_____

_____

DOBSON, Margaret
  Candlelight Ecstasy:
    145 Cactus Rose
    173 Restless Wind
    211 Tender Journey
  Candlelight Ecstasy Supreme:
    30 Eventide
_____

_____

DOMINIQUE, Meg
                    [Annette Sanford]
  Harlequin Temptation:
    2 When Stars Fall Down
_____

_____

DOMNING, Joan J.
  Loveswept:
    12 Hunter's Payne
    13 Tiger Lady
    19 Pfarr Lake Affair
    39 Kirsten's Inheritance
    54 Gypsy And The
          Yachtsman, The
    63 Lahti's Apple
_____

_____

DONALD, Robyn
  Harlequin Presents:
    567 Mansion For My Love
    623 Guarded Heart, The
    631 Return To Yesterday
    649 An Old Passion
    665 Gates Of Rangitatau, The
    696 Durable Fire, A
_____

_____

DONNE, John
  Love Poems Of John Donne
_____

_____

DONNELLY, Jane
  Harlequin Romance:
    2552 Call Up The Storm
    2576 Face The Tiger
    2635 Fierce Encounter, A
    2649 Moonlady
_____

_____

DORE, Christy
                    [Jim Plagakis]
  Torchlite:
    Passionate Awakening
_____

_____

DORIEN, Ray   <GOT>
  House Of Dread, The
  Noonday Nurse
_____

_____

DORSETT, Daniella   <GOT>
                    [Dorothy Daniels]
  Dueling Oaks, The
_____

_____

DOUGLAS, Carole Nelson
  Lady Rogue   <HR>
  Love & Life:
    Bestman, The
_____

_____

DOUGLAS, Casey
                    [June E. Casey]
  SuperRomance:
    56 Proud Surrender
    75 Dance-Away Lover
                          (cont'd)

45

DOUGLAS, Casey (continued)
  Harlequin SuperRomance:
    107 Edge Of Illusion

_____

_____

DOUGLASS, Billie
                    [Barbara Delinsky]
  Silhouette Desire:
    38 Sweet Serenity
    56 Flip Side Of Yesterday
    74 Beyond Fantasy
  Silhouette Special Edition:
    80 Fast Courting
    123 An Irresistible Impulse
   ●133 Carpenter's Lady, The

_____

_____

DOWNES, Kathleen
  Loveswept:
    49 Man Next Door, The

_____

_____

DOYLE, Emily
                    [Betty L. Henrichs]
  Silhouette Special Edition:
    95 Matter Of Trust, A

_____

_____

DRAKE, Asa
            [C. Dean Andersson w/
               Nina R. Andersson]
  Crimson Kisses
  Lair Of Ancient Dreams, The

_____

_____

DRAKE, Bonnie
                    [Barbara Delinsky]
  Candlelight Ecstasy:
    114 Lover From The Sea
    132 Silver Fox, The
  ● 146 Passion And Illusion
                          (cont'd)

DRAKE, Bonnie (continued)
    186 Gemstone
    219 Moment To Moment

_____

_____

DRUMMOND, Emma   <HO>
  Beyond All Frontiers

_____

_____

DRUMMOND, June   <RS>
  Farewell Party

_____

_____

DRUMMOND, William   <GOT>
  Gaslight

_____

_____

DRURY, Rebecca   <HO>
  Women At War Series: (continued)
    8 Sisters Of Battle
                [Robert Thompson]
    9 Savage Beauty
                [Jane Toombs]
    10 Splendid Victory
                [Greg Hunt]
    11 Darkness At Dawn
                [Will Holt]
    12 Courage At Sea
                [Ward Damio]
    13 Valient Wings
                [Neal Barrett, Jr.]
    14 Distant Thunder

    15 Desert Battle
                [Hugh Zachry]
    16 Bitter Victory
                [Hugh Zachry]
    17 Inchon Diary
                [Adrien Lloyd]
    18 Mission To Darkness
                [Greg Hunt]

_____

_____

DRYMON, Kathleen   <HR>
   Texas Blossom
   Wild Desires

   _____

   _____

DUBAY, Sandra
   Whispers Of Passion

   _____

   _____

DUKORE, Jesse
   Sweet Dreams: <YA>
      29 Never Love A Cowboy
      44 Long Distance Love

   _____

   _____

DUNAWAY, Diane
   Candlelight Ecstasy:
      158 Desire And Conquer

   _____

   _____

DUNCAN, Judith
             [Judith Mulholland]
   SuperRomance:
      51 Tender Rhapsody
      77 Hold Back The Dawn
   Harlequin SuperRomance:
      114 Reach The Splendor

   _____

   _____

DUNN, Carola   <RE>
   Angel
   Lavender Lady

   _____

   _____

DUNNE, Marjo
   First Love From Silhouette: <YA>
      61 Here Comes Kary

   _____

   _____

DUPREY, Richard
   Silver Wings

   _____

   _____

DUREAU, Lorena
   Lynette
   Tapestry: <HR>
      9 Iron Lace

   _____

   _____

DURHAM, Marilyn
   Flambard's Confession

   _____

   _____

DUVALL, Aimee
             [Aimee Martel Thurlo]
   Second Chance At Love:
      159 Loving Touch, The
      179 After The Rain
      211 One More Tomorrow

   _____

   _____

DWYER-JOYCE, Alice   <RS>
   Penny Box, The
   Strolling Players, The
   Unwinding Corner, The
   Gibbet Fen

   _____

   _____

DYMOKE, Juliet: <HO>
   The Plantagenets:
      Pride Of Kings, The
      Royal Griffin, The
      Lady Of The Garter
      Lion Of Mortimer, The
      Lord Of Greenwich, The
      Sun In Splendour, The

   _____

   _____

E

EADE, Charles w/ Ursula BLOOM
(Lozania Prole)

EATON, Evelyn   <HO>
[Evelyn Sybil Mary Eaton]
Restless Are The Sails

EATON, Laura
Second Chance At Love:
181 Rushing Tide

EBERT, Alan w/ Janice ROTCHSTEIN
Traditions

ECKERSLEY, Jill
[Helen Beaumont]
Sapphire Romance: <ENG>
Little Loving, A

ECKERT, Allan W.   <HO>
Gateway To Empire

EDEN, Laura
[Claire Harrison]
Silhouette Romance:
210 Flight Of Fancy

EDGAR, Josepine
[Mary Mussi]
Margaret Normanby   <HO>

EDGEWORTH, Ann
Sapphire Romance: <ENG>
Barriers Of Love

EDMONDS, Walter D.
Young Ames

EDWARDS, Adrienne
[Anne Kolaczyk
w/ Ed Kolaczyk]
To Have And To Hold:
29 Honorable Intentions

EDWARDS, Andrea
[Anne Kolaczyk
w/ Ed Kolaczyk]
The Avon Romance:
Corporate Affair
Now Comes The Spring
Power Play

EDWARDS, Cassie   <HR>
Elusive Ecstasy
Forbidden Embrace (title was
changed from "Enchanted Enemy"
Passion's Web
Secrets Of My Heart
Silken Rapture
In sequence:
Savage Obsession
Savage Innocence

EDWARDS, Estelle
[Mollie Gregory]
Rapture Romance:
21 Moonslide
47 Knave Of Hearts, The

EDWARDS, Kathryn
  Torch:
    Broken Promises
  Torchlite:
    Surrender Of Wills

_____

_____

ELIOT, Winslow
                    (Ellie Winslow)

ELLERBECK, Rosemary
                  (Anna L'Estrange)
                  (Nicole Thorne)
                  (Katherine Yorke)

ELLINGSON, Marnie   <RE>
  Dolly Blanchard's Fortune
  Wicked Marquis, The

_____

_____

ELLIOT, Douglass   <HO>
  American Patriot Series:
   (continued)
    Bold Destiny

_____

_____

ELLIOTT, Nancy
                  (Ellen Langtry)

ELLIOTT, Emily
                  [Emily Mims]
  Candlelight Ecstasy:
    140 Portrait Of My Love
    182 Delicate Balance
    200 Midnight Memories
    223 Morning's Promise
    252 Matter Of Judgement, A
  Candlelight Ecstasy Supreme:
    20   Just His Touch
    34   Dangerous Attraction, A

_____

_____

ELLIS, Audrey
  Jenetta

_____

_____

ELLIS, Julie
                    (Susan Marino)
  East Wind

_____

_____

ENDERLE, Judith
  Caprice Romance: <YA>
    30   When Wishes Come True
         Sealed With A Kiss
         Programmed For Love
         Someone For Sara
         Cheer Me On
    39   Sing A Song Of Love

_____

_____

ENFIELD, Carrie
  First Love From Silhouette: <YA>
    38   Secret Admirer
    54   Picture Perfect
    62   Secret Admirer

_____

_____

ENGELS, Mary Tate
                    (Tate McKenna)

ENGLISH, Genevieve
                    [Sarah Patton]
  Silhouette Romance:
    259 French Confection, The

_____

_____

ERICKSON, Lynn   <HR>
                  [Carla Peltonen
                   w/ Molly Swanton]
  Dawnfire
  Woman Of San Francisco, A<AWD:#1>

_____

_____

49

ERICKSON, Roger
  Maggie And David

ERNEST, Jeanette
            [Judy Wells Martin]
  Rapture Romance:
     3 Lover's Liar   *
    12 Dear Doubter

ERSKINE, Andra
            [Judy Wells Martin]
  Rapture Romance:
    84 Priority Affair

ESSEX, Marianna
  Rapture Romance:
    41 Torrent Of Love
    92 Love Came Courting

ESTRADA, Rita Clay
                    (Rita Clay)
                    (Tira Lacy)

EVANS, Claire
            [Claire DeLong]
  Second Chance At Love:
   115 Come Winter's End

EVANS, Laurel
  Silhouette Desire:
   144 Business After Hours

EVENS, Lori
  Avalon:
    Autumn Kisses

EYERLY, Jeannette   <YA>
  More Than A Summer Love

F

FABIAN Erika
  Harlequin SuperRomance:
   116 Sky Riders

FAIN, Michael w/ Judith BARNARD
                    (Judith Michael)

FAIRBAIRNS, Zoe   <HO>
  Stand We At Last   <Saga>

FAIRFAX, Gwen
            [Mary Jo Territo]
  Candlelight Ecstasy:
   213 Lover In Disguise

FAIRFAX, Kate
            [Irene Ord]
  Sweet Fire (Eng: 'Wild Honey')

FAIRFAX, Lynn
  Second Chance At Love:
    96 Guarded Moments

FAIRMAN, Paula
                    [Robert Vaughn]
   Passion's Promise
   River Of Passion

_____

_____

FAITH, Barbara
   [Barbara Faith de Covarrubias]
   Silhouette Intimate Moments:
      16 Promise Of Summer, The
      47 Wind Whispers
      63 Bedouin Bride

_____

_____

FARNES, Eleanor
   Harlequin Classic:
      131 Magic Symphony   (998)
      138 Happy Enterprise, The(487)
      149 Dream And The
              Dancer, The   (912)

_____

_____

FARNSWORTH, Mona   <GOT>
   House Of Whispering Death, The

_____

_____

FARRAR, Helen Graham   <GOT>
   How Evil The Word
   Web Begun

_____

_____

FASSHAUER, Susan C.
                    (Susan Chatfield)

FAST, Howard   <HO>
   Max

_____

_____

FAULKNER, Florence
   Avalon:
      Challenge For Two, A

_____

_____

FAULKNER, Whitney
                    [Elaine Bissell]
   The American Dream:<5-Book> <HO>
      In sequence:
         Emily's Destiny
         Jane's Promise
         Kathryn's Quest

_____

_____

FEDDERSEN, Connie
                     (Carol Finch)

FEIFFER, Judy   <YA>
   Lovecrazy

_____

_____

FELDHAKE, Susan C.
   Serenade/Serenata: <INSP>
      2 Love's Sweet Promise
      3 For Love alone

_____

_____

FELDMAN, Ellen 'Bette'
                    (Amanda Russell)
                   (Elizabeth Villars)

FERGUSON, Janet
   Sister Of Musgrave Ward   <M&B>

_____

_____

FERRARI, Ivy
   Sister At Ryeminster   <M&B>

_____

_____

FERRIS, Rose Marie
                    (Valerie Ferris)
                    (Robin Francis)
                   (Michelle Roland)
   Candlelight Ecstasy:
      207 Bristol's Law

_____

_____

FIANDT, Mary K.
  Willow Cabin.

_____

_____

FIELD, Penelope   <GOT>
              [Dorothy Giberson]
  Someone Is Watching

_____

_____

FIELD, Sandra
              (Jocelyn Haley)
  Harlequin Presents:
    568 Walk By My Side
    639 An Attraction Of Opposites
    681 Mistake In Identity, A
  Harlequin Romance:
    2577 Tides Of Summer, The

_____

_____

FIELD, Sandra w/ Anne MacLEAN
              (Jan MacLean)

FIELDING, Joy
  Other Woman, The

_____

_____

FILICHIA, Peter
  Two By Two Romance: <YA>
      8 Falling In Love

_____

_____

FILLINGHAM, Jan
  Lover's Landscape

_____

_____

FINCH, Carol   <HR>
              [Connie Feddersen]
  Dawn's Desire
  Endless Passion

                    (cont'd)

FINCH, Carol (continued)
  Passion's Vixen

_____

_____

FINLEY, Glenna
  Finley Series: (continued)
    32 Business Affair, A
    33 Wanted For Love
    34 Bridal Affair
    35 Weekend For Love, A

_____

_____

FIRTH, Susanna
  Harlequin Presents:
    624 Master Of Shadows
  Harlequin Romance:
    2564 Lions Walk Alone

_____

_____

FISCH, Mildred
              (Megan Alexander)

FISHER, Fran
              [Frances Copeland]
  First Love From Silhouette: <YA>
    50 Stay, Sweet Love

_____

_____

FISHER, Lois I.
  Sweet Dreams: <YA>
    30 Little White Lies
    54 I Can't Forget You

_____

_____

FITZGERALD, Amber
              (Nancy T. Smith)
  Starlight Romance:
    Reluctant Lover   *

_____

_____

```
FITZGERALD, Arlene          <HR>
  Windfire

_____

_____

FITZGERALD, Julia           <HR>
                   [Julia Watson]
  Fallen Woman              <ENG>
  Firebird
  Jeweled Serpent, The
  Princess And The Pagan, The
  Salamander
  Venus Rising
  In sequence:
    Royal Slave                 *
    Slave Lady              <ENG>
  Habsburg Series:          <ENG>
    Changeling Queen
    Emperor's Daughter
    Habsburg Inheritance
    Pearl Of Habsburg
    Snow Queen

_____

_____

FITZGERALD, Maeve
                   [Maura Seger]
  Circle Of Love:
    Once And Forever        <ENG>

_____

_____

FLANDERS, Rebecca
                   [Donna Ball]
  Harlequin American Romance:
    Twice In A Lifetime <PROM>
     6  Matter Of Trust, A
    24  Best Of Friends
    41  Suddenly Love
    51  Gilded Heart
    58  Second Sight
    66  Desert Fire
    74  Third Time, The
    83  Daydreams
    89  Sometimes It's Forever
  Harlequin Intrigue:
     1  Key, The
        Silver Threads

                     (cont'd)

FLANDERS, Rebecca (continued)
  Harlequin Presents:
   632  Morning Song
   666  Falkone's Promise
  Harlequin Romance:
  2623  Modern Girl, A

_____

_____

FLEMING, Lee
                   (Ginny Haymond)

FLEMING, Thomas             <HO>
  Dreams Of Glory

_____

_____

FLETCHER, Aaron             <HO>
  In sequence:
    Outback                     *
    Capricorn People, The
  New Zealanders Series:
    In sequence:
    Castaway, The

_____

_____

FLOURNOY, Sheryl
           [Sheryl Hines Flournoy]
                   (Sherry Dee)
  Tapestry:                 <HR>
    33  Destiny's Embrace

_____

_____

FOLEY, June
  Young Love:               <YA>
    Love By Any Other Name

_____

_____

FOOTE, Victoria
  Tapestry:                 <HR>
    21  Snow Princess

_____

_____
```

FORBES, Cabot L.   <HO>
  The Bradford Saga: *
    No. 14 Washington Place   1
    Two West 57th Street   2
    Seven Fifty Park Avenue   3
  _____

  _____

FORREST, Chelsey
                     [Jan Cunningham]
  Silhouette Romance:
    272 An Artist's Touch
  _____

  _____

FORVE, Guy
                     [Guy Cimbalo]
  Alexander MacKenzie: Lone
    Courage   <AES:#12>
  _____

  _____

FOSTER, Stephanie
  Sweet Dreams: <YA>
    58 Rhythm Of Love
  _____

  _____

FOWLER, Penny w/ Dennis FOWLER
                     (Lauren Fox)

FOX, Gardner   <HO>
                     (Lynna Cooper)
  Savage Passage
  _____

  _____

FOX, Lauren
                     [Penny Fowler w/
                      Dennis Fowler]
  Second Chance At Love:
    177 Sparring Partners
    197 Country Pleasures
  _____

  _____

FOXX, Rosalind
                     [June Haydon w/
                      Judy Simpson]
  Flame Against The Wind
  _____

  _____

FRANCIS, Clare
  Night Sky
  _____

  _____

FRANCIS, Dorothy
           [Dorothy Brenner Francis]
                     (Ellen Goforth)
                        (Pat Louis)
  First Love From Silhouette: <YA>
    41 Just Friends?
    82 Kiss Me, Kit
  _____

  _____

FRANCIS, Robin
                  [Rose Marie Ferris]
  Harlequin American Romance:
    38 Memories Of Love
    88 Season Of Dreams, A
  _____

  _____

FRANCIS, Sara
  Harlequin Romance:
    2624 Kate's Way
  _____

  _____

FRANCIS, Sharon
                     [Maureen Wartski]
  Second Chance At Love:
    161 Earthly Splendor
    212 Silken Longing
  _____

  _____

FRANKEL, Ruby
                     (Rebecca Bennett)
                     (Constance Conrad)
                     (Lillian Marsh)

FRASER, Alison
  Harlequin Presents:
    697 Princess
    721 Price Of Freedom
_____

_____

FRASER, Jane
                (Rosamunde Pilcher)
  Harlequin Classic:
    135 Young Bar   (958)
_____

_____

FRASER, Kathleen   <HR>
                [Margaret Ball]
  Highland Flame
_____

_____

FREDERICK, Thea
                [Barbara Keiler]
  Second Chance At Love:
    204 Beloved Adversary
_____

_____

FREED, Lynn
  Heart Change   <CO>
_____

_____

FREEMAN, Joy
                (Beverly Sommers)

FREMANTLE, Anne
                (Lady Caroline Lamb)

FRENCH, Janie
  Starlight Romance:
    Candidate For Love
_____

_____

FRIENDS, Jalynn   <HR>
                [Rosalyn Alsobrook
                 w/ Jean Haught]
  Texas Rapture
_____

_____

FRITCH, Elizabeth   <HO>
  Tides Of Rapture
  California Series: In sequence:
    Passion's Trail
    Golden Fires
_____

_____

FRITZGERALD, Nancy
  Grover Square
  Mayfair
_____

_____

FROST, Eleanor
                [Elsa Frohman]
    53 Elusive Paradise
    68 Public Affair, A
_____

_____

FROST, Joan
  Masque Of Chameleons, A
_____

_____

FULFORD, Paula
  Silhouette Desire:
    54 If Ever You Need Me
_____

_____

FURSTENBERG-FORBES, Lyn
  Hanover Heritage
_____

_____

G

GADDIS, Peggy
                [Peggy Gaddis Dern]
  Changing Heart, The (Nurse was
    Juliet, The)
  Frost In April
  Lady Doctor
  Harlequin Classic:
    City Nurse
    Doctor Sara   (544)*

GADSDEN, Angela
  Dawnstar Romance:
    Cinderella Charade

GAZDAK, D. H. w/ Karen RAY
               (Ann Bernadette)

GAIR, Diana
  Harlequin Romance:
   2530 Jungle Antagonist

GALIARDI, Spring
            (Spring Hermann)

GALT, Serena
  Silhouette Desire:
   149 Double Game

GAMEL, Nona
  Candlelight Ecstasy:
   265 Love's Secret Garden

GANN, Ernest K.   <HO>
  Benjamin Lawless
                (cont'd)

GANN, Ernest K. (continued)
  Blaze Of Noon
  Encounter, The
  Fiddler's Green
  Of Good And Evil
  Trouble With Lazy Ethel

GARDNER, Joy
               [Joy Aumente]
  Tapestry: <HR>
    Fortune's Bride

GARDNER, Majorie H.
  Avalon:
    Forbidden Reunion
    Heart Song
    Question Of Loving, A

GARLAND, Nicholas
  Crime Of Innocence, A   <CO>

GARLAND, Sherry
             (Lynn Lawrence)

GARLOCK, Dorothy
         (Dorothy Phillips)
         (Johanna Phillips)
  Annie Lash
  Forever Victoria
  Wild, Sweet Wilderness
  Loveswept:
    6 Love For All Time, A
   13 Dangerous Embrace
   33 Planting Season, The

GARRETT, George   <HO>
  Succession, The

GARRETT, Sally
  SuperRomance:
    90 Until Forever

GARRISON, Joan
         [William Arthur Neubauer]
  This Remembered Glory
  When The Moon Laughs

GARTNER, Chloe   <HR>
  Still Falls The Rain

GARVICE, Charles   (deceased)
                     (Caroline Hart)
                   (Carolyn G.Hart)

GAYLE, Margaret
  SuperRomance:
    52 Precious Interlude
  Harlequin SuperRomance:
    118 To Catch The Wind

GAYNOR, Anne   <HR>
  Rebel Rapture

GELLIS, Roberta   <HO>
                (Max Daniels <SF>)
                (Priscilla Hamilton)
  Heiress Series: (continued)
    Fortune's Bride, (title was   *
      changed from "Indian Heiress")

GELMAN, Jan
  Follow Your Heart Romance: <YA>
    1 Summer In The Sun
                          (cont'd)

GELMAN, Jan (continued)
    5 Faraway Loves

GEORGE, Catherine
  Harlequin Presents:
    640 Gilded Cage
    698 Imperfect Chaperone
    722 Devil Within
  Harlequin Romance:
    2535 Reluctant Paragon
    2571 Dream Of Midsummer

GIBBONS, Marion Chesney
                (Marion Chesney)
                (Helen Crampton)
                (Ann Fairfax)
                (Jennie Tremaine)

GIBERSON, Dorothy
                (Penelope Field)

GILBERT, Anna   <RS>
            [Marguerite Lazarus]
  Flowers For Lilian

GILBERT, Jacqueline
  Harlequin Presents:
    600 House Called Bellevigne, A
  Harlequin Romance:
    2631 Chequered Silence, The

GILES, Raymond   <HO>
  Sabrehill Plantation: *
    In sequence:
      Sabrehill
      Slaves Of Sabrehill
      Rebels Of Sabrehill
      Storm Over Sabrehill
      Hellcat Of Sabrehill

GILLESPIE, Jane
  Ladysmead (sequel to Mansfield
    Park By Jane Austen)
  Teverton Hall (sequel to Pride
    And Prejudice By Jane Austen)

_____

_____

GILMER, Ann
                        [W. E. D. Ross]
  Nurse On Call

_____

GILZEN, Elizabeth
                (Elizabeth Houghton)
                (Mary Hunton)
  Arctic Nurse   <M&B>

_____

_____

GISCARD, Valerie   <HR>
                [Emily Mesta]
  Rapture's Embrace

_____

_____

GLADSTONE, Eve
                [Herma Werner w/
                 Joyce Gleit]
  Silhouette Desire:
    108 Ballinger's Rule
  Silhouette Intimate Moments:
    55 Power Play
  Silhouette Special Edition:
    78 Fortune's Play

_____

_____

GLADSTONE, Maggie
                [Arthru M. Gladstone]
  Laceridge Ladies: (continued)
    Reluctant Debutante, The   *

_____

_____

GLASCO, Gordon
  Days Of Eternity, The

_____

_____

GLAZE, Eleanor
  Fear And Tenderness

_____

_____

GLEIT, Joyce w/ Herma WERNER
                (Eve Gladstone)

GLENN, Elizabeth
                [Martha Gregory]
  Harlequin American Romance:
    14 Dark Star Of Love
    36 Taste Of Love
  SuperRomance:
    67 What Love Endures

_____

_____

GLENN, Victoria
  Silhouette Romance:
                Not Meant For Love

_____

_____

GLICK, Ruth w/ Eileen BUCKHOLTZ
                (Amanda Lee)

GLICK, Ruth w/ Eileen BUCKHOLTZ and
  Louise TITCHENOR
                (Alyssa Howard)

GLICK, Ruth w/ Louise TITCHENOR
                (Alexis Hill Jordan)

GLUYAS, Constance   <HR>
  Brandy Kane   <CO>
  In sequence: *
    Savage Eden
    Rogue's Mistress

_____

_____

GODDEN, Rumer
  Breath Of Air, A
  Peacock Spring, The

GODWIN, Gail
  Mother And Two Daughters, A

GOLDENBAUM, Sally w/ Adrienne STAFF
               (Natalie Stone)

GOLDREICH, Gloria   <HO>
  This Burning Harvest

GOLDRICK, Emma
  Harlequin Presents:
    688 And Blow Your House Down

GOODMAN, Irene w/ Alex KAMAROFF
              (Diana Morgan)

GOODWIN, Hope
  Avalon:
    Acts Of Love

GORDON, Barbara
  Defects Of The Heart

GORDON, Deborah
          (Brooke Hastings)

GORDON, Lucy
         (Christine Sparks)
  Silhouette Romance:
    306 Carrister Pride, The
  Silhouette Special Edition:
    148 Legacy Of Fire
              (cont'd)

GORDON, Lucy (continued)
    185 Enchantment In Venice

GORDON, Ruth
  Shady Lady

GORDON, Susan   <RE>
  Match Of The Season

GORDON, Victoria
  Harlequin Presents:
    689 Blind Man's Buff
  Harlequin Romance:
    2531 Dinner At Wyatt's
    2540 Battle Of Wills

GOUDGE, Eileen
  Seniors: <YA>
    1 Too Much, Too Soon

GOWAR, Antonia
  Cashing In   <CO>

GOWER, Iris   <HR>
  Beloved Captive
  Copper Kingdom

GRADY, Liz
            [Pat Coughlin]
  Second Chance At Love:
    198 Too Close For Comfort
    210 Touch Of Moonlight

GRAHAM, Elizabeth
                    [E. Schattner]
  Harlequin Presents:
    583 Vision Of Love
    617 Highland Gathering

GRAHAM, Heather
        [Heather Graham Pozzessere]
  Candlelight Ecstasy:
    117 When Next We Love
    125 Tender Taming
    154 Season For Love, A
    177 Quiet Walks The Tiger
    214 Tender Deception
    241 Hours To Cherish
    271 Serena's Magic
  Candlelight Ecstasy Supreme:
     1   Tempestuous Eden
    10   Night, Sea And Stars
    17   Red Midnight
    37   Arabian Nights

GRAHAM, Leslie
  First Love From Silhouette: <YA>
    55 Love On The Run
    91 Rx For Love

GRAHAM, Marteen   <HR>
  Ariane

GRAHAM, Olivia
  McFadden Romance:
    36 Twilight Interlude   *

GRANGE, Peter   <HO>
              [Christopher Nicole]
  Devil's Emissary, The
                         (cont'd)

GRANGE, Peter (continued)
  Golden Goddess, The
  King Creole
  Tumult At The Gate, The

GRANGER, Katherine
              [Mary Sederquest]
  Second Chance At Love:
    206 Wanton Ways
  To Have And To Hold:
     13 Moments To Share

GRANT, Charles L.
                  (Felicia Andrews)
                  (Deborah Lewis)

GRANT, Jeanne
                    [Alison Hart]
  Second Chance At Love:
    119 Man From Tennessee
    149 Daring Proposition, A
    167 Kisses From Heaven
    184 Wintergreen
    220 Silver And Spice
  To Have And To Hold:
     14 Sunburst
     28 Trouble In Paradise

GRANT, Kathryn
                  (Kathleen Maxwell)

GRANTLEY, Samantha
  All That Glisters

GRAVES, Tricia
  Rapture Romance:
    38 Heart On Trial

GRAY, Alicia
  Enchanted Circle

GRAY, Alison
                         [Alma Moser]
  Dawnstar Romance:
    Porter's Designs

GRAY, Brenna
  Seasoned To Taste

GRAY, Ginna
                      [Virginia Gray]
  Silhouette Romance:
    285 Gentling, The
    311 Perfect Match, The
  Silhouette Special Edition:
    171 Golden Illusion

GRAY, Vanessa   <RE>
                   [Jacqueline Aeby]
  Accessible Aunt, The

GRAY, Virginia
                        (Ginna Gray)

GREEN, Billie
  Loveswept:
      7 Tryst With Mr. Lincoln, A
     16 Very Reluctant Knight, A
     26 Once In A Blue Moon
     38 Temporary Angel
     43 To See The Daisies..First
     65 Last Hero, The

GREENBERG, Jan
                       (Jill Gregory)

GREENFIELD, Irving A.   <HO>
                      (Riva Charles)
                      (Alicia Grace)
                      (Anita Grace)
                     (Gail St. John)
  No Better World

GREENLEA, Denice   <RE>
  Birchwood Hall

GREER, Francesca
                  [Frankie-Lee Janas]
  Bright Dawn

GREGG, Jess   <GOT>
  Other Elizabeth, The

GREGORY, Jill
                     [Jan Greenberg]
  Promise Me The Dawn

GREGORY, Lisa   <HR>
                     [Candace Camp]
  Bitterleaf

GREGORY, Martha
                    (Elizabeth Glenn)

GREGORY, Mollie
                   (Estelle Edwards)
          (see Terry Nelsen Bonner)

GRICE, Julia
           [Julia Haughey]
  Satin Embraces
  Scarlet Ribbons: <HR>
    Enchanted Nights
    Kimberly Flame
    Season Of Desire

GRIFFIN, Jocelyn
          [Laura Sparrow]
  Harlequin Romance:
  2543 White Wave, The   <PROM>
  SuperRomance:
   69 Battle With Desire

GRIMES, Frances Hurley
  First Love From Silhouette: <YA>
   84 Sunny Side Up

GROSECLOSE, Elgin
  Olympia

GROSS, Joel
  Four Sisters
  This Year In Jerusalem

GROSS, Susan Ellen
         (Sue Ellen Cole)
       (Susanna Collins)
      (Susan deLyonne)

GROVE, Joan
  Candlelight Ecstasy:
  277 One In A Million

GRUNDMAN, Donna
  Days To Remember   *

GUNTRUM, Suzanne
      (Suzanne Simmons)
       (Suzanne Simms)

H

HAASE, John
  Big Red
  San Francisco

HADARY, Simone
  Second Chance At Love:
  108 Spring Fever

HAGAN, Patricia   <HR>
  Golden Roses
  Dark Journey Home   <RS>*
  This Savage Heart
  Winds Of Terror   <RS>*

HAGER, Jean
          (Leah Crane)
        (Marlaine Kyle)
      (Jeanne Stephens)
  Candlelight Ecstasy:
  258 Promise Of Spring
  Judy Sullivan Books:
    Terror In The Sunlight <RS>
  Velvet Glove:
    Dangerous Enchantment <RS>

HAHN, Lynn Lowery
                    (Lynn Lowery)

HAILEY, Elizabeth Forsythe
  *Life Sentences
  * Woman Of Independent Means, A
  _____

  _____

HAINES, Pamela
  Diamond Waterfall, The

  _____

  _____

HALE, Antoinette
            [Antoinette Stockenberg]
  Candlelight Ecstasy:
    233 Trouble In Paradise

  _____

  _____

HALE, Arlene
              [Mary Arlene Hale]
                  (Tracy Adams)
                (Gail Everette)
                    (Mary Tate)
                (Lynn Williams)
  Candlelight Romance:
    222 When Dreams Come True
        (Nurse Rogers Discovery) *
  Wildfire: <YA>
    Lisa

  _____

  _____

HALE, Dorthea
              [Dorothy Weller]
  Harlequin American Romance:
    29 Woman's Prerogative, A
    50 Flight Of Fancy

  _____

  _____

HALE, Katherine   <HO>
  Madness

  _____

  _____

HALEY, Jocelyn
                    [Sandra Field]
  SuperRomance:
    54 Serenade For A Lost Love
    88 Cry Of The Falcon
  Harlequin SuperRomance:
    122 Shadows In The Sun

  _____

  _____

HALL, Bennie C.
  Sharon Romance:
    Coronation For Cinderella

  _____

  _____

HALL, Carolyn
                    (Carol Halston)

HALL, Gillian   <HR>
  This Shining Promise

  _____

  _____

HALL, Gimone
  Rules Of The Heart

  _____

  _____

HALL, Olivia M.
                    (Laurie Paige)

HALLDORSON, Phyllis
  Silhouette Inspirations:
    3 Honor Bright
  Silhouette Romance:
    247 Mountain Melody
    282 If Ever I Loved You

  _____

  _____

HALLIDAY, Ena
                [Sylvia Baumgarten]
  Tapestry: <HR>
    10 Lysette
    19 Delphine

  _____

  _____

HALLIN, Emily W.
                 (Elaine Harper)

HALL OF FAME SERIES <HofFS>   <HO>
  Each Bright River   *
                Noel B. Gerson
  Yankee Brig   *
            Carter A. Vaughan

_____

_____

HALSTON, Carole
               [Carolyn Hall]
  Silhouette Romance:
    208 Sunset In Paradise
  Silhouette Special Edition:
    86 Marriage Bonus, The
   115 Summer Course In Love
   139 Hard Bargain, The
   163 Something Lost, Something
        Gained

_____

_____

HAMILTON, Daphne
  SuperRomance:
    48 Prelude To Paradise

_____

_____

HAMILTON, Julia   <ENG><HO>
                [Julia Watson]
  Anne Of Cleves
  Katherine Of Aragon
  Last Of The Tudors
  Son Of York

_____

_____

HAMILTON, Lucy
             [Julia A. Rhyne]
  Silhouette Special Edition:
    92 All's Fair
   172 Shooting Star

_____

_____

HAMILTON, Paula
  Candlelight Ecstasy:
   231 Kiss And Tell

_____

_____

HAMILTON, Priscilla   *
             [Roberta Gellis]
  Love Token, The

_____

_____

HAMILTON, Steve w/ Melinda HOBAUGH
                (Linda Vail)

HAMLIN, Dallas
  Candlelight Ecstasy:
   260 Desperate Yearning

_____

_____

HAMMETT, Lafayette
  Captain's Doxy, The

_____

_____

HAMMILL, Grandin   *
  Woman Of Destiny, A   <CO>*

_____

_____

HAMMOND, Mary Ann
        [Mary Ann Slojkowski]
  Tapestry: <HR>
    40 Land Of Gold

_____

_____

HAMMOND, Rosemary
  Harlequin Romance:
   2601 Full Circle

_____

_____

HAMPSON, Anne
  Silhouette Romance:
    190 Another Eden   *
    196 When Love Comes
    202 Dreamtide
    214 Love So Rare
    220 Dawn Is Golden, The
    226 Sweet Second Love
    232 Spell Of The Island
    250 There Must Be Showers
    256 Soft Velvet Night

_____

_____

HANCOCK, Lucy Agnes
  Harlequin Classic: <PROM>
    Blood Of Her Ancestors   (502)
    Calling Nurse Blair   (284)
    Community Nurse   (264)
    District Nurse   (338)
    Doctor Bill   (346)
    General Duty Nurse   (235)
    Hospital Nurse   (313)
    Meet The Warrens   (372)
    Nurse Barlow   (292)
    Nurse In White   (496)
    Nurse's Aid   (356)
    Nurses Are People   (339)
    Pat Whitney, R. N.   (347)
    Resident Nurse   (333)
    Shorn Lamb, The   (397)
    Staff Nurse   (332)
    Village Doctor   (344)

_____

_____

HANNA, Evelyn
                   [Michael Dyne
                   w/ Ethel Frank]
  Woman Against The World, A

_____

_____

HANSON, Mary Catherine
  Starlight Romance:
    Captured Hearts   *

_____

_____

HARDING, Christina
  McFadden Romance
    35 Flight Of The Fury   *
    35 Yesterday's Promise   *

_____

_____

HARDWICK, Mollie
  Shakespeare Girl, The

_____

_____

HARDY, Antoinette
  Silhouette Special Edition:
      Fit To Be Loved

_____

_____

HARDY, Laura
                    [Sheila Holland]
  Silhouette Romance:
    309 Men Are Dangerous

_____

_____

HARPER, Elaine
                    [Emily W. Hallin]
  First Love From Silhouette: <YA>
    39 Be My Valentine
    53 Light Of My Life
    65 Mystery Kiss, The
    73 Short Stop For Romance
    89 Bunny Hug

_____

_____

HARPER, Karen   <HR>
                    [Karen Harris]
  Passion's Reign
  Sweet Passion's Pain

_____

_____

HARPER, Madeline
                    [Shannon Harper w/
                    Madeline Porter]
  Love Dance
                            (cont'd)

HARPER, Madeline (continued)
  Harlequin Temptation:
        Every Intimate Detail

HARPER, Olivia
                    (Jolene Adams)

HARPER, Olivia And Ken
            [Olivia Harper
              w/ Ken Harper]
            (JoAnna Brandon)
  Loveswept:
    52 Casey's Cavalier

HARPER, Shannon w/ Madeline PORTER
                (Madeline Harper)
                (Anna James)

HARRELL, Janice
  First Love From Silhouette: <YA>
    67 Puppy Love
    95 Heavens To Bitsy
  Two By Two Romance: <YA>
     5 One Special Summer

HARRINGTON, Sharron w/ Rick
  HARRINGTON
                    (Rianna Craig)

HARRIS, Karen
                    (Karen Harper)

HARRIS, Melinda
            [Melinda Snodgrass]
  Second Chance At Love:
    98 Wind's Embrace, The
   152 Once More With Feeling

HARRIS, Norma
  Sons Of Ada Stone, the

HARRIS, Sandra
                    (Abigail Wilson)
                    (Brittany Young)

HARRISON, Barbara
  This Cherished Dream

HARRISON, Claire
                    (Laura Eden)
                    (Ellen Harris)
                    (Claire St. John)
  Harlequin Presents:
   671 Prophecy Of Desire
   705 Dance While You Can
   727 Leading Man

HARROD-EAGLES, Cynthia   <HO>
  Moreland Dynasty: (continued)
     4 Crystal Crown, The
     5 Black Pearl, The
     6 Long Shadow, The

HARROWE, Fiona   <HR>
                [Florence Hurd]
  Bittersweet Afternoons   <CO>
  In sequence:
    Passion's Child
    Pride's Folly
  Love & Life:
    Separate Ways

HART, Alison
                    (Jeanne Grant)
                    (Jessica Massey)

HART, Carolyn G.
            [Charles Garvice]
  Escape From Paris

HART, Nicole
  First Love From Silhouette: <YA>
    94 Lead On Love

HART, Shirley
                [Shirley Larson]
  Candlelight Ecstasy:
    116 Caught In The Rain
    123 Wild Rhapsody
    144 Surrender To The Night
    161 Dangerous Haven, A
    183 Night To Remember, A
    208 Play To Win
    290 Balance Of Power
  Candlelight Ecstasy Supreme:
    26 Suspicion And Seduction

HART, Susannah
  Silhouette Desire:
    72 Nobody's Baby

HARTE, Marjorie   <RS>
                [Marjorie McEvoy]
  Strange Journey

HARTE, Samantha
  Hurricane Sweep   <Saga>

HARVEY, Judy
  Harlequin American Romance:
    23 In Loving Regret

HARVEY, Marianne
                (see Mary Williams)

HARVEY, Samantha
  Harlequin Romance:
    2522 Distant Man, The
    2541 Boy With Kite

HASKELL, Mary
                [Mary Curtis]
  Second Chance At Love:
    124 Song For A Lifetime
    144 Reach For Tomorrow
    176 Crazy In Love
    203 Heaven On Earth
  To Have And To Hold:
     8 Hold Fast 'Til Dawn
    17 All That Glitters
    37 Anniversary Waltz

HASTINGS, Brooke
                [Deborah Gordon]
  Silhouette Intimate Moments:
    37 Interested Parties
    64 Reasonable Doubts
  Silhouette Special Edition:
    79 An Act Of Love
    156 Tell Me No Lies

HASTINGS, Charlotte
                (Charlotte Wisely)

HATCHER, Robin Lee   <HO>
  The Spring Haven Saga:
    In sequence:
      Stormy Surrender
      Heart's Landing

HATHAWAY, Jan
                [William Arthur Neubauer]
  Coming Of Eagles, The
                              (cont'd)

HATHAWAY, Jan (continued)
  Junior Nurse
  Robynn's Way
  Treasure Of The Redwoods
  Sharon Contemporary Teens:
    Bright Morning
    Key Of Gold, The

  _____

  _____

HAUGHEY, Julia
                      (Julia Grice)

HAUGHT, Jean   <HR>
  Ecstasy's Treasure
  Flaming Ecstasy

  _____

  _____

HAUGHT, Jean w/ Rosalyn ALSOBROOK
                  (Jalynn Friends)

HAVILAND, Diana   <HR>
              [Florence Hershman]
  Proud Surrender

  _____

  _____

HAWKESWORTH, John
  Upstairs Downstairs

  _____

  _____

HAWKINS, Laura
  First Love From Silhouette: <YA>
    58 Double Exposure

  _____

  _____

HAYCRAFT, Molly Costain   <HO>
  Reluctant Queen, The

  _____

  _____

HAYDON, June w/ Judy SIMPSON
                  (Rosalind Foxx)
                  (Sara Logan)

HAYMOND, Ginny
                   [Lee Fleming]
  Love & Life:
    Someone Special

  _____

  _____

HAYNES, Barbara
  First Love From Silhouette: <YA>
    35 People Like Us

  _____

  _____

HAZARD, Barbara   <RE>
  Calico Countess, The
  Singular Miss Carrington, The
  Surfeit Of Suitors, A

  _____

  _____

HEALY, Catherine
  Harlequin SuperRomance:
    111 Private Corners

  _____

  _____

HEATH, Sandra   <RE>
               [Sandra Wilson]
  Commercial Enterprise, A
  Makeshift Marriage, The
  My Lady Domino
  Rakehell's Widow

  _____

  _____

HEATON, Dorothy
  Gratefully Yours
  To Cherish My Beloved

  _____

  _____

HEAVEN, Constance   <RS>
                 (Constance Fecher)
                 (Christina Merlin)
  Daughter Of Marignac
  Wildcliffe Bird, The
                         (cont'd)

HEAVEN, Constance (continued)
In sequence: *
  Lord Of Ravensley
  Ravensley Touch, The

_____

_____

HEERMANN, Lydia
  Serenade/Serenata: <INSP>
    4 Love's Late Spring

_____

_____

HELAND, Victoria
                    (Josephine Janes)

HENAGHAN, Rosalie
  Harlequin Romance:
  2572 Man From Ti Kouka, The
  2621 For Ever And A Day

_____

_____

HENLEY, Virginia
  The Avon Romance:
    Bold Conquest

_____

_____

HENRICHS, Betty L.
                    (Emily Doyle)
                    (Amanda Kent)
  Candlelight Ecstasy Supreme:
    46 Behind Every Good Woman
  Finding Mr. Right:
    More Than Friends
  Velvet Glove: <RS>
    Love's Suspects

_____

_____

HENRY, Anne
                    [Judith Wall]
  Harlequin American Romance:
    72 Cherokee Summer
    90 Glory Run, The

_____

_____

HEPBURNE, Melissa
               [Craig Howard Broude]
  In sequence: *
    Passion's Proud Captive
    Passion's Blazing Triumph

_____

_____

HERBERT, Kathleen
  Queen Of The Lightning

_____

_____

HERBERT, Nan   <RS>
  Shadow Over Heldon Hall

_____

_____

HERMAN, Nancy
                    (Jessica Jeffries)
                    (Renee Russell)
                    (Samantha Scott)

HERMAN, Spring   <CO>
  Taking Chances

_____

_____

HERRICK, Susannah
  Harlequin Temptation:
    Healing Passion, A

_____

_____

HERRINGTON, Terri
  Silhouette Romance:
    Blue Fire

_____

_____

HERSHMAN, Florence
                    (Diana Haviland)

HERSHMAN, Morris
                    (Evelyn Bond)
                    (Ian Kavanaugh)
                    (Janet Templeton)
                    (Jessica Wilcox)

HERTER, Lori
                [Loretta M. Herter]
  Candlelight Ecstasy:
   118 To Have And To Hold
   212 All Our Tomorrows
  Candlelight Ecstasy Supreme:
   27 Private Screenings

HEWITT, Elizabeth   <RE>
            [Mary Jeanne Abbott]
  Captain Black
  Fortune Hunter, The
  Sporting Proposition, A

HIBBERT, Eleanor Burford
              (Philippa Carr)
              (Victoria Holt)
              (Jean Plaidy)

HIGH, Monique Raphel
  Eleventh Hour, The

HILL, Alexis
           [Ruth Glick w/
           Louise Titchenor]
  Candlelight Ecstasy:
   115 In The Arms Of Love

HILL, Fiona
          [Ellen Jane Pall]
  Stanbroke Girls, The

HILL, Johanna
  Tapestry: <HR>
   41 Daughter Of Liberty

HILL, Pamela
  Bride Of Ae   <GOT>
  House Of Cray, The
  Place Of Ravens, A

HILL, Ruth Livingston
  A Hearth Romance:
   16 This Side Of Tomorrow

HILLIARD Nerina
  Harlequin Classic:
   107 House Of
         Adriano, The   (840)

HILLS, Ida
  Harlequin American Romance:
   34 Heartbreaker Mine

HIMROD, Brenda
              (Megan Lane)
            (Brenda Trent)
  Torch:
   Her Sister's Man

HINCMAN, Jane
  Starlight Romance:
   To London, To London

HINE, Al
  Liberty Belle

HINES, Charlotte
             [Judith McWilliams]
  Second Chance At Love:
    160 Tender Trap
  To Have And To Hold:
    38 Sweet Nothings

_____

_____

HINES, Jeanne   <GOT>
         (Rosamond Royal)
        (Valerie Sherwood)
  Bride Of Terror

_____

_____

HINKEMEYER, Michael T.
          (Vanessa Royall)

HOBAUGH, Melinda w/ Steve HAMILTON
          (Linda Vail)

HODGE, Jane Aiken   <RE>
 Lost Garden, The

_____

_____

HODGSON, Eleanor
         (Eleanor Howard)
          (Norah Parker)

HOHL, Joan
          (Amii Lorin)
        (Paula Roberts)
  Silhouette Intimate Moments:
    35 Moments Harsh, Moments
       Gentle

_____

_____

HOLDEN, Joanne   <GOT>
  Dangerous Legacy
  Nurse Of King's Grant

_____

_____

HOLDER, Nancy
      [Nancy L. Jones Holder]
        (Laurel Chandler)
          (Wendi Davis)
       (Nancy L. Jones)
  Loveswept:
    30 Winner Take All
    47 Greatest Show On
       Earth, The

_____

_____

HOLDING, Vera w/ John CHRISTY
  Sharon Contemporary Teens:
  Love Has Silent Wings

_____

_____

HOLLAND, Cecelia   <HO>
  Belt Of Gold

_____

_____

HOLLAND, Isabelle   <YA>
  In sequence: *
    After The First Love
    Summer Of My First Love

_____

_____

HOLLAND, Sarah
  Harlequin Presents:
    576 Deadly Angel
    601 Fever Pitch

_____

_____

HOLLAND, Sheila
         (Sheila Coates)
         (Laura Hardy)
       (Charlotte Lamb)
      (Sheila Lancaster)
       (Victoria Woolf)
  Sophie
  In sequence:
    Secrets

_____

_____

HOLLIDAY, Dolores
    Harlequin Romantic Suspense:
      Seventh Gate, The   *

HOLLINS, Mary
    Cold Blows The Winds
    Sacrifice, The

HOLMES, Deborah Aydt
    Family Ties   <Saga>

HOLMES, Mary Mayer   <HO>
    Wind-Rose, The

HOLT, Victoria
        [Eleanor Burford Hibbert]
    Time Of The Hunter's Moon, The
    The Landower Legacy

HOLT, Will
        (see Rebecca Drury)

HOOPER, Kay
          (Kay Robbins)
    Candlelight Ecstasy:
     153 On Wings Of Magic
    Loveswept:
      32 C. J.'s Fate
      46 Something Different
      62 Pepper's Way
      71 If There Be Dragons

HOOVER, Mab Graff
    Serenade/Serenata: <INSP>
     5 In Comes Love

HOPLEY, George   *
        [Cornell Woolrich]
    Night Has A Thousand Eyes, The

HORSMAN, Jennifer   <HR>
    Passion Flower

HORTON, Marian   <RE>
        (Marian Lorraine)
    Mischievous Spinster

HORTON, Naomi
        [Susan Horton]
    Silhouette Desire:
      Dream Builder

HOTCHKISS, Bill   <HO>
    Spirit Mountain

HOTCHKISS, Bill w/ Judith SHEARS
    Pawnee Medicine   <AIS:#14>
    Shoshone Thunder   <AIS:#12>

HOWARD, Alyssa
        [Eileen Buckholtz W/ Ruth
          Glick & Louise Titchenor]
    Silhouette Desire:
     100 Southern Persuasion

HOWARD, Eleanor
                    [Eleanor Hodgson]
  Tapestry: <HR>
    Cloak Of Fate

_____

_____

HOWARD, Guy
  A Hearth Romance:
    17 Give Me Thy Vineyard

_____

_____

HOWARD, Jessica   <HR>
                    [Monroe Schere]
  Prairie Flame

_____

_____

HOWARD, Joy
  SuperRomance:
    60 Stormy Paradise

_____

_____

HOWARD, Julia
          [Patricia K. Adams-Manson]
  Candlelight Ecstasy:
    165 Passionate Venture, A
    194 Lasting Image, A
    247 Working It Out

_____

_____

HOWARD, Linda
                  [Linda Howington]
  Silhouette Intimate Moments:
    22 Against The Rules

_____

_____

HOWARD, Linden
                [Audrie Manley-Tucker]
  Silhouette Special Edition:
    177 Come Lie With Me

_____

_____

HOWARD, Lyn
                      (Lynde Howard)
                      (Lynsey Stevens)

HOWARD, Lynde
                      [Lyn Howard]
  All I Ever Wanted   <ENG>

_____

_____

HOWARD, Mary   <RS>
                      [Mary Mussi]
  Anna Heritage
  Clouded Moon, The
  Cottager's Daughter, The (Eng:
    Sew A Fine Seam)
  Crystal Villa, The (Eng: House
    Of Lies)
  Devil In My Heart
  Family Orchestra
  Far Blue Horizons
  First Star
  Fool's Haven
  Gay Is Life
  Intruder, The
  Mist On The Hills
  Promise Of Delight
  Return To Love
  Sixpence In Her Shoe
  Strangers In Love
  There Will I Follow
  Unchartered Romance
  Wise Forget, The
  Young Lady, The (Eng: Bow To
    The Storm)

_____

_____

HOWATCH, Susan   <GOT>
  ● Wheel Of Fortune, The

_____

_____

HOWE, Margaret
  Debutante Nurse

_____

_____

73

HOWE, Susanna
                    (Bree Thomas)

HOWELL, Jessica
  First Love From Silhouette: <YA>
    37 Love Note

HOWINGTON, Linda
                 (Linda Howard)

HOY, Elizabeth
      [Alice 'Nina' Conarain]
  Harlequin Classic:
    120 Homeward The Heart   (925)
    129 Who Loves Believes   (959)
    140 My Heart Has Wings   (483)

HUDSON, Anna
         [JoAnn Algermissen]
  Candlelight Ecstasy:
    156 Kiss The Tears Away
    197 Design For Desire
    240 Taking A Chance
    269 Take My Hand
    286 Prize Catch, A
  Candlelight Ecstasy Supreme:
    13 Body And Soul

HUDSON, Meg
      [Margaret Hudson Koehler]
  Harlequin American Romance:
    25 To Love A Stranger
  SuperRomance:
    52 Return To Rapture
    64 Though Hearts Resist
    70 Charm For Adonis, A
    79 Two Worlds, One Love
    94 Beloved Stranger
                 (cont'd)

HUDSON, Meg (continued)
  Harlequin SuperRomance:
    106 Rising Road, The
         Now In September

HUFF, Tom E.
           (Edwina Marlow)
           (Beatrice Parker)
     (Katherine St. Clair)
         (Jennifer Wilde)

HUFFORD, Susan
        (Samantha Hughes)

HUGHES, Cally
             [Lass Small]
  Second Chance At Love:
    112 Lasting Treasure, A
    140 Innocent Seduction
    173 Cupid's Revenge
  To Have And To Hold:
    15 Whatever It Takes
    25 Treasure To Share, A (a
         sequel to Second Chance
         #112)
    33 Never Too Late

HUGHES, Rose
  Stranger In Paradise

HUGHES, Samantha
           [Susan Hufford]
  Candlelight Ecstasy:
    122 Silent Wonder, A
    179 Desert Splendor
  Candlelight Ecstasy Supreme:
    11 Politics Of Passion
    29 Diamonds In The Sky

HUNT, Greg   <HO>
                 (see Rebecca Drury)
John Bozeman: Mountain Journey
                           <AES:#13>

_____

_____

HUNT, Jena
                [Helen Manak Conrad]
Second Chance At Love:
   127 Jade Tide
   147 Proud Possession

_____

_____

HUNTER, Damion   <HO>
Roman Saga: (continued)
   3 Emperor's Games, The

_____

_____

HUNTER, Elizabeth
                     (Isobel Chace)
                 (Elizabeth deGuise)
Silhouette Romance:
   198 London Pride
   218 Fountains Of Paradise
   240 Shared Destiny
   257 Tower Of Strength, A
   268 Kiss Of The Rising Sun
   278 Time To Wed, A
   290 Rain On The Wind
   298 Song Of Surrender
   310 Loving Relations

_____

_____

HUNTER, Margaret   <HR>
                    [Ronald Singer]
Love's Secret Journey

_____

_____

HUNTER, Terry
Caprice Romance: <YA>
   31 Heartbreaker

_____

_____

HURD, Florence
                    (Fiona Harrowe)
                    (Flora Hiller)

HURLEY, Ann
   Silhouette Special Edition:
   98   Touch Of Greatness
   167 Heart's In Exile

_____

_____

HYATT, Betty Hale
   Starlight Romance:
   Jade Pagoda, The   *
   Sapphire Lotus, The

_____

_____

HYLTON, Sara
   Caprice
   Jacintha

_____

_____

HYMAN, Jackie   <RE>
                  [Jacqueline Hyman]
                (Jacqueline Diamond)
                (Jacqueline Topaz)
   Lady In Disguise
   Song For A Lady

_____

_____

I

INNES, Jean
                [Jean Innes Saunders]
   Circle Of Love:
   32   Scent Of Jasmine
        Silver Lady   <ENG>
   Dawnstar Romance:
   Silver Lady

                                 (cont'd)

INNES, Jean (continued)
  Torch:
    Captive Heart

  _____

  _____

IRELAND, Jane
                    [Jacqueline Potter]
  Second Chance At Love:
    169 Silver Enchantment

  _____

  _____

IRWIN, Sarita
  Simplicity Of Love, The

  _____

  _____

ISAACS, Susan
  Almost Paradise

  _____

  _____

IVES, Averil
  Harlequin Classic:
    141 Master Of Hearts   (1047)

  _____

  _____

J

JACKSON, Betty
  Candlelight Ecstasy Supreme:
    8 Handle With Care

  _____

  _____

JACKSON, Lisa
  Silhouette Intimate Moments:
    39 Dark Side Of The Moon
  Silhouette Special Edition:
    118 Twist Of Fate, A
    189 Shadow Of Time

  _____

  _____

JAGGER, Brenda   <HO>
  Days Of Grace
  A Family Saga:
    Verity
    Barforth Women, The
    An Independent Woman

  _____

  _____

JAHN, Michael
  (see Lee Davis Willoughby <MOAS>)

JAMES, Amalia
                    [Carla Neggars]
  Dawnstar Romance:
    Dream Images

  _____

  _____

JAMES, Anna
                    [Madeline Porter w/
                     Shannon Harper]
  Silhouette Intimate Moments:
    13 Edge Of Love
    42 Her Own Rules
    Love On The Line

  _____

  _____

JAMES, Arlene
                    [Deborah Rather]
  Silhouette Inspirations:
    2 Proud Spirit
    11 Wish For Always, A
  Silhouette Romance:
    235 No Easy Conquest
    253 Two Of A Kind

  _____

  _____

JAMES, B. J.
  Loveswept:
    60 When You Speak Love
    73 More Than Friends

  _____

  _____

JAMES, Dana
  Harlequin Romance:
    2632 Desert Flower

JAMES, Deana   <HR>
                        [Mona Sizer]
  Love Stone
  Love Spell

JAMES, Elizabeth   <CO>
  Secrets

JAMES, Kristin
                     [Candace Camp]
  Silhouette Intimate Moments:
     1 Dreams Of Evening
    17 Amber Sky, The (4th book
        in Sky Series)
    45 Morning Star

JAMES, Leigh Franklin   <HO>
                      [Paul Little]
  Saga Of The Southwest:(continued)
    Night Of the Hawk

JAMES, Livia
  Emerald Land, The

JAMES, Melanie
  Love Forever   <CO>

JAMES, Robin
                     [Sharon Curtis w/
                       Thomas D. Curtis]
  To Have And To Hold:
     1 Testamony, The

JAMES, Sarah
             [Mildred Havill Juskevice]
  Harlequin American Romance:
    67 Public Affair

JAMES, Stephanie
                  [Jayne Ann Krentz]
  Silhouette Desire:
    31 Reckless Passion   *
    37 Price Of Surrender
    49 Affair Of Honor
    55 To Tame The Hunter
    67 Gamemaster
    85 Silver Snare, The
    97 Battle Prize
   103 Body Guard
   115 Gambler's Woman
   127 Fabulous Beast
   145 Night Of The Magician
        Nightwalker
  Silhouette Intimate Moments:
     9 Serpent In Paradise
    21 Raven's Prey

JAMES, Susannah   <HR>
  Lucia's Legacy

JAMESON, Claudia
  Harlequin Premiere III:
    29 Escape To Love
  Harlequin Presents:
   690 Gentle Persuasion
   712 For Practical Reasons
                         (cont'd)

JAMESON, Claudia (continued)
  Harlequin Romance:
    2523 Lesson In Love
    2565 Melting Heart, The
    2578 Never Say Never
    2594 Yours...Faithfully

_____

_____

JAMESON, Storm   <HO>
  Captain's Wife, The (Eng:Farewell
    Night, Welcome Day)   *

_____

_____

JANAS, Frankie Lee
                (Francesca Greer)
                (Sailee O'Brien)

JANES, Josephine
                [Victoria Heland]
  Second Chance At Love:
    117 London Frolic   <RE>

_____

_____

JARRETT, Amanda Jean   <HO>
            [Robert Derek Steeley]
  Southerners Series: (continued)
    This Traitor Moon
    Where My Love Lies Dreaming
    Passion And The Fury, The
    Red Roses Forever

_____

_____

JEFFREY, Elizabeth
  Harlequin Premiere III:
    30 Jordan's Castle

_____

_____

JEFFRIES, Jessica
                [Nancy Herman]
  Harlequin American Romance:
    22 All In The Game
                          (cont'd)

JEFFRIES, Jessica (continued)
  SuperRomance:
    71 Certain Sunrise, A

_____

_____

JEKEL, Pamela   <HR>
  Sea Star

_____

_____

JENKINS, Sara Lucille
                (Joan Sargent)

JENNINGS, Sara
                [Maura Seger]
  Candlelight Ecstasy:
    202 Reach For The Stars
    256 Game Plan
    287 Loves Not The Enemy

_____

_____

JENSEN, Dorthea w/ Catherine R.
  ALLEN   (Catherine Moorhouse)

JENSEN, Muriel
  Harlequin American Romance:
    73 Winter's Bounty

_____

_____

JERINA, Carol
  Tapestry: <HR>
    39 Lady Raine
        Gallagher's Lady

_____

_____

JESSUP, Kathryn   <MED>
  Karen Evans, M. D.: Transplant
                [Anne w/ Ed Kolaczyk]

_____

_____

JOHANSEN, Iris
  Loveswept:
    14 Stormy Vows
    17 Tempest At Sea

                          (cont'd)

JOHANSEN, Iris (continued)
   24 Reluctant Lark, The
   27 Bronzed Hawk, The
   29 Lady And The Unicorn, The
   31 Golden Valkyrie, The
   35 Trustworthy Redhead, The
   40 Return To Santa Flores
   44 No Red Roses
   55 Capture The Rainbow
   59 Touch The Horizon

JOHN, Nancy
              [Nancy Sawyer w/
               John Sawyer]
Silhouette Desire:
  119 Night With A Stranger
Silhouette Romance:
  192 Make-Believe Bride   *
  262 Window To Happiness
Silhouette Special Edition:
   75 Summer Rhapsody
  106 Never Too Late
  166 Dream Of Yesterday

JOHNS, Janetta
  Sweet Dreams: <YA>
   41 Truth About Me And
       Bobby V., The

JOHNSON, Audrey
  Avalon:
   Hush Winifred Is Dead   <RS>*
   Nurse Of The Thousand Islands

JOHNSON, Barbara Ferry   <HR>
  In sequence: *
   Delta Blood
   Homeward Winds The River
   Heirs Of Love

JOHNSON, Maud/Maude
  First Love From Silhouette: <YA>
   33 You And Me   *
   59 Rainbow For Alison, A
  Wildfire:
   Kiss For Tomorrow, A
   Sixteen Can Be Sweet

JOHNSON, Norma
  Judy Sullivan Books:
   Inca Gold   <RS>

JOHNSON, Renate
         (Ellen Tanner Marsh)

JOHNSTON, Velda
         (Veronica Jason)
  Other Karen, The   <RS>

JONES, Jan
          (Caron Welles)

JONES, Marian
  SuperRomance:
   68 Bonds Of Enchantment

JONES, Nancy L.
      [Nancy L. Jones Holder]
  Jessie's Song   <CO>

JORDAN, Alexis Hill
         [Ruth Glick w/
         Louise Titchener]
  Candlelight Ecstasy:
  163 Brian's Captive
  195 Reluctant Merger
  250 Summer Wine

             (cont'd)

JORDAN, Alexis Hill (continued)
    291 Beginner's Luck

_____

_____

JORDAN, Joanna
  SuperRomance:
    72 Never Say Farewell

_____

_____

JORDAN, Penny
  Harlequin Presents:
    562 Bought With His Name
    569 Escape From Desire
    584 Flawed Marriage, The
    591 Phantom Marriage
    602 Rescue Operation
    609 Desire's Captive
    618 Sudden Engagement, A
    633 Passionate Protection
    641 Island Of The Dawn
    650 Savage Atonement
    655 Man-Hater
    667 Forgotten Passion
    706 Shadow Marriage
    713 Inward Storm, The
    728 Response

_____

_____

JOSEPH, Joan   <HO>
  World For The Taking, A

_____

_____

JOURDAIN, Rose   <HO>
  Those The Sun Has Loved

_____

_____

JOYCE, Deborah
                    [Joyce Porter w/
                     Deborah Bryson]
  SuperRomance:
    61 Questing Heart, A
  Harlequin SuperRomance:
    108 Dream To Share, A
    125 Never Look Back

                        (cont'd)

JOYCE, Deborah (continued)
  Second Chance At Love:
    109 In The Arms Of A Stranger

_____

_____

JOYCE, Janet
                    [Janet Bieber w/
                     Joyce Thies]
  Silhouette Desire:
    53 Winter Lady
    71 Man Of The House
    98 Man Of Glory
    116 Controlling Interest
    140 Run Of Gold
         Rare Breed
  Silhouette Romance:
    287 Permanent Fixture
  Tapestry: <HR>
    11 Libertine Lady
    34 Fields Of Promise
         Over The Boundry
         Invading Forces

_____

_____

JUSKEVICE, Mildred Havill
                    (Antonio Blake)
                    (Sarah James)

JUSTIN, Jennifer
                    (Jennifer West)
  Silhouette Special Edition:
    90 Passion's Victory

_____

_____

K

KACHELMEIER, Glenda   <HO>
  Rose

_____

_____

KAHN, Mary
                    (Miranda Cameron)
                    (Amanda Troy)

KAIL, Robert
          (see Richard Hale Curtis)

KAKU, Louzana
                (Christina Dair)

KALMAN, Yvonne
  In sequence: *
    Greenstone
    Silver Shores
    Passion's Gold

_____

_____

KAMAROFF, Alex w/ Irene GORDON
                (Diana Morgan)

KANIN, Garson
  Cordelia?

_____

_____

KAPLAN, Barry Jay   <HO>
  That Wilder Woman

_____

_____

KATZ, Carol
              (Penny Allison)
            (Rosalynn Carroll)

KAUFMAN, Pamela
  Shield Of Three Lions

_____

_____

KAVANAUGH, Cynthia   <GOT>
          [Dorothy Daniels]
  Deception, The

_____

_____

KAVANAUGH, Ian   <HO>
        [Morris Hershman]
  O'Donnell Saga: (continued)
    Far From The Blessed Land
    Waltz On The Wind, A
          (end)

_____

_____

KAY, Catherine
        [Catherine Dees w/
           Kay Croissant]
  SuperRomance:
    80 Interlude
  Harlequin SuperRomance:
      Critic's Choice

_____

_____

KAYE, Barbara
        [Barbara K. Walker]
  Harlequin American Romance:
    19 Call Of Eden
  SuperRomance:
    46 Heart Divided, A
  Harlequin SuperRomance:
    124 Come Spring

_____

_____

KAYE, Joanne
  World Of High Fashion: <MOD-NO>
    4 Satin & Stars   *

_____

_____

KAYE, M. M. (Mollie)
  Death In Cyprus   <MY>
  Death In Kenya   <MY>
  Death In Zanzibar   <MY>

_____

_____

KAZAN, Elia
  In sequence: *
    America, America
    Anatolian, The

_____

_____

KEAST, Karen
  Second Chance At Love:
    225 Suddenly The Magic

_____

_____

KEILER, Barbara
           (Ariel Berk)
       (Thea Frederick)

KELLEY, Leo P.
  (see Lee Davis Willoughby <MOAS>)

KELLS, Susannah   <HO>
  Crowning Mercy, A

KENNEDY, Adam   <HO>
  In A Far Country

KENNEDY, Jr. Cody   <HO>
           [John Reese]
  This Wild Land
  Warrior Flame, The

KENNEDY, Kim
  Two By Two Romance: <YA>
    7 In-Between Love

KENNEDY, Lena
  Lizzie

KENNEDY, M. L.   <YA>
  Turning Points:
    2 Kerry's Dance

KENNEDY, Marilyn
  Silhouette Desire:
    81 Opening Bid

KENNEDY, Nancy M.
      [Nancy MacDougall Kennedy]
  Summer Frost

KENT, Amanda
         [Betty L. Henrichs]
  Second Chance At Love:
    111 Ardent Protector, The <RE>

KENT, Deborah   <YA>
  Caprice Romance:
    36 Heartwaves
  Sweet Dreams:
    47 Te Amo Means I Love You
  Wildfire:
    Cindy

KENT, Jean Salter
         (Kathryn Kent)

KENT, Katherine
          [Joan Dial]
  Judy Sullivan Books:
    Tawny Rose   <HR>

KENT, Kathryn
      [Jean Salter Kent]
  Rapture Romance:
    28 Precious Possession
    52 Silk And Steel
    63 Reluctant Surrender
    77 Orchid Of Love
    90 An Affair Of Interest

KENT, Pamela
                    [Susie Barrie]
  Harlequin Classic:
    125 Desert Doorway   (909)
    152 Moon Over Africa   (983)

_____

_____

KENYON, Bruce
                    (Daisy Vivian)

KENYON, F. W.   <HO>
  Duke's Mistress, The
  That Spanish Woman

_____

_____

KENYON, Joanna
                    [Janet K. Clarke]
  Silhouette Intimate Moments:
    32 Dangerous Paradise

_____

_____

KER, Madeleine
  Harlequin Presents:
    642 Aquamarine
    656 Virtuous Lady
    672 Pacific Aphrodite
    699 Winged Lion, The
  Harlequin Romance:
    2595 Voyage Of The Mistral
    2636 Street Of The Fountain,
          The

_____

_____

KETTER, Pam   <YA>
                    [Pamela Browning]
  Caprice Romance:
    37 Stardust Summer
  First Love From Silhouette:
    36 One On One

_____

_____

KIDD, Elizabeth   <RE>
                    [Linda Triegel]
  Dancer's Land, The   <HR>
  LadyShip, The

_____

_____

KIDD, Flora
  Harlequin Presents:
    577 Tempted To Love
    592 Dark Seduction
    643 Tropical Tempest
    657 Dangerous Encounter
    682 Passionate Pursuit
    729 Desperate Desire

_____

_____

KIEHL, Claire w/ Susan PHILLIPS
                    (Justine Cole)

KIHLSTROM, April   <RE>
  An Improper Companion
  Mysterious Governess, The
  Wary Spinster, The
  Avalon:
    Paris Summer

_____

_____

KILMER, Wendella
                    (Karen Van der Zee)

KIMBRO, John M.
                    (Kym Allyson)
                    (Ann Ashton)
                    (Charlotte Bramwell)
                    (Jean Kimbro)
                    (Katheryn Kimbrough)

KIMBROUGH, Coleen
                    [Kay Porterfield]
  Harlequin Temptation:
    Swept Off Her Feet

_____

_____

KINCAID, Katharine   <HR>
                    [Pamela Daoust]
  In sequence:
    Crimson Desire
    Crimson Embrace

_____

_____

KINCAID, Nell
                    [Janet K. Clarke]
  Candlelight Ecstasy:
    129 Love On Any Terms
    149 With Every Loving Touch
    185 Turn Back The Dawn
    268 Compromising Passion, A
  Candlelight Ecstasy Supreme:
     7   Whisper On The Wind
    15   Where These's Smoke
    33   Fateful Embrace
    45   Silent Partner

_____

_____

KING, Christine
                        (Thea Lovan)

KING, Dianne
  Harlequin Temptation:
    10   Friend Of The Heart
  SuperRomance
    101 When Dreams Come True

_____

_____

KING, Josie
  Silhouette Romance:
    228 Dance At Your Wedding

_____

_____

KING, Peggy E.
            (see Velma S. Daniels)

KINGSBURY, Dawn
  First Love From Silhouette: <YA>
    93   South Of The Border

_____

_____

KINGSTON, Meredith
            [Meredith Babeaux Brucker]
  Second Chance At Love:
    126 Longing Unveiled

_____

_____

KIRBY, Susan E.
  Avalon:
    Blizzard Of The Heart
    Chasing A Dream
    Lessons Of The Heart
    Love's Welcome Home
    Reach For Heaven

_____

_____

KITT, Sandra
                        (Bree Saunders)
  Harlequin American Romance:
    43   Rites Of Spring
  Starlight Romance:
    All Good Things

_____

_____

KLEVIN, Jill Ross   <YA>
  Wildfire:
    Best Of Friends, The
    Summer Of The Sky-Blue
      Bikini, The
    That's My Girl

_____

_____

KNIGHT, Alanna   <RS>
                        (Margaret Hope)
    Castle Of Foxes

_____

_____

KNIGHT, Alicia
                        (Lucretia Wright)

KNIGHT, Doris   <RS>
  Nurse By Night

_____

_____

KNIGHT, Sali
                    [Tina Serafini]
  Starlit Surrender
_____

_____

KNOWLES, Mable Winnifred
                    (Wynne May)
KOEHLER, Margaret Hudson
                    (Maggie Charles)
                    (Meg Hudson)

KOHAKE, Rosanne   <HR>
  For Honor's Lady
_____

_____

KOLACZYK, Anne w/ Ed KOLACZYK
                    (Adrienne Edwards)
                    (Andrea Edwards)
                    (see Kathryn Jessup)

KOVACS, Katherine
                    (Katherine Coffaro)

KRAFT-MACOY, Lia
  To Love And Honor
_____

_____

KRAHN, Betina M.   <HR>
  Rapture's Ransom
_____

_____

KRAMER, Kathryn   <HR>
  Beloved Conqueror
_____

_____

KRASNER, William   <HO>
  Francis Parkman: Dakota Legend
                    <AES:#9>
_____

_____

KRAUZER, Steve
                    (see Terry Nelsen Bonner)

KRENTZ, Jayne Ann
                    (Jayne Bentley)
                    (Jayne Castle)
                    (Stephanie James)
                    (Jayne Taylor)*
  Harlequin Temptation:
    11 Uneasy Alliance
        Call It Destiny
_____

_____

KUCZKIR, Mary w/ Roberta ANDERSON
                    (Fern Michaels)

KUHLIN, Suzanne J.
                    (Jennifer Mikels)

KWOCK, Laureen
                    (Clarice Peters)

KYLE, Susan Spaeth
                    (Diana Blayne)
                    (Diana Palmer)

L

LACEY, Anne
                    [Martha Corson]
  Silhouette Special Edition:
    98 Love Feud   *
    155 Softly At Sunset
        Song In The Night
_____

_____

LACHLAN, Edythe
                    (Julia Alcott)
                    (Bettina Montgomery)
                    (Nicole Norman)
                    (Maureen Norris)
                    (Rinalda Roberts)

LACY, Tira
                    [Rita Clay Estrada]
  Candlelight Ecstasy:
    133 With Time And Tenderness
         (title changed from
         "Shamed Honor")
    225 Only For Love

_____

_____

LADAME, Cathryn
        [Cathryn J. L. Baldwin]
  Silhouette Romance:
    209 Trail Of The Unicorn

_____

_____

LADD, Linda   <HR>
                    (Jillian Roth)
  The Avon Romance:
    Wildstar

_____

_____

LADD, Veronica
  First Love From Silhouette: <YA>
    57 Some Day My Prince

_____

_____

LA FARGE, Oliver   <HO>
  Long Pennant
  Sparks Fly Upward

_____

_____

LAING, Alexander   <HO>
  Jonathan Eagle
  Sea Witch, The

_____

_____

LAKE, Patricia
  Harlequin Presents:
    570 Step Backward, A
    578 Silver Casket, The
    593 Moment Of Madness
    634 Fated Affair
                    (cont'd)

LAKE, Patricia (continued)
    707 Illusion Of Love
    730 Fidelity

_____

_____

LAKER, Rosalind   <HR><RS>
                  [Barbara Ovstedal]
  Jewelled Path
  What The Heart Keeps

_____

_____

LAMB, Charlotte
                    [Sheila Holland]
  Harlequin Presents:
    585 Betrayed
    635 Sex War, The
    644 Haunted
    658 Secret Intimacy, A
    668 Darkness Of The Heart
    700 Infatuation
    731 Scandalous
  Other:
    Violation, A

_____

_____

LAMB, Lady Caroline   <GOT>
                  [Anne Fremantle]
  Glenarvon

_____

_____

LAMBERT, Bill
                    (Willa Lambert)

LAMBERT, Derek   <HO>
  Great Land, The

_____

_____

LAMBERT, Willa
                    [Bill Lambert]
  SuperRomance:
    59 Love's Golden Spell

_____

_____

LANCASTER, Bruce   <HO>
  Big Knives, The
  Blind Journey
  Night March
  No Bugles Tonight
  Phantom Fortress
  Scarlet Patch
  Secret Road, The
  Trumpet To Arms
  Venture In The East

_____

_____

LANCASTER, Lydia   <HO>
                    [Eloise Meaker]
  Heaven's Horizon

_____

_____

LANE, Allison
  Revelations

_____

_____

LANE, Elizabeth   <HO>
  China Song
  China Quest

_____

_____

LANE, Kami
                  [Elaine C. Smith]
  Harlequin American Romance:
    47 Fantasy Lover

_____

_____

LANE, Marina
  Doctor At Happy End, The

_____

_____

LANE, Megan
                  [Brenda Himrod]
  Candlelight Ecstasy:
    171 Hold Love Tightly
                        (cont'd)

LANE, Megan (continued)
    263 Tomorrow Will Come
    292 Live Together As
           Strangers
  Candlelight Ecstasy Supreme:
    5 Tenderness At Twilight

_____

_____

LANE, Roumelia
  Harlequin Premiere III:
    31 Second Spring
  Harlequin Romance:
    2536 Lupin Valley
  Other:
    Brightest Star, The
    Himalayan Moonlight
    Second Spring
    Where The Moon Flower Weaves

_____

_____

LANG, Eve
                  [Ruth Ryan Langan]
  Dawnstar Romance:
    Cross His Heart

_____

_____

LANG, Heather
                    [Darlene Baker]
  Harlequin American Romance:
    31 Thorn In My Side

_____

_____

LANG, Miriam
                      (Margot Leslie)

LANGAN, Ruth
                  [Ruth Ryan Langan]
                        (Eve Lang)
  Silhouette Romance:
    224 Hidden Isle
    303 No Gentle Love
         Eden Of Temptation
                        (cont'd)

LANGAN, Ruth (continued)
  Silhouette Special Edition:
  119 Beloved Gambler

LANG-CARLIN, Alexandra   <HR>
  Dark Destiny

LANGFORD, Sandra
                    (Olivia Sinclair)

LANGTRY, Ellen
                    [Nancy Elliott]
  Silhouette Desire:
  66 Fierce Gentleness, The

LANIGAN, Catherine
                    (Joan Wilder)

LANTZ, Francess Lin
  Caprice Romance: <YA>
  28 Surfer Girl
  40 Rock 'n' Roll Romance

LARKIN, Rochelle
  Crystal Heart, The   <CO>

LARSON, Shirley
                    (Shirley Hart)
  Silhouette Desire:
  131 To Touch The Fire

LARSON, Susan w/ Barbara MICHELS
                    (Suzanne Michelle)

LARUE, Brandy
  Second Chance At Love:
  97 Ecstasy Reclaimed

LATHAM, Robin
                    (Robin Lynn)

LA TOURRETTE, Jacqueline   <HR>
  Patarran
  Pompeii Splendor, The (The
    Pompeii Scroll)   *

LATOW, Roberta
  Tidal Wave

LAVARRE, Deborah   <HR>
  Captive Mistress

LAVENDER, William   <HO>
  Stone Hill

LAWRENCE, Amy
                    [Joyce Schenk]
  Andrea
  Blues For Cassandra
  Color It Love

LAWRENCE, Fred   <HO>
                    [Fred Feldman]
  Jed Smith: Freedom River
                    <AES:#1>*
  Joseph Walker: Frontier Sheriff
                    <AES:#14>

88

LAWRENCE, Lynn
          [Sherry Garland]
  Second Chance At Love:
    157 Deep In The Heart

_____

_____

LAYMON, Richard
  (see Lee Davis Willoughby <MOAS>)

LAYTON, Edith   <RE>
  Disdainful Marquis, The
  Duke's Wager, The
  Mysterious Heir, The
  Red Jack's Daughter

_____

_____

LAZARUS, Marguerite
          (Anna Gilbert)

LEA, Constance
  Nurse In New York   <M&B>

_____

_____

LEATHER AND LACE: <L&L>   <HO>
  1 Lavender Blossoms, The
               Dorothy Dixon
  2 Trembling Heart, The
               Dorothy Dixon
  3 Belle Of The Rio Grande
               Dorothy Dixon
  4 Flame Of The West
               Dorothy Dixon
  5 Cimarron Rose
               Dorothy Dixon
  6 Honeysuckle Love
          Carolyn T. Armstrong
  7 Diamond Queen
               Dorothy Dixon
  8 Texas Wildflower
            Tammie Lee
            [Tom Townsend]
  9 Yellowstone Jewel
               Dorothy Dixon

_____

_____

LECOMPTE, Jane
          (Jane Ashford)

LEDERER, Paul Joseph   <HO>
  Indian Heritage Series:
  (continued)
    2 Shawnee Dawn
    3 Seminole Skies

_____

_____

LEE, Amanda
        [Eileen Buckholtz w/
          Ruth Glick]
  Silhouette Special Edition:
    165 End Of Illusion

_____

_____

LEE, C. Y.
  Flower Drum Song, The

_____

_____

LEE, Doris
  Silhouette Special Edition:
    131 Fire In The Soul, A

_____

_____

LEE, Elsie   <GOT><HO>
        (Elsie Cromwell)
        (Jane Gordon)
  Barrow Sinister (Eng: Romantic
    Assignment)   *
  Blood Red Oscar
  Curse Of Carranca, The (Eng: The
    Second Romance)   *
  Doctor's Office
  Fulfillment
  Masque Of Red Death
  Mystery Castle
  Satan's Coast (Eng: Mystery
    Castle)   *
  Season Of Evil (Eng: Two Hearts
    Apart - By Jane Gordon)   *
  Second Romance
  Sinister Abbey (Eng: Romance On
    The Rhine)   *
              (cont'd)

LEE, Elsie (continued)
  Spy Of The Villa Miranda (Eng:
    The Unhappy Parting)   *

LEE, Lucy
                    [Charlene Talbot]
  SuperRomance:
    93 Heart's Paradise

LEE, Maureen
  Lila

LEE, Tammie
                    [Tom Townsend]
  Texas Wildflower   <L&L:#8>

Le GRAND, Sybil
                    [Kaa Byington]
  Second Chance At Love:
    148 Silken Tremors

LEHR, Helene   <HR>
  Capture The Dream
  The Avon Romance:
    Gallant Passion, A

LEIGH, Susannah
  Scarlet Ribbons: <HR>
    Cheyenne Star

LEMERY, Alysse
                    [Alysse S. Rasmussen]
  Harlequin American Romance:
    46 Twilight Dawn

L'ENGLE, Madeleine
                    [Madeleine L'Engle Franklin]
  Small Rain, The
  Winter's Love, A
  In sequence: <RS>   *
    Love Letters, The
    Other Side Of The Sun, The

LENZ, Jeanne R.
  Caprice Romance: <YA>
    24 Do You Really Love Me?

LEONARD, Phyllis
                    [Isabel Ortega]
  Mariposa   <HO>
  Prey Of The Eagle   *
  Beloved Stranger

LEROE, Ellen
  First Love From Silhouette: <YA>
    87 Enter Laughing

LESLIE, Alice
  Torch:
    Stormy Obsession

LESLIE, Margot
                    [Miriam Lang]
  Second Chance At Love:
    156 Lovestruck

LESTER, Teri   <GOT>
    Everything But Love (Hawaiian
        Cruise)   *

_____

_____

Le VARRE, Deborah   <HR>
                [Deborah Varlinsky]
    Captive Mistress

_____

_____

LEVINSON, Len
            (see Richard Hale Curtis)

LEWENSOHN, Leone
                    (Frances Davies)

LEWI, Charlotte Armstrong
                (Charlotte Armstrong)

LEWIS, Canella   <GOT>
                [Jonathan Richards]
    Sensitive Encounter

_____

_____

LEWIS, Carrie
    First Love From Silhouette: <YA>
        100 Head In The Clouds

_____

_____

LEWIS, Deborah   <GOT>
                [Charles L. Grant]
    Eve Of The Hound, The

_____

_____

LEWTY, Marjorie
    Harlequin Romance:
        2546 Makeshift Marriage
        2579 One Who Kisses
        2587 Dangerous Male
        2650 Riviera Romance

_____

_____

LEY, Alice Chetwynd   <RE>
    ◆Beloved Diana (Eng: Tenant Of
        Chesdene Manor)   *
    ◆Courting Of Joanna, The (Eng: The
        Guinea Stamp)   *
    Intrepid Miss Haydon, The
    ◆Master And The Maiden (Eng:
        Master Of Liversedge)   *
    ◆Sentimental Spy, The (Eng:
        Letters For A Spy)   *

_____

LIDE, Mary   <HR>
    Ann Of Cambray

_____

_____

LIND, Pamela
    Silhouette Desire:
        51 Shadow Of The Mountain

_____

_____

LINDSAY, Rachael
                    (Roberta Leigh)
    Harlequin Classic:
        148 Heart Of A Rose   (888)

_____

_____

LINDSEY, Johanna   <HR>
    ◆Gentle Feuding, A
    Heart Of Thunder
    So Speaks The Heart

_____

_____

LINZ, Cathie
                [Cathie Baumgardner]
    Candlelight Ecstasy:
        157 Wildfire
        178 Summer's Embrace, A
        203 Charming Strategy, A
                            (cont'd)

LINZ, Cathie (continued)
  242 Private Account
  266 Winner Takes All

LISTON, Robert
          (Elizabeth Bright)

LITTLE, Paul
          (Marie de Jourlet)
      (Leigh Franklin James)
           (Paula Minton)

LIVINGSTON, Georgette
         (Diane Crawford)
  SuperRomance:
   92 Serengeti Sunrise

LLEWELLYN, Richard   <HO>
  How Green Was My Valley
  Night Of Bright Stars, A
  Tell Me Now & Again

LLOYD, ADRIEN
       (see Rebecca Drury)

LLOYD, Frances
  Silhouette Romance:
  200 Savage Moon
      Desert Rose

LLOYD, Marta
      [Marta Buckholder]
  Torchlite:
  Lion's Shadow, The
  Winds Of Love, The

LOCKWOOD, Ethel
  Sands Of Destiny

LOFTS, Norah   (deceased)
          (Juliet Astley)
          (Peter Curtis)
  Afternoon Of An Autocrat
  Calf For Venus, A
  Colin Lowrie
  Eternal France
        w/ Margery Weiner
  Little Wax Doll, The (Devil's
   Own, The - by Peter Curtis)   *
  Madselin
  Pargetters

LOGAN, Daisy
         [Sara Orwig]
  Second Chance At Love:
  138 Southern Pleasures
  163 Sweet Bliss

LOGAN, Jessica
      [Lawrence Foster w/
        Pauline Foster]
  SuperRomance:
   99 Awakening Touch, The

LOGAN, Mark
      [Christopher Nicole]
  Trilogy: (in sequence)   *
  Captain's Woman, The
   (Tricolour)
  French Kiss (Guillotine)
  December Passion (Brumaire)

LONDON, Hilary
        [John Sawyer w/
        Nancy Sawyer
  Harlequin American Romance:
   27 Scent Of Gold

LONDON, Laura   <HR>
          [Sharon Curtis w/
           Thomas Dale Curtis]
Windflower, The
_____

_____

LONG, Gabrielle Margaret (deceased)
                (Marjorie Bowen)
              (Margaret Campbell)
               (Joseph Shearing)

LONG, William Stuart   <HO>
          [Vivian Stuart Mann]
  Australian Series: (continued)
    5 Adventurers, The
    6 Colonists, The
_____

_____

LONGSTREET, Stephen   <HO>
  Delilah's Fortune
_____

_____

LOOK, Jane H.
                      (Lee Damon)

LORD, Bette Bao
  Eighth Moon
_____

_____

LORD, Graham   <RS>
  Spider And The Fly, The
_____

_____

LORD, Vivian
          [Pat Wallace Strother]
  Summer Kingdom
_____

_____

LORIN, Amii
                      [Joan M. Hohl]
  Come Home to Love   *
    (original by Paula Roberts)
  Candlelight Ecstasy Supreme:
    32 While The Fire Rages
  Other:
    Candleglow   <M&B>
_____

_____

LORING, Jenny
                      [Marty Sans]
  SuperRomance:
    74 Stranger's Kiss, A
  Harlequin SuperRomance:
    Right Woman, The
_____

_____

LORING, Lynn
  Avalon:
    Snow Kisses
_____

_____

LORRAINE, Marian   <RE>
              [Marian L. Horton]
  Mischievous Spinster, The
_____

_____

LORRIMER, Claire
          [Patricia Denise Robins]
  In sequence:
    Chatelaine, The   *
    Wilderling, The
_____

_____

LOTTMAN, Eileen   <HO>
  Brahmins, The
_____

_____

LOUIS, Jacqueline
                    [Jacqueline Hacsi]
    SuperRomance:
      84 Love's Stormy Heights

LOVAN, Thea
                    [Christine King]
    Silhouette Romance:
      281 Tender Passion, A

LOVELACE, Jane   <RE>
    Eccentric Lady

LOWE, Susan L.
                    (Andrea Davidson)
                    (Elise Randolph)

LOWELL, Elizabeth
                    [A. E. 'Ann' Maxwell]
    Silhouette Desire:
      77 Summer Thunder
    Silhouette Intimate Moments:
      18 Danvers Touch, The
      34 Lover In The Rough
      57 Summer Games
          Conspiracy Of Love

LOWERY, Lynn
                    [Lynn Lowery Hahn]
    In sequence:
      Moonflower
      Starflower

LUEDTKE, Julie
    Avalon:
      Dare To Love

LUKE, Mary   <RS>
    Ivy Crown, The

LUPTON, Mary
    Avalon:
      Dangerous Kisses
      Fantasy At Midnight
      Fear To Love
      House Of Vengeance   <GOT>

LUTYENS, Mary
                    (Esther Wyndham)

LYLE, Elizaeth
    Claire

LYNCH, Frances   <GOT>
    In The House Of Dark Music

LYNDELL, Catherine
                    [Margaret Ball]
    Tapestry: <HR>
      31 Alliance Of Love
          Masquerade

LYNN, Barbara   *
                    [Charles R. MacKinnon]
                    (Charles Stuart-Vernon)
                    (Vivian Stuart **)
    ** (DO NOT confuse this pseudonym
       with that of another author)

LYNN, Karen
                    [Lynn Taylor w/
                     Karen Maxfield]
    Starlight Romance:
      Dual Destiny

LYNN, Robin
                              [Robin Latham]
    Second Chance At Love:
    209 Dreams Of Gold And Amber

_____

_____

LYONS, Maggie   <HR>
    Heirs Of Rebellion
    In sequence: *
        Flame Of Savannah
        Flame Of Charleston

_____

_____

LYONS, Mary
    Harlequin Presents:
        625 Passionate Escape, the
        673 Caribbean Confusion
        701 Desire In The Desert
        714 Spanish Serenade

_____

_____

LYONS, Ruth
    Love Has Two Faces   <CO>

_____

_____

M

MacDONALD, Elizabeth
    Harlequin Temptation:
    19 Love Me Again

_____

_____

MACDONALD, Malcolm
    Stevenson Family: (Continued)
        Abigail   *

_____

_____

MacDONNEL, Megan
                          [Serita Stevens]
    Dream Forever, A   <YA><85>

_____

_____

MACE, Gertrude
    Avalon:
        Elusive Memory

_____

_____

MACK, Dorothy   <RE>
                        [Dorothy McKittrick]
    Blackmailed Bridegroom, The
    Luckless Elopement, The

_____

_____

MacKENZIE, Maura
    SuperRomance:
        76 Mirror Of The Heart

_____

_____

MacKINNON, C. R.
    Happy Hostage, The

_____

_____

MacKINNON, Charles R.   *
                        (Vivian Donald)
                        (Barbara Lynn)
                        (Charles Stuart)
                  (Charles Stuart-Vernon)
                        (Iain Torr)
                     (Vivian Stuart **)
    ** (DO NOT confuse this pseudonym
        with that of another author)

MacLEAN, Jan
                        [Sandra Field w/
                          Anne MacLean]
    Harlequin Romance:
    2547 All Our Tomorrows

_____

_____

MacLEOD, Jean S.
                    (Catherine Airlie)
  Harlequin Classic:
    116 Sugar Island   (853)

_____

_____

MacLEOD, Robert
  Daring Destiny

_____

_____

MacNEILL, Anne   <RE>
                    [Maura Seger]
  Mind Of Her Own, A

_____

_____

MACOMBER, Debbie
  Silhouette Inspirations:
    1 Heartsong
    9 Undercover Dreamer
  Silhouette Romance:
       That Wintery Feeling
  Silhouette Special Edition:
    128 Starlight

_____

_____

MacPHERSON, A. D. L.
                    (Sara Seale)

MacWILLIAMS, Margaret
  Starlight Romance:
    Beau Rivage

_____

_____

MADISON, Winifred   <YA>
  First Love From Silhouette:
    45 Touch Of Love
    64 Mix And Match
  Wildfire:
    Dance With Me
    Suzy Who?

_____

_____

MAGER, Marcia
  Woman Of New York   <AWD:#4>

_____

_____

MAGNER, Laura
                    (Laura Paige)

MAJOR, Ann
            [Margaret Major Cleaves]
  Silhouette Desire:
    35 Meant To Be
    99 Love Me Again
    151 Wrong Man, The
  Silhouette Intimate Moments:
    54 Seize The Moment
  Silhouette Special Edition:
    83 Brand Of Diamonds

_____

MAKING OF AMERICA SERIES <MOAS><HO>
            (see Lee Davis Willoughby)

MAKRIS, Kathryn
  First Love From Silhouette: <YA>
    98 One Of The Guys
  Two By Two Romance: <YA>
    4 Only A Dream Away
    9 Weekends For Us

_____

_____

MALCOLM, Aleen   <HR>
  Sinclair Trilogy: *
    In sequence:
      Taming, The
      Ride Out The Storm
      Daughters Of Cameron, The

_____

_____

MALEK, Doreen Owens
                    (Faye Morgan)
  First Love From Silhouette: <YA>
    71 That Certain Boy
    83 Where The Boys Are
                         (cont'd)

MARDON, Deirdre (continued)
   33 Destiny's Sweet Errand
Harlequin Intrigue:
   2 In For A Penny
Harlequin Temptation:
  15 Jealous Mistress, A

_____

_____

MARINO, Susan   <GOT>
            [Julie M. Ellis]
Vendetta Castle

_____

_____

MARITANO, Adela
                (Jane Converse)
                  (Adela Gale)
                 (Kay Martin)

MARK, Polly
  Avalon:
    Nurse At Seaview
    Nurse In Singapore
    Nurse Molly's Search

_____

_____

MARKHAM, Patricia
  Candlelight Ecstasy:
   280 River Rapture

_____

_____

MARLISS, Deanna
                (Diana Mars)
              (Diana Moore)

MARLOWE, Stephen   <HO>
  Deborah's Legacy   <Saga>

_____

_____

MARS, Diana
           [Deanna Marliss]
  Second Chance At Love:
   95 Sweet Surrender
                (cont'd)

MARS, Diana (continued)
  122 Sweet Abandon
  182 Sweet Trespass
  214 Sweet Splendor

_____

_____

MARSH, Ellen Tanner
          [Renate Johnson]
Wrap Me In Splendor

_____

_____

MARSH, Lillian
           [Ruby Frankel]
Second Chance At Love:
  99 Forgotten Bride, The <RE>

_____

_____

MARSH, Rebecca
      [William Arthur Neubauer]
Always In Her Heart
Assistant Angel
Backhand To Love (Trial By Love)*
But Love Remains
Girl For Him, The
Girl In Love
Hill Top House
Home For Mary, A
Lady Detective
Library Lady
Million Dollar Nurse
Nurse Annette
Nurse Ann's Emergency
Recovery Room Nurse
Redwood Valley Romance
Remembered Heritage
Summer In Vermont
Tiger In Her Heart
Walks Of Dreams, The
When Love Wakes
Willow Tree, The
Sharon Romance:
  Maverick Heart

_____

_____

MARSHALL, Andrea
  First Love From Silhouette: \<YA\>
    99 Written In The Stars

MARTEL, Aimee
              [Aimee Thurlo]
  Silhouette Desire:
    136 Fires Within, The

MARTEN, Jacqueline
        [Jacqueline Stern Marten]
  Tapestry: \<HR\>
    26 English Rose
    37 Irish Rose
    French Rose

MARTIN, Ethel Bowyer   \<GOT\>
  Nightmare House

MARTIN, Ione
  Silhouette Romance:
    260 Goldenrain Tree, The

MARTIN, Judy Wells
             (Jeanette Ernest)
             (Andra Erskine)

MARTIN, Liz
  Rage To Live, A   \<CO\>

MARTIN Malachi   \<HO\>
  King Of Kings

MARTIN, Marian
  Harlequin Gothic Romance:
    Ravens Of Rockhurst, The

MARTIN, Nancy
             (Elissa Curry)
  Silhouette Intimate Moments:
    60 Black Diamond

MARTIN, Pam
  First Love From Silhouette: \<YA\>
    43 Knight To Remember

MARTIN, Prudence
        [Prudence Bingham Lichte]
  Candlelight Ecstasy:
    119 Heart's Shadow
    137 Love Song
    148 Moonlight Rapture
    168 Champagne Flight
    234 Better Fate, A
    279 Sinner And Saint
  Candlelight Ecstasy Supreme:
    4 Lovers And Pretenders
    12 No Strings Attached

MARTIN, Wendy
             [Teri Martini]
  Avalon:
    Love's Journey

MARTINI, Teri
             (Alison King)
             (Wendy Martin)
             (Therese Martini)
  Avalon:
    Two Hearts Adrift

MARTINI, Therese   <HR>
                [Teri Martini]
   Love's Lost Melody
   _____
   _____

MASCOTT, Holly Anne
   Cherish The Dream
   _____
   _____

MASCOTT, Trina   <RS>
   Wife Who Ran Away, The
   _____
   _____

MASSEY, Jessica
                [Alison Hart]
   Candlelight Ecstasy:
   218 Stormy Surrender
   _____
   _____

MASTIN, Venita
   Avalon:
      Heart Of Winter
   _____
   _____

MATHER, Anne
                [Mildred Grieveson]
   Harlequin Presents:
    35 Seen By Candlelight (Eng:
         Design For Loving)   *
   563 Passionate Affair, A
   586 An Elusive Desire
   610 Cage Of Shadows
   626 Green Lightning
   683 Sirocco
   715 Moondrift
   Other:
      Enchanted Isle (Innocent
       Invader - by Caroline Fleming)
      Tangled Tapestry
      Wild Concerto
   _____
   _____

MATHEWS, Jan
                [Jan Milella]
   Second Chance At Love:
   141 Season Of Desire
   185 No Easy Surrender
   _____
   _____

MATHEWS, Michelle
   First Love From Silhouette: <YA>
   75   Under The Mistletoe
   _____
   _____

MATTHEWS, Laura   <RE>
                [Elizabeth Walker Rotter]
   Ardent Lady Amelia, The
   Emotional Ties   <CO>
   Lord Greywell's Dilemma
   Very Proper Widow, A
   _____
   _____

MATTHEWS, Patricia
      (a joint pseudo: Patty Brisco)
                (Laura Wiley)
   Dancer Of Dreams
   Enchanted
   _____
   _____

MAXAM, Mia
   Silhouette Romance:
   205 Race The Tide
   236 Lost In Love
   _____
   _____

MAXFIELD, Karen w/ Lynn TAYLOR
                (Karen Lynn)

MAXWELL, A. E.
                [Ann Maxwell]
                (Elizabeth Lowell)
   Golden Empire
   Another Day In Paradise
   _____
   _____

MAXWELL, Kathleen
     [Kathryn Grant]
 Scarlet Ribbons: <HR>
  Devil's Heart, The
  Winter Masquerade

_____

_____

MAXWELL, Patricia
     (Jennifer Blake)
     (Maxine Patrick)
     (Patricia Ponder)

MAY, Wynne
   [Mabel Winnifred Knowles]
 Harlequin Romance:
  2532 Peacock In The Jungle
  2548 Wayside Flower

_____

_____

MAYO, Margaret
 Harlequin Premiere III:
  32 Unwilling Wife, The
 Harlequin Romance:
  2557 Dangerous Journey
  2602 Return A Stranger

_____

_____

Mc

McALLISTER, Amanda <RS>
 McAllister Series: *
  Pretty Enough To Kill
    [Dorothy Dowdell]
  Waiting For Caroline
    [Eloise Meaker]
  Look Over Your Shoulder
    [Eloise Meaker]

_____

_____

McBAIN, Laurie   <HR>
 Wild Bells To The Wild Sky

_____

_____

McBRIDE, Harper
     [Judith Weaver]
 Candlelight Ecstasy:
  175 Tender Torment

_____

_____

McCAFFREE, Sharon
     [Jean Wisener w/
      J. J. Nether]
 Harlequin American Romance:
  4 Now And Forever
  80 Misplaced Destiny
 SuperRomance:
  85 Passport To Passion

_____

_____

McCALL, Virginia Nielsen
     (Virginia Nielsen)

McCARTHY, Gary   <HO>
 Silver Winds

_____

_____

McCARTNEY, Brenna <HR>
 Passion's Blossom

_____

_____

McCARTY, Betsy   <HR>
 The Avon Romance:
  Passionate Flower, A

_____

_____

McCLURE, Anna
      [Roy Sorrels]

 Rapture Romance:
  80 Chanson D'Amour

McCONNELL, Lisa
    [Lorena McCourtney]
 Rapture Romance:
  2 River Of Love   *

McCOURTNEY, Lorena
      (Jocelyn Day)
      (Lisa McConnell)
      (Rena McKay)

McCOY, Cathlyn
      [Fran Baker]
 Silhouette Desire:
  132 On Love's Own Terms

McCUE, Noelle Berry
     (Nicole Monet)
 Loveswept:
  3 Joining Stone, The
  11 Beloved Intruder
  50 In Search Of Joy

McDONALD, Kay L.   <HO>
 Trilogy: *
  Journey On The Wind
  Vision Of The Eagle
  Vision Is Fulfilled, The

McDONNELL, Margie
     (Margie Michaels)
 Loveswept:
  72 Conflict Of Interest

McELFRESH, Adeline
     (Jennifer Blair)
      (Jane Scott)
    (Elizabeth Wesley)

McEVOY, Marjorie
     (Marjorie Harte)
 Brazilian Stardust   <RS>
 Starlight Romance:
  Calabrian Summer   *
  Sleeping Tiger, The
  Star Of Randevi

McGAUREN, Joanna
     (Christa Merlin)

McGIVENY, Maura
 Harlequin Presents:
  674 Grand Illusion, A
  723 Promises To Keep

McGRATH, Kay
 Seeds Of Singing, The

McGRATH, Laura
 Harlequin Romance:
  2588 Mayan Magic

McINTYRE, Hope
 Silhouette Desire:
  Moon On East Mountain

McKAY, Rena
    [Lorena McCourtney]
 Silhouette Romance:
  239 Valley Of Broken Hearts
  291 Singing Stone, The

McKAY, Simon   <HO>
          [Christopher Nicole]
     Seas Of Fortune, The

McKEE, Janice   <HR>
     Heirs Of Destiny

McKENNA, Lindsay
          [Eileen Nauman]
     Silhouette Desire:
       75 Chase The Clouds
      134 Wilderness Passion
           Too Near The Fire
     Silhouette Intimate Moments:
       44 Love Me Before Dawn
     Silhouette Special Edition:
       82 Captive Of Fate

McKENNA, RoseAnne
          [Patricia Pinianski]
     First Love From Silhouette: <YA>
       88 Change Of Heart, A

McKENNA, Tate
          [Mary Tate Engels]
     Candlelight Ecstasy:
      126 Legacy Of Love
      142 Kindle The Fires
      172 Enduring Love
      201 Daring Proposal
      229 Perfect Touch, The
      295 Love's Dawning

McKENZIE, Melinda
          [Melinda Snodgrass]
     Rapture Romance:
       48 Beyond All Stars
                         (cont'd)

McKENZIE, Melinda (continued)
       62 Blue Ribbon Dawn
       78 Romantic Caper
       91 Gentle Diplomacy, A

McKITTRICK, Dorothy
                         (Dorothy Mack)

McMAHAN, Ian
     (see Lee Davis Willoughby - MOAS)

McMAHON, Barbara
     Harlequin Romance:
     2643 Come Into The Sun

McMAHON, Kay   <HR>
     Passion's Slave
     The Pirate's Slave

McMICKLE, Barbara   <GOT>
     Secret Of The Weeping Monk, The

McNAUGHT, Judith
     Harlequin Temptation:
       16 Double Standards
     SuperRomance:
       86 Tender Triumph

McNICOL, Amanda
     Make Your Dreams Come True: <YA>
        2 Winning At Love
        4 Dream Date

McWILLIAMS, Judith
                         (Charlotte Hines)

MEACHAM, Leila
  Judy Sullivan Books:
    Crowning Design   <RS>
    Ryan's Hand   <CO>

_____

_____

MEADOWS, Alicia
                [Linda Burak w/
                    Joan Zeig]
  Woman Of Boston, A   <AWD:#3>
  Finding Mr. Right:
    Opposites Attract

_____

_____

MEAKER, Eloise
                (Lydia Benson Clark)
                (Valancy Hunter)
                (Lydia Lancaster)
        (see Amanda McAllister)

MELDAL-JOHNSEN, Trevor   <HR>
  This Cruel Beauty

_____

_____

MELVILLE, Anne
    [Margaret Edith Newman Potter]
  Lorimer Family Saga: *
    Alexa
    Blaize
    Family Fortunes
    Lorimer Line, The

_____

_____

MERCER, Charles   <HO>
  Murray Hill

_____

_____

MERIWETHER, Kate
                [Patricia Ahearn]
  Silhouette Special Edition:
     89 Sweet Adversity
    144 Courting Game, The
                        (cont'd)

MERIWETHER, Kate (continued)
    179 Strictly Business

_____

_____

MERLIN, Christa
                [Joanna McGauren]
  Second Chance At Love:
    199 Kisses Incognito

_____

_____

MERLIN, Christina   <RS>
                [Constance Heaven]
  Spy Concerto, The
  Sword Of Mithras   <ENG>

_____

_____

MERRITT, Emma
                (Emma Bennett)

MERTZ, Barbara
                (Barbara Michaels)
                (Elizabeth Peters)

MERWIN, Lucy
  McFadden Romance:
    11 Island Of Dreams   *

_____

_____

MERWIN, Marjorie   <GOT>
  And Thereby Hangs

_____

_____

MESTA, Emily
                (Valerie Giscard)
  SuperRomance:
    73 Forbidden Destiny

_____

_____

METZGER, Barbara   <RE>
  Earl And The Heiress, The

_____

_____

MEYER, Donna
                    (Megan Daniel)

MEYER, Karl
(see Lee Davis Willoughby - MOAS)

MICHAEL, Judith
                    [Judith Barnard w/
                    Michael Fain]
● Possessions   <CO>
_____

_____

MICHAEL, Marie
      [Marie Rydzynski-Ferrarella]
Loveswept:
    9 December 32nd...And Always
   37 Irresistible Forces
_____

_____

MICHAELS, Anne   <RE>
An Amicable Arrangement
_____

_____

MICHAELS, Barbara
                    [Barbara Mertz]
Here I Stay   <OCC>
_____

_____

MICHAELS, Fern
                    [Roberta Anderson w/
                    Mary Kuczkir]
Cinders To Satin
Love & Life:
    Free Spirit
_____

_____

MICHAELS, Kasey   <RE>
                    [Kathie Seidick]
Rambunctious Lady Royston, The
In sequence: *
    Belligerent Miss Boynton, The
                         (cont'd)

MICHAELS, Kasey (continued)
    Lurid Lady Lockport, The
_____

_____

MICHAELS, Leigh
Harlequin Presents:
   702 Kiss Yesterday Goodbye
_____

_____

MICHAELS, Margie
                    [Margie McDonnell]
Harlequin Temptation:
    12 Untamed Desire
_____

_____

MICHELLE, Suzanne
                    [Barbara Michels w/
                    Susan Larson]
Silhouette Desire:
    47 Silver Promises
    57 No Place For A Woman
    76 Stormy Serenade
    87 Recipe For Love
   106 Fancy Free
   128 Political Passions
   152 Sweetheart Of A Deal
_____

MIKELS, Jennifer
                    [Suzanne J. Kuhlin]
Silhouette Special Edition:
    66 Sporting Affair, A
   124 Whirlwind
_____

_____

MILAN, Angel
                    [Elizabeth Neibor]
Silhouette Desire: *
    34 Snow Spirit
    64 Sonatina
    96 SummerSon
                         (cont'd)

MILAN, Angel (continued)
    118 Out Of Bounds
    153 Danielle's Doll

MILBURN, Cynthia
  Sharon Contemporary Teens:
    Spin A Dream

MILELLA, Jan
                        (Jan Mathews)

MILES, Cassie
                   [Kay Bergstrom]
  To Have And To Hold:
    35 Fortune's Smile

MILLER, Ann
                     (Leslie Morgan)
                     (Anne London)

MILLER, Caroline
  Lamb In His Bosom

MILLER, Cissie
              [Stanlee Miller Coy]
  Starlight Romance:
    Tish

MILLER, Linda Lael
  Silhouette Intimate Moments:
    59 Snowflakes On The Sea
  Tapestry: <HR>
    22 Fletcher's Woman
    30 Desire And Destiny
        Tanner's Bane
        Banner O'Brien

MILLER, Marica   <GOT>
                    [Marceil Baker]
  Waiting Heart, The

MILLER, Merle
  Day In Late September, A

MILLER, Valerie
                        (Hilary Cole)

MILLER, Victor
  Glory Sharers, The

MIMS, Emily
                      (Emily Elliott)

MINER, Jane Claypool
  Wildfire: <YA>
    Senior Class

MINGER, Elda
  Harlequin American Romance:
    12 Untamed Heart
    95 Touched By Love
    Velvet Fires

MITCHELL, Allison   <HR>
  Wild Harvest

MITCHELL, Ann
  Sapphire Romance: <ENG>
    Amberly Cure, The

MITCHELL, Erica
  Tapestry: <HR>
    32 Jade Moon

MITTERMEYER, Helen
                        (Ann Cristy)
                    (Hayton Monteith)
                      (Danielle Paul)
  Loveswept:
    2 Surrender
   15 Brief Delight
   57 Unexpected Sunrise
   67 Vortex

MONET, Nicole
              [Noelle Berry McCue]
  Silhouette Desire:
    39 Shadow Of Betrayal
    62 Passionate Silence
   133 Love And Old Lace

MONSON, Christine   <HR>
  Stormfire
  Surrender the Night

MONTAGUE, Jeanne
        [Jeanne Betty Frances Yarde]
  Passion Flame (Eng: Touch Me
    With Fire)   *

MONTEITH, Hayton
              [Helen Mittermeyer]
  Candlelight Ecstasy:
   210 Lover's Knot
  Candlelight Ecstasy Supreme:
    47 Pilgrim's Soul

MOON, Modean
  Harlequin American Romance:
    77 Dare To Dream

MOORE, Anne   <RE>
  Passion's Glory

MOORE, Aurora   <HR>
                   [Arthur Moore]
  Raging Heart

MOORE, Diana
                  [Deanna Marliss]
  Torch:
    Blossoms In The Wind

MOORE, Jill
  Dawnstar Romance:
    Moonlight In Aspen

MOORE, Lisa
                [Elizabeth Chater]
  Rapture Romance:
    45 September Song

MOORE, Mary
  Harlequin Premiere III:
    33 Hills Of Amethyst
  Harlequin Romance:
   2606 Spring Of Love

MOORE, Paula
                [Robert Vaughn]
  Dark Desire Romance:
    Hostage Of Desire

MOORE, Rayanne
  Harlequin American Romance:
    8   Thin White Line
    65 Images On Silver

MOORHOUSE, Catherine   <RE>
                [Dorothea Jensen w/
                 Catherine R. Allen]
  In sequence:
    Adriana
    Louisa
    Dorothea

MORGAN, Alice
  Harlequin American Romance:
    35 Branded Heart
    68 Deception For Desire
  Candlelight Ecstasy Supreme:
    35 Man In Control

MORGAN, Alyssa
                [Edith G. Delatush]
  Candlelight Ecstasy:
    191 No Other Love

MORGAN, Diana
                [Alex Kamaroff w/
                 Irene Goodman]
  Rapture Romance:
    9   Crystal Dreams
    20 Emerald Dreams
    43 Amber Dreams

                        (cont'd)

MORGAN, Diana (continued)
    72 Lady In Flight
    86 Ocean Fire
  Silhouette Romance:
    293 Behind Closed Doors

MORGAN, Faye
                [Doreen Owens Malek]
  Second Chance At Love:
    104 Trial By Fire

MORGAN, Leslie
                [Ann Miller]
  Rapture Romance:
    18 Silken Webs
    34 Against All Odds

MORGAN, Raye
                [Helen Manak Conrad]
  Silhouette Desire:
    52 Embers Of The Sun
    101 Summer Wind
    141 Crystal Blue Horizon

MORGAN, Stanley
  Laura Fitzgerald

MORRIS, Janet   <HO>
  I, The Sun

MORRIS, Terry
  Wildfire: <YA>
    Just Sixteen

MORSE, Nancy   <HR>
  Race Against Love

_____

_____

MORTIMER, Carole
  Harlequin Presents:
    564 Passion From The Past
    571 Perfect Partner
    579 Golden Fever
    587 Hidden Love
    594 Love's Only Deception
    603 Captive Loving
    611 Fantasy Girl
    619 Heaven Here On Earth
    627 Lifelong Affair
    636 Love Unspoken
    645 Undying Love
    651 Subtle Revenge
    659 Pagan Enchantment
    669 Trust In Summer Madness
    675 Failed Marriage, The
    684 Sensual Encounter
    716 Everlasting Love
    724 Hard To Get

_____

_____

MORTON, Joyce   <GOT>
  Avalon:
    Edge Of Fear
    Speak No Evil

_____

_____

MOSCO, Maisie
  Trilogy: In sequence:
    From The Bitter Land
    Scattered Seed, The
    Glittering Harvest
  Trilogy:
    Between Two Worlds

_____

_____

MOSER, Alma
                        (Alison Gray)

MOSS, Jan   <HR>
  Onyx Flame

_____

_____

MOUNTJOY, Roberta Jean   <HO>
                            [Jerry Sohl]
  In sequence: (Indian)
    Night Wind
    Black Thunder

_____

_____

MOWERY, Betty Chezum
  Avalon:
    Echoing Heart, The
    Voice Of Terror   <GOT>

_____

_____

MULHOLLAND, Judith
                        (Judith Duncan)

MULLEN, Dore   <HO>
                        [Dorothy Mullen]
    Shanghai Bridge   <Saga>

_____

_____

MUMM, Vella
  Harlequin American Romance:
    42   Summer Season
    76   River Rapture

_____

_____

MURRAY, Annabel
                         [Marie Murray]
  Harlequin Romance:
    2549 Roots Of Heaven
    2558 Keegan's Kingdom
    2596 Chrysanthemum And The
            Sword
    2612 Villa Of Vengeance
    2625 Dear Green Isle

_____

_____

MURRAY, Frances   <HO>
     [Rosemary Booth]
   Brave Kingdom

_____

_____

MURRAY, Marie
                 (Annabel Murray)

MURREY, Jeneth
   Harlequin Premiere III:
      34 Time Of Wanting, A
   Harlequin Romance:
      2559 Tame A Proud Heart
      2567 Forsaking All Others
      2637 Road To Forever, The

_____

_____

MUSSI, Mary
                 (Josephine Edgar)
                 (Mary Howard)

MYERS, Barry
                 (Jeanne Sommers)
   (see Lee Davis Willoughby <MOAS>)

MYERS, Mary Ruth   *
   Captain's Pleasure
   Friday's Daughter
   Love & Life:
      Insights
      Private Matter, A

_____

_____

MYERS, Virginia
   Harlequin SuperRomance:
      105 Sunlight On Sand

_____

_____

MYRUS, Joyce   <HR>
   Sweet Fierce Fires

_____

_____

N

NAPIER, Priscilla   <HR>
   Imperial Winds   <Saga>

_____

_____

NASH, Jean
   The Avon Romance:
      Forever, My Love

_____

_____

NATHAN, Robert
   Portrait Of Jennie
   Stonecliff

_____

_____

NAUMAN, Eileen
                 (Beth Brookes)
                 (Lindsay McKenna)

NEELS, Betty
   Harlequin Premiere III:
      35 Heaven Round The Corner
   Harlequin Romance:
      2542 All Else Confusion
      2550 Dream Come True, A
      2566 Midsummer Star
      2597 Roses And Champagne
      2626 Never Too Late
   Other:
      Fate Is Remarkable   <M&B>

_____

_____

NEELY, Esther Jane   <RS>
   Chateau Laurens
   Moon Cat Tex
   South Wind   <Saga>

_____

_____

NEELY, Richard
  Shadows From The Past

_____

_____

NEGGERS, Carla
                    (Amalia James)
  Candlelight Ecstasy:
    296 Southern Comfort
  Finding Mr. Right:
    Dancing Season
  Loveswept:
     5 Matching Wits
    20 Heart On A String
    36 Touch Of Magic, A
  Rapture Romance:
    69 Delinquent Desire
  Velvet Glove:
    Venus Shop, The   <RS>

NEGGERS, Carla A.   <HR>
  Outrageous Desire

_____

_____

NEIBOR, Elizabeth
                    (Angel Milan)

NEILSON, Eric
  Haakon Series:
    Golden Ax, The
    Viking Revenge, The

_____

_____

NELSON, Louella
  SuperRomance:
    96 Sentinel At Dawn
  Harlequin SuperRomance:
    Freedom's Fortune

_____

_____

NERI, Penelope   <HR>
  Jasmine Paradise
  In sequence: *
    Passion's Rapture
    Beloved Scoundrel

_____ Sea Jewel _____

NETHER, J. J. w/ Jean WISENER
                    (Sharon McCaffree)

NEUBAUER, William Arthur
                    (Christine Bennett)
                    (Joan Garrison)
                    (Jan Hathaway)
                    (Rebecca Marsh)
                    (Norma Newcomb)
  Assignment: Romance   *
  Blue Waters
  Duel Of Hearts
  Girl Of Big-Mountain
  Golden Heel, The
  High-Country Dreamer, The
  Love Came Along
  Love Remains
  Old Covered Bridge
  River Song
  Roses For Carol (Roses Of Goose
    Bay, The)
  Summer Of The Shore
  Sweetheart Of The Air
  This Darkling Love
  Trouble In Ward J
  Wing Of The Blue Air
  Sharon Romance:
    Beckoning Star

_____

_____

NEVIN, David   <HO>
  Dream West   <Saga>

_____

_____

NEVINS, Kate
  Second Chance At Love:
    162 Midsummer Magic
    191 Spellbound
    215 Breakfast With Tiffany

_____

_____

NEWCOMB, Kerry   <HO>
  Morning Star

_____

_____

NEWCOMB, Kerry w/ Frank SCHAEFER
                    (Shana Carrol)
                    (Peter Gentry)
                    (Christina Savage)

NEWCOMB, Norma
        [William Arthur Neubauer]
  Angel Of The Hills
  Forest Creek
  Green Bench, The
  Large Land, The
  Love Comes Riding
  Memo Of The Heart
  Nurse To Marry, A
  Questing Heart, A
  Singing Heart,A
  Sparkles In The Water
  Sharon Romance:
    Bright Stars
    Eve's Hour

_____

_____

NICHOLS, Carolyn w/ Stanlee
  Miller COY
                    (Iona Charles)

NICHOLS, Pamela
  Escape To Romance (Mexican
    Interlude)   *
_____

_____

NICHOLS, Sarah   <GOT>
                    [Lee Hays]
  Serpents Tooth
_____

_____

NICHOLSON, Christina   <HO>
              [Christopher Nicole]
  Queen Of Paris, The
_____

_____

NICHOLSON, Peggy E.
  Harlequin Presents:
    732 Darling Jade, The

_____

_____

NICKSON, Hilda
  Kiss For Elaine, A (Love Is The
    Anchor)   *
_____

_____

NICOLAYSEN, Bruce   <HO>
  New York Series: (continued)
      Pirate Of Grammercy Park, The
      Gracie Square
                    (end)
_____

_____

NICOLE, Christopher   <HO>
                    (Daniel Adams)
                    (Leslie Arlen)
                    (Robin Cade)
                    (Peter Grange)
                    (Mark Logan)
                    (Simon McKay)
              (Christina Nicholson)
                    (Alison York)
  Amyot Series: *
    Amyot's Cay
    Blood Amyot
    Amyot Crime, The
  Crimson Pagoda, The
  Darknoon
  Face Of Evil, The
  Heroes
  Longest Pleasure, The
  Self-Lovers, The
  Shadows In The Jungle
  Thunder And The Shouting, The
  White Boy
_____

_____

NICOLE, Marie
     [Marie Rydzynski-Ferrarella]
  Silhouette Desire:
    112 Tried And True
    142 Buyer Beware
        Through Laughter and Tears

NIELSEN, Virginia   <HR>
     [Virginia Nielsen McCall]
  Traitor for Love
  Harlequin SuperRomance:
    110 Trusting

NIXON, Agnes
        (Rosemarie Santini)
      (Rosemary Anne Sisson)

NOBILE, Jeanette
  First Love From Silhouette: <YA>
    37 Portrait Of Love

NOBISSO, Josephine
          (Nadja Bride)
          (Nuria Wood)

NOGA, Helen
  Ayisha

NOLAN, Frederick   <HO>
  Carver's Kingdom
  White Night's, Red Dawn <Saga>

NORBY, Lisa
  Turning Points: <YA>
    1 Friends Forever
  Two By Two Romance: <YA>
    10 Just The Way You Are

NORMAN, David   <HO>
  The Frontier Rakers: (continued)
    Santa Fe Dream   <Saga>

NORMAN, Yvonne
  Avalon:
    Leaves On The Wind   <GOT>

NORRIS, Carol
        [Carolyn Brimley Norris]
  Candlelight Ecstasy:
    246 Secrets For Sharing

NORRIS, Maureen
        [Edythe Lachlan]
  Second Chance At Love:
    165 Starry Eyed
    205 Seaswept

NORTON, Andre   <HO>
        [Alice Mary Norton]
  Stand And Deliver
  Ralstone Luck, The

NUNN, Rebecca
  Candlelight Ecstasy Supreme:
    38 Another Day Of Loving

O

OATES, Joyce Carol
  Mysteries Of Winterthurn

O'BANYON, Constance   <HR>
                   [Evelyn Gee]
  Enchanted Ecstasy
  Rebel Temptress
  In sequence:
    Savage Desire
    Savage Splendor

O'BRIAN, Gayle   <HR>
  Reckless Rapture

O'BRIEN, Saliee   <HR>
          [Frankie-Lee Janas]
  Cayo
  In sequence: *
    Bayou
    Cajun
    Creole

O'DONNELL, Jan
  Wildfire: <YA>
    Funny Girl Like Me, A

O'DONOGHUE, Maureen   <HR>
  Jedder's Land
  Wild Honey Time

O'FLAHERTY, Louise   <HO>
  Dreamers, The

OGILVIE, Elisabeth   <RS>
  Dawning Of The Day   *
  No Evil Angel
  Silent Ones, The
  Scottish Trilogy: <HO>
    Jennie About To Be
  Wildfire: <YA>
    Beautiful Girl
    Too Young To Know

O'GRADY, Leslie
  Lord Raven's Widow   <RE>
  In sequence: *
    Artist's Daughter
    Raven's Court

O'GRADY, Rohan   <GOT>
               [June Skinner]
  Curse Of The Montrolfes, The

O'HALLION, Sheila
            [Sheila R. Allen]
  Tapestry: <HR>
    35 Fire And Innocence

O'HARA, Kate
  Harlequin Romance:
  2560 Summerhaze

OLDEN, Marc
     (see Terry Nelsen Bonner)

OLDFIELD, Elizabeth
  Harlequin Presents:
    604 Dream Hero
    608 Second Time Around
    637 Florida Fever
    652 Beloved Stranger
    676 Take It Or Leave It
    685 Fighting Lady
    691 Submission

OLDHAKER, Thelma
  Intimate Strangers   <CO>

OLMSTEAD, Lorena Ann
  Candlelight: (also Avalon)
    145 Faithful Promise, The
        (Christie Comes Through) *

O'MORE, Peggy
             (Betty Blockinger)
             (Jeanne Bowman)
  Nurse Involved, A
  Sharon Romance:
    Disastrous Love
  Sharon Contemporary Teens:
    Laughing Girl, The
    Tall Girl, The

O'NEILL, Olivia   <HR>
  Dragon Star

OPPENHEIMER, Joan
  Wildfire: <YA>
    Voices Of Julie, The

ORDE, Lewis   <HO>
  Eagles
  Rag Trade

ORR, Alice Harron
           (Elizabeth Allison)

ORR, Zelma
  Harlequin American Romance:
     7 Miracles Take Longer
    18 In The Eyes Of Love
    55 Love Is A Fairy Tale
    82 Measure Of Love
    94 From This Day

ORWIG, Sara
             (Daisy Logan)
  Spy For Love, A   <RE>
  Harlequin Regency Romance:
    Fairfax Brew, The
    Revenge For A Duchess
  Loveswept:
    18 Autumn Flames
    42 Heat Wave
    48 Beware The Wizard
    58 Oregon Brown
    70 Midnight Special, The
  SuperRomance:
    57 Magic Obsession

OSBORNE, Juanita Tyree   <GOT>
  Avalon:
    Darkness At Middlebrook
    Hand Of Evil
    Hidden Fury, The
    Menace At Brackstone
    Menace At The Gate
    Mists Of Revilla
    Walk With A Shadow

OSBORNE, Maggie
  Rapture Romance:
      66 Flight Of Fancy
      92 Castles In The Sand
  Scarlet Ribbons: <HR>
    Rage To Love

_____

_____

OUTLAW, Louise Lee
                        (Juliet Ashby)
                        (Lee Canaday)

OVSTEDAL, Barbara
                    (Barbara Douglas)
                    (Rosalind Laker)
                    (Barbara Paul)**
  ** (DO NOT confuse this pseudonym
      with that of another author)

OWEN, Ann
  Silhouette Romance:
      41 Sands Of Time, The

_____

_____

OWEN, Wanda   <HR>
  Golden Gypsy
  Texas Wildfire

_____

_____

P

PADE, Victoria
  The Avon Romance:
    When Love Remains

_____

_____

PAGE, Betsy
                    [Bettie Wilhite]
  Harlequin Romance:
    2627 Bonded Heart, The
                            (cont'd)

PAGE, Betsy (continued)
  Other:
    Darknight Stranger   <M&B>

_____

_____

PAIGE, Laurie
                    [Olivia M. Hall]
  Silhouette Desire:
    123 Gypsy Enchantment
  Silhouette Romance:
    296 South Of The Sun
  Silhouette Special Edition:
    170 Lover's Choice

_____

_____

PALL, Ellen Jane
                        (Fiona Hill)

PALMER, Diana
                    [Susan Spaeth Kyle]
  Silhouette Desire:
     50 Friends And Lover's
     80 Fire & Ice
    102 Snow Kisses
    110 Diamond Girl
         Rawhide Man
         Lady Love   <TMC>
  Silhouette Romance:
    254 Darling Enemy
    301 Roomfull Of Roses
    314 Heart Of Ice, The
         Passion Flower   <TMC>
  Silhouette Special Edition:
     33 Heather's Song   *

_____

_____

PALMER, Rachel
                        [Ruth Potts]
  SuperRomance:
     58 No Sweeter Song

_____

_____

PAPAZOGLOU, Orania
                    (Nicola Andrews)

PARENTEAU, Shirley
  Love & Life:
    Hot Springs

PARETTI, Sandra   <HO>
  Fields Of Battle
  Rose And The Sword, The

PARGETER, Margaret
  Harlequin Presents:
    572 Prelude To A Song
    580 Substitute Bride
    588 Clouded Rapture
    595 Man From The Kimberleys
    620 Demetrious Line, The
    638 Caribbean Gold
    653 Chains Of Regret
    660 Storm In The Night
  Harlequin Romance:
    2613 Silver Flame, The

PARK, Anne
  Sweet Dreams: <YA>
    43 Tender Loving Care

PARKER, Cynthia
  SuperRomance:
    100 Tiger Eyes

PARKER, Laura
                   [Laura Castoro]
          (see Terry Nelsen Bonner)
  Finding Mr. Right:
    Until Love Is Enough
  Silhouette Special Edition:
    137 Perfect Choice, The
         Dangerous Company
  Tapestry: <HR>
    16 Emerald And Sapphire
                        (cont'd)

PARKER, Laura (continued)
    36 Moth And Flame

PARKER, Norah   <HR>
                   [Eleanor Hodgson]
  Wild Splendid Love

PARKER, Robert B.
  Love & Glory

PARKIN, Bernadette   <HR>
  Sweet Barbarian

PARRIS, Laura
                   [Laura Magner]
  Harlequin American Romance:
    60 High Valley Of The Sun

PARRISH, Patt
                   [Patt Bucheister]
  Dawnstar Romance:
    Gift To Cherish, A

PARV, Valerie
  Harlequin Romance:
    2589 Tall Dark Stranger
    2628 Remember Me, My Love
    2644 Dreaming Dunes, The

PASCAL, Francine
  Sweet Valley High: <YA>
    1 Double Love
    2 Secrets
                        (cont'd)

117

PASCAL, Francine (continued)
3 Playing With Fire
4 Power Play
5 All Night Long
6 Dangerous Love
7 Dear Sister
8 Heart Breaker
9 Racing Hearts

_____

_____

PATRICK, DeAnn
              [Dorothy Corcoran w/
              Mary Ann Slojkowski]
Tapestry: <HR>
18 Montana Brides

_____

_____

PATRICK, Lynn
              [Patricia Pinianski w/
              Linda Sweeney]
Candlelight Ecstasy:
276 Perfect Affair, The

_____

_____

PATTON, Sarah
              (Genevieve English)

PAUL, Barbara   <RS>*
              [Barbara Ovstedal]
Devil's Fire, Love's Revenge
Frenchwoman, The
Seventeenth Stair, The
To Love A Stranger (Eng: A Wild
  Cry Of Love)

_____

_____

PAUL, Barbara   *
An Exercise For Madmen
Bibblings
Fourth Wall, The
Pillars Of Salt
Under The Canopy

_____

_____

PAUL, Danielle
              [Helen Mittermeyer]
Harlequin Temptation:
13 Chameleon

_____

_____

PAULOS, Sheila
Candlelight Ecstasy:
189 Love's Madness
230 Heaven's Embrace
261 Give And Take

_____

_____

PAYNE, Oliver   <HO>
Northwest Territory: (continued)
  Defiance
  Rebellion

_____

_____

PAYNE, Tiffany
Silhouette Romance:
283 Stirring's Of The Heart

_____

_____

PEAKE, Lilian
Harlequin Presents:
612 Passionate Intruder
Harlequin Romance:
2603 Night Of Possession
2614 Come Love Me
2651 Woman In Love, A

_____

_____

PEARCE, Mary E.
Polsinney Harbour
In Sequence: *
  Apple Tree Lean Down
  Land Endures, The

_____

_____

PEARL, Jack
              (Stephanie Blake)

118

PEARSON, Michael
  Store, The

PETERS, Ellis   <HO>
  Virgin In The Ice, A

PECK, Maggie
                [Marjorie Price]
  Second Chance At Love:
    151 Moonlight On The Bay

PETERS, Natasha
  Darkness Into Light
  Immortals, The

PELFREY, Judy
                (Rhett Daniels)

PETERS, Othello   <GOT>
  Whispers From The Dark Side
    Of Tomorrow

PELLICANE, Patricia   <HR>
  Embers Of Desire
  Tapestry: <HR>
    42 Charity's Pride

PETERS, Sue
                (Angela Carson)
  Harlequin Romance:
    2583 Lightning Strikes Twice

PELTON, Sonya T.   <HR>
  Awake Savage Heart
  Bittersweet Bondage
  Wild Island Sands

PETRATUR, Joyce
                (Joyce Verrette)

PETRI, David
  Curtain Of Night, The

PELTONEN, Carla w/ Molly SWANTON
                (Lynn Erickson)

PEMBERTON, Margaret
  Flower Garden, The

PETRON, Angela
  Prelude To Happiness

PEPLOE, Dorothy Emily
                (D. E. Stevenson)

PETTY, Elizabeth
  Love Of Sister Nichole, The <M&B>

PETERS, Clarice   <RE>
                [Laureen Kwock]
  Samantha

PHILLIPS, Erin
   First Love From Silhouette: <YA>
      96 Research For Romance

PHILLIPS, Johanna
                [Dorothy Garlock]
   Second Chance At Love:
      125 Hidden Dreams

PHILLIPS, Patricia
   Marie Fleur   <RE>

PHILLIPS, Susan w/ Claire KIEHL
                (Justine Cole)

PHILLIPSON, Sandra
   McFadden Romance:
      11 Moonlight Interlude   *

PICANO, Felice   <RS>
   House Of Cards

PICKART, Joan E.
   Loveswept:
      61 Breaking All Rules
      74 Charade

PIEPER, Kathleen
   Avalon:
      Summer Kisses

PILCHER, Rosamunde   <HO>
                (Jane Fraser)
   Carousel, The

PINCHOT, Ann
   Luck Of The Linscotts, The

PINES, Nancy
   Sweet Dreams: <YA>
      55 Spotlight On Love

PINIANSKI, Paticia
                (RoseAnne McKenna)
                (Patricia Rosemoor)

PINIANSKI, Patricia w/ Linda
SWEENEY
                (Lynn Patrick)

PLAGAKIS, Jim
                (Christy Dore)

PLAIDY, Jean   <HO>*
            [Eleanor Burford Hibbert]
   General Historical Novels:
      Beyond The Blue Mountains
      Daughter Of Satan (The Unholy
        Woman)
      Defenders Of The Faith
      Goldsmith's Wife, The (The
        King's Mistress)
      Scarlet Cloak, The
   Stories Of Victorian England:
      It Began In Vauxhall Gardens
      Lilith
   Tudor Novels:
      Katharine Of Aragon:
         Katharine, The Virgin Widow
         Shadow Of The
           Pomegranate, The
         King's Secret Matter
      Murder Most Royal
      St. Thomas's Eve

                        (cont'd)

PLAIDY, Jean (continued)
    Sixth Wife, The
    Thistle And The Rose
    Mary, Queen Of France
    Spanish Bridegroom, The
    Gay Lord Robert
    Uneasy Lies The Head
    Myself, My Enemy
  Ferdinand And Isabella Trilogy:
    Castle For Isabella
    Spain For The Sovereigns
    Daughter Of Spain
  French Revolution Trilogy:
    Louis The Well-Beloved
    Road To Compiegne, The
    Flaunting, Extravagent Queen
  Georgian Saga:
    Princess Of Celle, The
    Queen In Waiting
    Caroline The Queen
    Prince And The Quakeress, The
    Third George, The
    Perdita's Prince
    Sweet Lass Of Richmond Hill
    Indiscretions Of The Queen
    Regent's Daughter, The
    Goddess Of The Green Room
    Victoria In The Wings
  Henri Of Navarre:
    Evergreen Gallant
  Lucrezia Borgia Series:
    Madonna Of The Seven Hills
    Light On Lucrezia
  Mary Queen Of Scots Series:
    Royal Road To Fotheringay
    Captive Queen Of Scots, The
  Medici Trilogy:
    Catherine De' Medici:
      Madame Serpent
      Italian Woman, The
      Queen Jezebel
  Norman Trilogy:
    Bastard King, The
    Lion Of Justice, The
    Passionate Enemies, The
  Plantagenet Saga:
    Plantagenet Prelude, The
    Revolt Of The Eaglets, The
    Heart Of The Lion, The
    Prince Of Darkness, The
    Battle Of The Queens, The
    Queen From Provence, The
    Edward Longshanks
    Follies Of The King, The
              (cont'd)

PLAIDY, Jean (continued)
    Vow On The Heron, The
    Passage To Pontefract
    Star Of Lancaster, The
    Epitaph For Three Women
    Red Rose Of Anjou
    Sun In Splendor, The
    Hammer Of The Scots
  Queen Victoria Series:
    Captive Of Kensington
      Palace, The
    Queen And Lord M, The
    Queen's Husband, The
    Widow Of Windsor, The
  Stuart Saga:
    Murder In The Tower, The
    Charles II:
      Wandering Prince, The
      Health Unto His Majesty, A
      Here Lies Our Sovereign Lord
    The Last Of The Stuarts:
      Three Crowns, The
      Haunted Sisters, The
      Queen's Favorites, The
  Non-Fiction:
    Mary Queen Of Scots:
      Fair Devil Of Scotland, The
    Triptych Of Poisoners, A
    The Spanish Inquisition:
      Rise Of The Spanish
        Inquisition
      Growth Of The Spanish
        Inquisition
      End Of The Spanish
        Inquisition
  Juvenile:
    Young Elizabeth, The
    Meg Roper, Daughter Of Sir
      Thomas More
    Young Mary Queen Of Scots, The

PLIMMER, Charlotte w/ Denis   <HO>
  Power Seekers, The

PLOWDEN, Judith
  Afterglow   <CO>

PLUMMER, Clare
  Destroying Limelight, The

  _____

  _____

POGNAY, Jean Coulter
                (Catherine Coulter)

POLLAND, Madeleine A.   <GOT>
  No Price Too High

  _____

  _____

POLLOWITZ, Melinda
  Sweet Dreams: <YA>
    34 Country Girl

  _____

  _____

POOLE, Helen Lee   <HO>
  Whitewater Dynasty: (continued)
    Wabash!, The

  _____

  _____

POPE, Pamela
  Harlequin Presents:
    628 Eden's Law
  Harlequin Romance:
    2573 Candleberry Tree, The

  _____

  _____

PORTER, Donald   <HO>
  Sioux Arrows   <AIS:#9>
  Kiowa Fires   <AIS:#11>

  _____

  _____

PORTER, Donald Clayton   <HO>
  Pony Express
  White Indian Series: (continued)
    War Cry
    Ambush
    Seneca

  _____

  _____

PORTER, Joyce w/ Deborah BRYSON
                (Deborah Joyce)

PORTER, Madeline w/ Shannon HARPER
              (Madeline Harper)
                (Anna James)

PORTERFIELD, Kay
              (Coleen Kimbrough)

POTTER, Jacqueline
                (Jane Ireland)

POTTER, Margaret E. Newman
              (Anne Betteridge)
              (Anne Melville)

POTTS, Ruth
                (Rachel Palmer)

POWERS, Nora
                [Nina Pykare]
  Silhouette Desire:
    33   Promise Me Tomorrow
    48   Dream Of The West
    59   Time Stands Still
    84   In A Moment's Time
    117 This Brief Interlude
    148 In A Stranger's Arms

  _____

  _____

PRATE, Kit
  Woman Of Chicago, A   <AWD:#5>

  _____

  _____

PRESSLEY, Hilda
  Harlequin Petite:
    3 Journey To Love
  Other:
    New Registrar   <M&B>

  _____

  _____

PRESTON, Fayrene
                (Jaelyn Conlee)
  Loveswept:
    4 Silver Miracles
                (cont'd)

PRESTON, Fayrene (continued)
    In sequence:
    21   Seduction Of Jason, The
    34   For The Love Of Sami
    45   That Old Feeling

_____

_____

PRICE, Eugenia   <HO>
    Savannah

_____

_____

PRICE, Marjorie
                    (Maggie Peck)
                    (Margot Prince)

PRIESTLEY, Lee
    Avalon:
        Sound Of Always

_____

_____

PRINCE, Margot
                    [Marjorie Price]
    Candlelight Ecstasy:
    206   Man Who Came To Stay, The
    264   Run To Rapture

_____

_____

PRINCE MICHAEL Of Greece   <HO>
    Sultana

_____

_____

PRITCHETT, Ariadne
    Mill Reef Hall

_____

_____

PROLE, Lozania
        [Ursula Bloom w/ Charles Eade]
    Princess Philander   *

_____

_____

PYATT, Rosina
    Sapphire Romance: <ENG>
        Wish Me Happy

_____

_____

PYKARE, Nina
                    (Ann Coombs)
                    (Nina Coombs)
                    (Nan Pemberton)
                    (Nora Powers)
                    (Regina Towers)

Q

QUIN-HARKIN, Janet   <YA>
    Caprice Romance:
        35   Tommy Loves Tina
    Sweet Dreams:
        32   Daydreamer
        53   Ghost Of A Chance
        61   Exchange Of Hearts

_____

_____

QUINN, Alison
    Harlequin Gothic Romance:
        Satyr Ring, The

_____

_____

QUINN, Christina
    Tender Price, A

_____

_____

R

RAE, Judie
    Caprice Romance: <YA>
        43   Prescription For Love

_____

_____

RAE, Patricia
               [Patricia Rae Walls]
  Hospital Nurse   \<DNS\>
  Maternity Nurse   \<MED\>
  Storm Tide   \<HR\>
  Student Nurse   \<CO\>
  Touch, The
  Ways Of The Wind   \<RW\>

RAEF, Laura/Laura C.
  Avalon:
    Dr. Terri's Project
    Miracle At Seaside   *
    Moonlight Kisses

RAESCHILD, Sheila   \<HO\>
        (see Terry Nelsen Bonner)
  Earthstones

RAFFAT, Donne   \<HO\>
  Caspian Circle, The

RAFFEL, Elizabeth
  Candlelight Ecstasy:
    180 Lost Without Love

RAGOSTA, Millie J.
        (Melanie Randolph)
  Starlight Romance:
    Dream Weaver, The
    Gerait's Daughter
    Sing Me A Love Song
    Winter Rose, The   *

RAINE, Nicole
  Candlelight Ecstasy Supreme:
    44 Secrets And Desire

RAINVILLE, Rita
  Silhouette Romance:
    313 Challenge The Devil

RAND, Suzanne
                 [Debra Brand]
  Sweet Dreams: \<YA\>
    49 Too Much To Loose
    57 On Her Own
    62 Just Like The Movies

RANDOLPH, Elise
               [Susan L. Lowe]
  Candlelight Ecstasy:
    143 Passionate Appeal
  Candlelight Ecstasy Supreme:
    19 Shadow Games

RANDOLPH, Ellen
               [W. E. D. Ross]
  Avalon:
    Nurse Martha's Wish

RANDOLPH, Melanie
          [Millie J. Ragosta]
  To Have And To Hold:
    9 Heart Full Of Rainbows

RANSOM, Candice F.
  Sunfire: <YA><HO>
    Susannah
    Amanda

RANSOM, Katherine
                [Mary Sederquist]
  Rapture Romance:
    37 O'Hara's Woman
    65 Wish On A Star

RASLEY, Alicia Todd
                (Elizabeth Todd)
                (Michelle Venet)

RASMUSSEN, Alysse
                (Alysse Lemery)
  Candlelight Ecstasy:
    221 Night In The Forest, A

RATHER, Deborah
                (Arlene James)

RAU, Margaret
  Starlight Romance:
    Hoyden Bride, The

RAWLINGS, Cynthia
  McFadden Romance: *
    48 Tiara
    48 Moonchild

RAY, Karen w/ G. H. GAZDAK
                (Anne Bernadette)

RAYE, Linda
                [Linda Turner]
  Second Chance At Love:
    222 Made In Heaven

REAVIN, Sara
  Elise

RECEVEUR, Betty Layman   <HR>
  In sequence: *
    Molly Gallagher
    Carrie Kingston

REECE, Colleen L.
  Avalon:
    Alpine Meadows Nurse
    Everlasting Melody
    Nurse Of The Crossroads   *

REED, Miriam
  Starlight Romance:
    Summer Song

REESE, John
                (Cody Kennedy, Jr.)

REEVES, Fionnuala   <RS>
  Deadly Inheritance

REID, Henrietta
  Harlequin Romance:
    2524 New Boss At Birchfields

REISSER, Anne N.
  Loveswept:
    28 Love, Catch A Wild Bird

_____

_____

REIT, Ann
  Wildfire: <YA>
    Yours Truly, Love, Janie

_____

_____

RETTKE, Marian Pope
                        (Anne Devon)

REVESZ, Etta
  Miss Fancy

_____

_____

RHODES, Evan H.   <HO>
  American Palace Series: <Saga>
    Bless This House
    Forged In Fury
    Valiant Hearts
    Distant Dream, A

_____

_____

RHODES, J. H.   <GOT>
  Avalon:
    Clouds Over Stormcrest
    Danger At Darkoaks
    Fear In The Night
    Menace In The Fog
    Shadow Over Hawkhaven
    Summer Mysteries

_____

_____

RHOME, Adah
                        [Ada Sumner]
    Silhouette Special Edition:
      This Cherished Land

_____

_____

RHYNE, Julia A.
                    (Lucy Hamilton)

RICE, Pat   <HR>
  Love's First Surrender

_____

_____

RICHARDS, Johnathan
                    (Canella Lewis)

RICHARDS, Penny w/ Sandra CANFIELD
                     (Sandi Shayne)

RICHARDS, Stephanie
  Rapture Romance:
    5 Chesapeake Autumn

_____

_____

RICHARDS, Tad
  (see Lee Davis Willoughby - MOAS)

RIEFE, Barbara
                        [Alan Riefe]
  Wicked Fire

_____

_____

RIFE, Ellouise A.   <GOT>
  House At Stonehaven, The

_____

_____

RIGDON, Charles   <CO>
  Caramour Woman, The

_____

_____

RILEY, Eugenia   <HR>
  Ecstasy's Triumph

_____

_____

RILEY, Sandra   <HO>
  Bloody Bay

_____

_____

RIPLEY, Alexandra
         [Alexandra Braid Ripley]
In sequence: <Saga>
   Charleston   *
   On Leaving Charleston

_____

_____

RIPY, Margaret
              [Margaret Daley]
Silhouette Special Edition:
    76 Tomorrow's Memory
   114 Rainy Day Dreams
   134 Matter Of Pride
   164 Firebird
        Feathers In The Wind

_____

_____

RIVERS, Francine   <HR>
  Sarina
This Golden Valley
Second Chance At Love:
   142 Hearts Divided
   208 Heart In Hiding

_____

_____

ROBARDS, Karen   <HR>
  Amanda Rose
  Forbidden Love
In sequence: *
   Island Flame
   Sea Fire

_____

_____

ROBB, JoAnn
              [JoAnn Ross]
Rapture Romance:
    29 Stardust And Diamonds
    49 Dreamlover
    61 Sterling Deceptions
    70 Secure Arrangement, A
    81 Tender Betrayal
    93 Touch The Sun

_____

_____

ROBBINS, JoAnn
              [JoAnn Ross]
Silhouette Desire:
    94 Winning Season

_____

_____

ROBBINS, Kay
              [Kay Hooper]
Second Chance At Love:
   110 Taken By Storm
   130 Elusive Dawn
   155 Kissed By Magic
   190 Moonlight Rhapsody

_____

_____

ROBERTS, Janet Louise   (deceased)
                 (Louise Bronte)
                (Rebecca Danton)
              (Janette Radcliffe)
Flower Of Love
Scarlet Poppies

_____

_____

ROBERTS, Leigh
Harlequin Temptation:
        Love's Circuits
SuperRomance:
    81 Moonlight Splendor

_____

_____

ROBERTS, Nora
          [Eleanor Aufdem-Brinke]
Promise Me Tomorrow
Silhouette Imtimate Moments:
     2 Once More With Feeling
    12 Tonight And Always
    25 This Magic Moment
    33 Endings And Beginnings
    49 Matter Of Choice, A
        Rules Of The Game
Silhouette Romance:
   199 From This Day
                        (cont'd)

127

ROBERTS, Nora (continued)
    215 Her Mothers Keeper
    252 Untamed
    274 Storm Warning
    280 Sullivan's Woman
    299 Less Of A Stranger
    Silhouette Special Editions:
        In sequence:
    100   Reflections
    116   Dance Of Dreams
    162 First Impressions
    175 Law Is A Lady
        Opposites Attract

_____

_____

ROBERTS, Suzanne
                        (Laurie Marath)
    Hearts Measure, The

_____

_____

ROBERTS, Willo Davis
    Sunfire: <YA><HO>
        Elizabeth

_____

_____

ROBERTSON, Carol
    First Love From Silhouette: <YA>
        52 Summer To Remember, A

_____

_____

ROBINS, Denise
                        (Ashley French)
                        (Harriet Gray)
                        (Julia Kane)
                        (Francesca Wright)
    All For You
    Bitter Core, The (orig under
        pseudo: Ashley French)
    Breaking Point, The (orig under
        pseudo: Ashley French)
    Dark Secret Love (orig under
        pseudo: Julia Kane)
    Family Holiday
    Gold For The Gay Masters (orig
        under pseudo: Harriet Gray)
                        (cont'd)

ROBINS, Denise (continued)
    Heavy Clay
    Moment Of Truth
    Once Is Enough (orig under
        pseudo: Ashley French)
    Sin Was Mine (orig under
        pseudo: Julia Kane)

_____

_____

ROBINS, Eleanor
    Starlight Romance:
        Tormenting Memories

_____

_____

ROBINS, Madeleine
    Coventry:
        175 Lady John

_____

_____

ROBINSON, Barbara   <YA>
    Temporary Times, Temporary Places

_____

_____

ROBY, Mary Linn
                    (Valerie Bradstreet)
                    (Pamela D'Arcy)
                    (Georgia Grey)
                    (Pauline Pryor)
                    (Elizabeth Welles)
                    (Mary Wilson)

ROGERS, Eleanor
                        (Eleanor Woods)

ROGERS, Rosemary
    Wanton, The

_____

_____

ROLAND, Michelle
                [Rose Marie Ferris]
    Second Chance At Love:
        102 Beloved Stranger

_____

_____

ROME, Margaret
  Harlequin Romance:
    2553 Rapture Of The Deep
    2561 Lord Of The Land
    2584 Bay Of Angels
    2615 Castle Of The Line

ROSE, Jennifer
                    [Nancy Webber]
  To Have And To Hold:
    2 Taste Of Heaven, A
   11 Keys To The Heart
   27 Kisses Sweeter Than Wine

ROSE, Marcia
            [Marcia Kamien w/
             Rose Novak]
  Connections
  Music Of Love

ROSEMOOR, Patricia
          [Patricia Pinianski]
  Torchlite:
   Tender Spirit

ROSENSTOCK, Janet
          (see Dennis Adair)

ROSS, Clarissa
         [W. E. D. Ross]
  Summer Of The Shaman

ROSS, Dana Fuller   <HO>
         [Noel B. Gerson]
  Yankee Rogue
  Wagons West Series: (continued)
   Montana!
   Dakota!
            (cont'd)

ROSS, Dana Fuller (continued)
   Utah!
   Idaho!

ROSS, Erin
       [Shirley Bennett Tallman]
  Silhouette Desire:
    89 Time For Tomorrow
   114 Fragrant Harbor
   137 Tide's End
   155 Odds Against
       This Time For Keeps
  Silhouette Special Edition:
   107 Flower Of The Orient

ROSS, JoAnn
           (JoAnn Robb)
          (JoAnn Robbins)
  Harlequin Temptation:
   Stormy Courtship

ROSS, Marilyn
         [W. E. D. Ross]
  Decision For Nurse Baldwin
  House Of Dark Shadows

ROSS, W. E./W. E. D.
       [W. E. Daniel Ross]
        (Leslie Ames)
         (Rose Dana)
        (Ruth Dorset)
         (Ann Gilmer)
       (Diana Randall)
      (Ellen Randolph)
          (Dan Ross)
         (Dana Ross)
       (Clarissa Ross)
       (Marilyn Ross)
       (Jane Rossiter)
       (Rose Williams)
  Avalon:
   Christopher's Mansion
            (cont'd)

ROSS, W. E./W. E. D. (continued)
    Flight In Romance
    Ghostly Jewels, The   <GOT>
    Let Your Heart Answer   *
    Midhaven   *
    Nurse Janice's Dream
    Rehearsal For Love
    This Dark Lane
    This Uncertain Love

_____

_____

ROSSEN, Steven
    Naked Angel

_____

_____

ROSZEL, Renee
                    [Renee Wilson]
    Harlequin American Romance:
        10 Hostage Heart
    Silhouette Desire:
        90 Wild Flight

_____

_____

ROTCHSTEIN, Janice
                    (see Alan Ebert)

ROTH, Jillian
                    [Linda King Ladd]
    Rapture Romance:
        55 Bittersweet Temptation
        71 On Wings Of Desire

_____

_____

ROTHWEILER, Joanne Metro w/
    Paul ROTHWEILER
    (see Lee Davis Willoughby <MOAS>)

ROTTER, Elizabeth Walker
                    (Laura Matthews)
                    (Elizabeth Walker)
                    (Elizabeth Neff Walker)
    Finding Mr. Right:
        Paper Tiger

_____

_____

ROWAN, Barbara
                    [Ida Pollock]
    Harlequin Classic:
        132 Mountain Of Dreams (902)

_____

_____

ROWE, Jack
    Brandywine   <Saga>

_____

_____

ROWE, Melaine
                    [Pamela Browning]
    Silhouette Special Edition:
        129 Sea Of Gold

_____

_____

ROWLAND, Susannah   <HR>
    Coral Winds

_____

_____

ROYALL, Vanessa
                    [M. T. Hinkemeyer]
    In sequence: *
        Wild Wind Westward
        Sieze The Dawn

_____

_____

RYAN, George
    (see Lee Davis Willoughby <MOAS>)

RYAN, Jeanette Miles   <YA>
    Reckless

_____

_____

RYAN, Nancy Henderson   <HR>
    Kathleen's Surrender

_____

_____

130

SAKOL, Jeanne
  Maiden Voyage

_____

_____

SALERNO, Jeanette
  Princessa

_____

_____

SALISBURY, Carola   <RS>
         [Michael Butterworth]
  Count Vronsky's Daughter

_____

_____

SALOFF-ASTAKHOFF, N. I.
  A Hearth Romance:
    19 Judith

_____

_____

SALVATO, Sharon
  Manning Family Saga: *
    In sequence:
      Fires Of July, The
      Drums Of December, The

_____

_____

SANDERS, Shirley F.
  Avalon:
    Search For Enchantment

_____

_____

SANDERSON, Jill
              [Helen Beaumont]
  Sapphire Romance: <ENG>
    Never Forget Me

_____

_____

SANFORD, Annette
                (Mary Carroll)
                (Meg Dominique)
                (Lisa St. John)
                (Anne Shore)
                (Anne Starr)

SANFORD, Ursula   <GOT>
  Poisoned Anemones, The

_____

_____

SANS, Marty
                (Jenny Loring)
                (Lee Sawyer)

SANTINI, Rosemarie
              [Agnes Nixon]
  All My Children Series:
    I   Tara & Philip
    II   Erica
    III Lovers, The

_____

_____

SARGENT, Katherine   <HO>
  Outcasts From Eden
  Rose And The Sword, The

_____

_____

SARGENT, Lynda   <HO>
  Judith Duchesne

_____

_____

SATRAN, Pamela   *
  Finding Mr. Right:
    Balancing Act

_____

_____

SAUCIER, Donna
              [Donna Schomberg]
  Harlequin SuperRomance:
    109 Amethyst Fire

_____

_____

SAUNDERS, Bree
                    [Sandra Kitt]
  Harlequin American Romance:
    86 Adam And Eve

SAUNDERS, Jean
                [Jean Innes Saunders]
                        (Jean Innes)
  Silhouette Romance:
    216 Love's Sweet Music
    243 Language Of Love, The
    261 Taste The Wine
    289 Partners In Love

SAVAGE, Elizabeth
  Willowwood

SAWYER, Nancy w/ John SAWYER
                    (Nancy Buckingham)
                    (Nancy John)
                    (Hilary London)
                    (Erica Quest - Eng)

SAXON, Antonia
  Silhouette Special Edition:
    88 Paradiso
    141 Above The Moon

SCAFIDEL, James
  (see Lee Davis Willoughby - MOAS)

SCANTLIN, Bea
                    (Ruth Stewart)

SCARIANO, Margaret M.
  Caprice Romance: <YA>
    27 Too Young To Know

SCHAEFER, Frank w/ Kerry NEWCOMB
                    (Shana Carrol)
                    (Peter Gentry)
                    (Christina Savage)

SCHAFER, Rosemary   <RS>
  Last Of The Whitcombers, The

SCHATTNER, E.
                    (Emma Church)
                    (Elizabeth Graham)

SCHELLENBERG, Helene Chambers
  Beth Adams, Private Duty Nurse
  Breath Of Life

SCHENK, Joyce
                    (Amy Lawrence)
                    (Jo Stewart - YA)
  Avalon: <GOT>
    Caves Of Darkness

SCHERE, Monroe
                    (Jessica Howard)
                    (Abigail Winter)

SCHOMBERG, Donna
                    (Donna Saucier)

SCHOONOVER, Shirley
  Mountain Of Winter

SCHULER, Candace
                    (Jeanette Darwin)

SCHULTE, Elaine L.
  Serenade/Serenata:
    1 On Wings Of Love

SCHULTZ, Duane   \<HO\>
  Sabers In The Wind

SCHULTZ, Janet
                       (Jan Stuart)

SCHULZE, Hertha
                  (Kate Wellington)

SCHURFRANZ, Vivian
  Sunfire: \<YA\>\<HO\>
    Danielle

SCHWARTZ, Paula
            (Elizabeth Mansfield)
               (Libby Mansfield)

SCHWARTZ, Shiela
  Wildfire: \<YA\>
    One Day You'll Go

SCOFIELD, Carin
  Silhouette Romance:
    249 Silverwood

SCOTT, Alexandra
  Harlequin Romance:
    2554 Catch A Star
    2585 Love Comes Stealing
    2604 Borrowed Girl

SCOTT, Alison
  World Full Of Secrets, A

SCOTT, Amanda   \<RE\>
           [Lynne Scott-Drennan]
  An Affair Of Honor
  Indomitable Miss Harris, The
  Kidnapped Bride, The
  Ravenwood's Lady

SCOTT, Celia
  Harlequin Romance:
    2568 Seeds Of April
    2638 Starfire

SCOTT, Elizabeth A.
  Rim Of The Tub, The

SCOTT, Joanna
  Silhouette Special Edition:
        Perfect Passion, A \<PROM\>*
    136 Exclusively Yours
    186 Corporate Policy

SCOTT, Melissa
  Silhouette Desire:
    147 Territorial Rights

SCOTT, Michael William
  Rakehell Dynasty: (continued)
    4 Mission To Cathay

SCOTT, Rachel
              (Ana Lisa de Leon)
              (Marisa de Zavala)
  Velvet Glove:
    In The Dead Of The Night

SCOTT, Samantha
                    [Nancy Herman]
  Candlelight Ecstasy:
    147 Love's Unveiling
    204 After The Loving
  Candlelight Ecstasy Supreme:
    22 All In Good Time
  _____

  _____

SCOTT-DRENNAN, Lynne
                    (Amanda Scott)
  Starlight Romance:
    Summer Sandcastle
  _____

  _____

SCRIMGEOUR, G. J.   <HO>
  Woman Of Her Times, A
  _____

  _____

SEALE, Sara
        [Mrs. A. D. L. MacPherson]
  Harlequin Classic:
    114 Child Friday   (896)
    122 Charity Child   (991)
    137 This Merry Bond   (583)
    146 Maggy   (469)
  _____

  _____

SEDERQUIST, Mary
                  (Katherine Granger)
                  (Katherine Ransom)

SEGAL, Harriet
  Susquehanna
  _____

  _____

SEGER, Maura
                    (Jenny Bates)
                (Maeve Fitzgerald)
                 (Sara Jennings)
                 (Anne MacNeill)
                 (Laurel Winslow)
  Empire Of The Heart   <HR>
                          (cont'd)

SEGER, Maura (continued)
  Silhouette Intimate Moments:
    61 Silver Zephyr
  Silhouette Special Edition:
    135 Gift Beyond Price, A
  Tapestry: <HR>
    13 Rebellious Love
    20 Forbidden Love (sequel to
        Tapestry 'Defiant Love')
    23 Flame On The Sun
  _____

  _____

SEIDEL, Kathleen Gilles
  Harlequin American Romance:
    2 Same Last Name, The
    17 Risk Worth Taking, A
    57 Mirrors And Mistakes
    84 When Love Is Not Enough
  Harlequin American Romance
  Premier Edition:
    After All These Years
  _____

  _____

SEIDICK, Kathie
                    (Kasey Michaels)
  Or You Can Let Him Go   <NF>
  _____

  _____

SEIFERT, Elizabeth
                [Elizabeth Gasparotti]
  Bright Scalpel (Eng: Healing
    Hands)   *
  Hillbilly Doctor (Eng:
    Doctor Bill)   *
  Thus Doctor Mallory (Eng: Doctor
    Mallory)   *
  Two Doctors, Two Loves
  Young Doctor Galahad (Eng: Young
    Doctor)   *
  _____

  _____

SELDEN, Neil
  Caprice Romance: <YA>
    38 Last Kiss In April
  _____

  _____

SELLERS, Alexandra
  Harlequin Temptation:
      6 Forever Kind, The
  SuperRomance:
     87 Season Of Storm

_____

_____

SELLERS, Con
        [Connie Leslie Sellers, Jr.]
                  (Lee Raintree)
  Keepers Of The House

_____

SELLERS, Lorraine
  Silhouette Intimate Moments:
     15 Shadow Dance

_____

_____

SERAFINI, Tina
                  (Sali Knight)

SEYMOUR, Janette
  Reckless Lady   <CO>

_____

SHAHEEN, Leigh
                  (Valerie Zayne)

SHANDS, Sondra   <HO>
  Time Of Passion

_____

_____

SHARMAT, Marjorie   <YA>
  How To Meet A Gorgeous Guy

_____

_____

SHAW, Linda
  Silhouette Special Edition:
    •67 After The Rain
                        (cont'd)

SHAW, Linda (continued)
     97 Way Of The Willow
    121 Thistle In The Spring
    151 Lovesong And You, A

_____

_____

SHAW, Susan
  Caprice Romance: <YA>
     25 Bicycle Built For Two, A

_____

_____

SHAYNE, Sandi
            [Sandra Cranfield w/
                 Penny Richards]
  Silhouette Intimate Moments:
      No Perfect Season

_____

_____

SHEARING, Joseph   <GOT>
          [Gabrielle Margaret Long]
  Abode Of Love, The
  Aunt Beardie
  Blanche Fury w/ Margaret Campbell
  Crime Of Laura Sarelle, The
    (Laura Sarelle)
  Golden Violet, The
  Moss Rose
  Spectral Bride, The (The Fetch)
  Spider In The Cup, The
    (Album Leaf)
  Strange Case Of Lucile Clery
    (Lucile Clery: Woman Of Int-
    rigue) (Forget-Me-Not)
  To Bed At Noon

_____

_____

SHEARS, Judith w/ Bill HOTCHKISS
  Pawnee Medicine   <AIS:#14>
  Shoshone Thunder   <AIS:#12>

_____

_____

SHELBY, Graham   <HO>
  The Cannaway saga: In sequence: *
    Cannaways, The
    Cannaway Concern, The

_____

_____

SHELL, Peggy
  Avalon:
    Dr. Lindsey's Strategy

_____

_____

SHELLABARGER, Samuel   <HO>
  King's Cavalier, The

_____

_____

SHERIDAN, Jane   <HR>
  Love At Sunset

_____

_____

SHERRILL, Suzanne
              [Sherryl Ann Woods]
  Candlelight Ecstasy:
    209 Desirable Compromise

_____

_____

SHERWOOD, Valerie   <HR>
              [Jeanne Hines]
  Born To Love
  Lovely Lying Lips

_____

_____

SHEWMAKE, Georgia M.
  Avalon:
    Beckoning Moon
    Ghosts Of Yesterday   <GOT>
    Ridge Of Fear   <GOT>
    Love's Sweet Victory

_____

_____

SHIELDS, Dinah
                        (Jane Clare)

SHIMER, Ruth   <GOT>
  Correspondent, The

_____

_____

SHIPLETT, June Lund   <HR>
  "Winds" series: (continued)
    Wild Winds Calling

_____

_____

SHOCK, Marianne
  Loveswept:
    69 Queen's Defense, The

_____

_____

SHORE, Francine
              [Maureen Crane Wartski]
  Rapture Romance:
    11 Flower Of Desire
    22 Golden Maiden, The
    36 Love's Gilded Mask
    51 Lover In The Wings
    75 Lover's Run

_____

_____

SHUB, Joyce   <RS>
  Moscow By Nightmare

_____

_____

SHURA, Mary Francis
              [Mary Francis Craig]
  Shop On Threnody Street, The

_____

_____

SILVERLOCK, Anne
  Candlelight Ecstasy:
    284 Casanova's Master

_____

_____

SIMMONS, Suzanne
                    [Suzanne Guntrum]
  MacFadden Romance: *
    140 From This Day Forward
    233 Ivory Satin (was not
           published)

SIMMS, Suzanne
                    [Suzanne Guntrum]
  Silhouette Desire:
     43 Wild Sweet Magic, A
     61 All The Night Long
     79 So Sweet A Madness
    109 Only This Night
    150 Dream Within A Dream

SIMPSON, Judith w/ June HAYDON
                    (Rosalind Foxx)
                    (Sara Logan)

SINCLAIR, Cynthia
            [Maureen Crane Wartski]
  Tapestry: <HR>
     27 Winter Blossom

SINCLAIR, Tracy
  Silhouette Romance:
    244 Stars In Her Eyes
  Silhouette Special Edition:
     68 Castles In The Air
    105 Fair Exchange
    140 Winter Of Love
    153 Tangled Web
    183 Harvest Is Love, The

SINCLAIRE, Francesca
  Second Chance At Love:
    143 Splendid Obsession, A

SINGER, June Flaum
  Debutantes, The
  Movie Set, The
  Star Dreams

SINGER, Ronald
                    (Margaret Hunter)
                    (Delphine Marlowe)

SINGER, Sally M.
                    (Amelia Jamison)
  Giver Of Song   <CO>

SIZER, Mona
                    (Deana James)

SKELTON, C. L.   <HO>
  Regiment Quartet: (continued)
    Beloved Soldiers   Vol IV

SKILLERN, Christine
  Silhouette Special Edition:
     71 Moonstruck

SKINNER, June
                    (Rohan O'Grady)

SLAUGHTER, Frank G.
                    (C. V. Terry)
  Doctor's Daughters

SLAUGHTER, Pamela   <RS>
  Ravished

138

SLOJKOWSKI, Mary Ann
                    (Mary Ann Hammond)

SLOJKOWSKI, Mary Ann w/ Dorothy
   CORCORAN   (DeAnn Patrick)

SMALL, BERTRICE   <HR>
   Beloved
   In sequence: *
      Skye O'Malley
      All The Sweet Tomorrows
      Enchantress Mine
   _____

   _____

SMALL, Lass
                    (Cally Hughes)
   Candlelight Ecstasy:
      192 Dedicated Man, The
   _____

   _____

SMILEY, Viginia K.
                    (Tess Ewing)
   Avalon: *
      Libby Williams Nurse -
         Practitioner
      Nurse Of The Grand Canyon
   _____

   _____

SMITH, Barbara Cameron
                    (Barbara Camermon)

SMITH, Bobbi   <HR>
   Forbidden Fires
   In sequence: <3-Books>
      Rapture' Rage
   _____

   _____

SMITH, Carol Sturm
   Love & Life:
      Emily's Place
   _____

   _____

SMITH, Clare Breton
   Doctor's Problem, The   <M&B>
   _____

   _____

SMITH, Elaine C.
                    (Kami Lane)

SMITH, Genell Dellin
                    (Gena Dalton)

SMITH, George
                    (Diana Summers)

SMITH, Harriet
   Two Against The World
   _____

   _____

SMITH, Joan
                    [Jennie Gallant]
   Lace For Milady
   Lady Madeline's Folly   <RE>
   Love Bade Me Welcome
   Love's Way   <RE>
   Prelude To Love   <RE>
   Dawnstar Romance:
      Strictly Business
   Silhouette Romance:
      234 Next Year's Blonde
      255 Caprice
      269 From Now On
      288 Chance Of A Lifetime
      302 Best Of Enemies
      315 Trouble In Paradise
   _____

   _____

SMITH, Julia Cleaver
   Morning Glory
   _____

   _____

SMITH, Kenn
                    (Robin Leigh Smith)

SMITH, Marion
               [Marion Smith Collins]
  Harlequin Romance:
    2598 Beachcomber, The

SMITH, Nancy Carolyn   <GOT>
  To Dwell In Shadows

SMITH, Robin Leigh   <HO>
                  [Kenn Smith]
  Georgia Dynasty Series:
    In sequence:
      Passage To Glory

SMITH, Ruth
                 (Eileen Bryan)
                 (Alana Smith)

SMITH, Sally Tyree
  Avalon:
    Return To Terror

SMITH, Wilbur
  Angels Weep, The
  In sequence:
    Falcon Flies, A   <ENG>
    Men Of Men   <ENG>

SNODGRASS, Melinda
              (Melinda Harris)
          (Melinda McKenzie)

SNOW, Dorothea J.
  Avalon:
    Garden Of Love
    Golden Summer

SNOW, Lucy
               [Rosemary Aubert]
  SuperRomance:
    83 Song Of Eden
  Harlequin SuperRomance:
    115 Red Bird In Winter, A

SOHL, Jerry
         (Roberta Jean Mountjoy)

SOMERS, Suzanne   <GOT>
              [Dorothy Daniels]
  Shadow Of A Man
  Tidemill
  Avalon:
    House Of Eve
    Image Of Truth

SOMMERFIELD, Sylvie F.   <HR>
  Cherish Me, Embrace Me
  Kristen's Passion
  Tame My Wild Heart

SOMMERS, Beverly
                [Joy Freeman]
  Candlelight Ecstasy:
    169 Interlude Of Love
  First Love From Silhouette: <YA>
    66 Up To Date
    74 Passing Game, A
  Harlequin American Romance:
    11 City Life, City Love
    26 Unscheduled Love
    62 Verdict Of Love
    69 Last Key, The
    85 Mix And Match

SOMMERS, Jeanne
                [Barry Myers]
  Dark Desire Romance:
    Heartbreak Hill

SORRELS, Roy
                  (Anna McClure)

SORTORE, Nancy   <HO>
  Border Gentry   <Saga>

_____

_____

SOULE, Maris
  Harlequin Temptation:
       First Impressions   <PROM>
       No Room For Love

_____

_____

SPARK, Natalie
  Harlequin Romance:
  2633 Once More With Feeling

_____

_____

SPARKS, Christine
                (Lucy Gordon)

SPARROW, Laura
            (Jocelyn Griffin)

SPECTOR, Debra
  Sweet Dreams: <YA>
    31 Too Close For Comfort
    39 First Love
    51 Magic Moments

_____

_____

SPELLMAN, Cathy Cash
  So Many Partings

_____

_____

SPENCER, Anne
  McFadden Romance:
    24 Midnight Jewel   *

_____

_____

SPENCER, LaVyrle
  •Hellion, The
  ✓Separate Beds   <85>
  •Sweet Memories
  Twice Loved
  Harlequin Temptation:
    • 1 Spring Fancy
  Second Chance At Love:
    100 Promise To Cherish, A

_____

_____

SPRINGER, Lacey
  Silhouette Inspirations:
    7 Wealth Of Love, A

_____

_____

STAFF, Adrienne w/ Sally
  GOLDENBAUM   (Natalie Stone)

STANCLIFFE, Elaine
                (Elisa Stone)

STANFORD, Sondra
  Silhouette Special Edition:
    91 Love's Gentle Chains
   161 Heart Knows Best, The
        For All Time

_____

_____

STANLEY, Edward   <HO>
  Rock Cried Out, The

_____

_____

STANLEY, Sandra   <GOT>
  Rogue's Castle

_____

_____

STANTON, Anna
          [Helen Beaumont]
  Sapphire Romance: <ENG>
    Journey's End

_____

_____

STARR, Cynthia
  Silhouette Romance:
    201 Tears Of Gold

STARR, Kate
                [Joyce Dingwell]
  Harlequin Classic:
    117 Ship's Doctor   (828)
    142 Enchanted Trap, The   (950)

STARR, Martha
  Harlequin American Romance:
    87 From Twilight To Sunrise

STATHAM, Frances Patton
  Trilogy: In sequence:
    Phoenix Rising
    From Love's Ashes

STEEBER, Sharon   <HO>
  Jews, The

STEEL, Danielle
          [Danielle Steel Traina]
  Changes
  Full Circle
  Thurston House

STEELE, Jessica
  Harlequin Presents:
    596 Price To Be Met
    605 Intimate Enemies
    621 No Quiet Refuge
                          (cont'd)

STEELE, Jessica (continued)
    661 Reluctant Relative
    717 Ruthless In All
    725 Gallant Antagonist
  Harlequin Romance:
    2555 Distrust Her Shadow
    2580 Tethered Liberty
    2607 Tomorrow - Come Soon

STEELEY, Robert Derek
              (Amanda Jean Jarrett)

STEIN, Toby
  Only The Best   <CO>

STEINER, Barbara
  Wildfire: <YA>
    Secret Love

STEINER, Irene Hunter
  Gentle Intruder, The

STEMBER, Sol
  Judith: A Love Story Of Newport

STEPHENS, Barbara
              (Barbara South)
  Starlight Romance:
    Toast To Love, A

STEPHENS, Jeanne
                [Jean Hager]
  Silhouette Imtimate Moments:
    14 Reckless Surrender
    38 Memories
                          (cont'd)

STEPHENS, Jeanne (continued)
  Silhouette Special Edition:
    84 Splendored Sky, The   *
   108 No Other Love   *

STEPHENS, Kay
  Silhouette Romance:
   300 Felstead Collection, The

STEVENS, Kimberly
  Love's Deception

STEVENS, Lynsey
                      [Lyn Howard]
  Harlequin Presents:
   606 Man Of Vengeance
   654 Forbidden Wine
   692 Starting Over
  Harlequin Romance:
  2574 Closest Place To Heaven
  2608 Ashby Affair, The
  Other:
  1558 Terebori's Gold   <M&B>
  1778 Starting Over   <M&B>

STEVENS, Serita
                  (Megan MacDonnell)
  Shrieking Shadows Of Penporth
    Island, The   <GOT>
  Tapestry: <HR>
    25 Tame The Wild Heart

STEVENS, Susan
  Silhouette Romance:
   230 Ivory Innocence

STEVENSON, D. E.
              [Dorothy Emily Peploe]
  Alister & Co.
  Five Windows
  Golden Days
  World In Spell, A

STEVENSON, Florence
                   (Zandra Colt)
                   (Lucia Curzon)
                   (Zabrina Faire)

STEWART, Edward
  For Richer, For Poorer

STEWART, ISOBEL
  Masqueade:
    78 Stranger In The Glen   *

STEWART, Jo   <YA>
  Andrea
  Magic Moments: <YA>
    1 Love Vote, The

STEWART, Mary   <RS>
  Wicked Day, The

STEWART, Ruth
                    [Bea Scantlin]
  Silhouette Desire:
    42 Ask Me No Secrets
  Silhouette Intimate Moments:
     Reckless Summer

STINE, Whitney
          (Constance F. Peale)
  Oklahomans Series: (continued)
    4 Survivors, The

_____

STIRLING, Jessica
          [Peggie Coghlan w/
            Hugh C. Rae]
  Dresden Finch, The (Eng:
    Beloved Sinner)
  Stalker Trilogy: In sequence:
    Strathmore (Eng: Spoiled Earth)
    Call Home The Heart (Eng:
      Hiring Fair)
    Dark Pasture, The   *
  Beckman Family Trilogy:
    In sequence:
    Drums Of Time, The (Eng: Deep
      Well At Noon)   *
    Blue Evening Gone, The
    Gates Of Midnight, The

_____

STOCKENBERG, Antoinette
          (Antoinette Hale)

STONE, Elisa
          [Elaine Stancliffe]
  Rapture Romance:
    31 Shared Love, A

_____

STONE, Karen
          (Karen Young)

STONE, Natalie
          [Sally Goldenbaum w/
            Adrienne Staff]
  Candlelight Ecstasy:
    198 Double Play
    235 Blue Ridge Autumn
    288 Summer Fling

_____

STONE, Sharon
  Second Chance At Love:
    114 Moonlight Persuasion

_____

STRATTON, Rebecca
          (Lucy Gillen)
  Harlequin Romance:
    2543 Man From Nowhere, The

_____

STREIB, Dan
          [Daniel Streib]
          (Louise Grandville)
      (see Richard Hale Curtis)

STRESHINSKY, Shirley   <HO>
  Hers The Kingdom

_____

STRINGFELLOW, Olga
  Gift For The Sultan, A

_____

STROTHER, Elsie W.
  Avalon:
    Love's Sweet Treasure
    Safari Into Danger

_____

STROTHER, Pat Wallace
          (Patricia Cloud)
          (Vivian Lord)
          (Pat Wallace)

STRUTT, Sheila
  Harlequin Premiere III:
    36 No Yesterdays
  Harlequin Romance:
    2333 Master Of Craighill, The *
          (cont'd)

STRUTT, Sheila (continued)
  2562 Flight Of The Golden
        Hawk, The

STUART, Anne
    [Anne Kristine Stuart Ohlrogge]
  Harlequin American Romance:
    30 Chain Of Love
    39 Heart's Ease
    52 Museum Piece
    93 Housebound

STUART, Becky   <HR>
        [Ann Elizabeth Bullard]
  First Love From Silhouette: <YA>
    70 More Than Friends
    81 Mockingbird, The
    97 Land's End

STUART, Casey   <HR>
        [Ann Elizabeth Bullard]
  Waves Of Passion

STUART, Doris
                    (Dee Stuart)
                    (Ellen Searight)

STUART, Florence
  Necklace, The
  Sharon Romance:
    I Love You Ruby Compton

STUART, Jan
                    [Janet Schultz]
  Candlelight Ecstasy:
    255 Risk Worth Taking

STUART, Jessica   <HR>
  Moonsong Chronicles: (continued)
    Shadows Of Moonsong, The

STUART, Sheila
  Harlequin Premiere III:
    36 No Yesterday

STUART, Vivian
                    [Vivian Stuart Mann]
                    (Barbara Allen)
                    (William Stuart Long)
                    (Alex Stuart)

STUART, Vivian **
                    [Charles R. MacKinnon]
                    (Charles Stuart-Vernon)
                    (Barbara Lynn)
  ** (DO NOT confuse this pseudonym
      with that of another author)

STUART-OHLROGGE, Anne Kristine
                    (Anne Stuart)

STUART-VERNON, Charles
                    [Charles R. MacKinnon]
                    (Barbara Lynn)
                    (Vivian Stuart **)
  ** (DO NOT confuse this pseudonym
      with that of another author)

STUBBS, Jean   <HO>
  Howarth Saga: (continued)
    Vivian Inheritance, The

SULLIVAN, Jo
  Harlequin Romance:
    2544 Suspicion

SUMMERS, ASHLEY
                    [Faye Ashley]
  Silhouette Desire:
    95 Marrying Kind, The
  Silhouette Romance:
    197 Season Of Enchantment
    223 Private Eden, A

SUMMERS, Diana   <HO>
                    [George Smith]
  Louisiana

SUMMERS, Essie
  Harlequin Classic:
    109 Moon Over The Alps   (862)
  Harlequin Romance:
    2525 Daughter Of The Misty
          Gorges
    2590 Mountain For Luenda, A
    2622 Lamp For Jonathan, A
    2645 Season Of Forgetfulness

SUMMERVILLE, Margaret   <RE>
                    [Pamela Wilson w/
                     Barbara Wilson]
  Scandal's Daughter

SUMNER, Ada
                    (Adah Rhome)

SWANTON, Molly w/ Carla PELTONEN
                    (Lynn Erickson)

SWATRIDGE, Charles w/ Irene Maude
  SWATRIDGE
                    (Theresa Charles)

SWEENEY, Linda w/ Patricia
  PINIANSKI
                    (Lynn Patrick)

SWINDLES, Madge   <HR>
  Summer Harvest

SWINNERTON, Frank
  Tigress In The Village, A

T

TAHOURDIN, Jill
  Harlequin Romance: <PROM>
    Hummingbird Island

TALBOT, Charlene
                    (Lucy Lee)

TALIAS, Angela
                    (Angela Alexie)

TALLMAN, Shirley Bennett
                    (Erin Ross)

TAX, Meredith
  Rivington Street

TAYLOR, Abra
                    [Barbara Brouse]
  Hold Back The Night   <CO>
  Harlequin Temptation:
        Summer Surrender
  Silhouette Special Editon:
    73 Season Of Seduction
    103 Wild Is The Heart
    127 Woman Of Daring, A
    157 Forbidden Summer
        Sea Spell

TAYLOR, Allison
  McFadden Romance:
    36 Winter White   *

TAYLOR, Dorothy E.   <HR>
  Fleur de Lis

TAYLOR, Janelle
  Daughters Of The Warring
    Winds   <85>
  Destiny's Temptress   <85>
  Ecstasy Saga: (continued)
    Seeds Of Fury   <85>
  First Love, Wild Love (title
    changed from "Silver Spurs &
    Red Satin")
  Harlequin American Romance:
    54 Valley Of Fire

TAYLOR, Mary Anne
                      (Kate Bowe)
  Apointment In Verona

TEMPLETON, Janet
              [Morris Hershman]
  Starlight Romance:
    Lady Fortune
    Lover's Knot   *
    Scapegrace, The   *

TERRITO, Mary Jo
                  (Kate Belmont)
               (Kathryn Belmont)
                 (Gwen Fairfax)

TERRY, Margaret
  Avalon:
    Last Of April, The
                        (cont'd)

TERRY, Margaret (continued)
    Love For Tomorrow

TEW, Marzee King
  Avalon:
    Fireside Love

THACKER, Cathy
  Second Chance At Love:
    153 Intimate Scoundrels

THACKER, Cathy Gillen
  Harlequin American Romance:
    37 Touch Of Fire
    75 Promise Me Today
  Velvet Glove:
    Wildfire Trace, The

THANE, Elswyth   <HO>
                    [Elswyth Beebe]
  Williamsburg Saga:
    In sequence: *
      Dawn's Early Light
      Yankee Stranger
      Ever After

THAYER, Nancy
  Stepping   <CO>
  Bodies And Souls

THIELS, Kathryn
  Silhouette Intimate Moments:
    51 Alternate Arrangements

THIES, Joyce w/ Janet BIEBER
               (Janet Joyce)

THIMBLETHORPE, J. S.
              (Sylvia Thorpe)

THOM, James Alexander   <HO>
  Follow The River
  From Sea To Shining Sea
  Long Knife

_____

_____

THOMAS, Bree
           [Susannah Howe]
  Rapture Romance:
    42 Love's Journey Home

_____

_____

THOMAS, Rosie
  Follies

_____

_____

THOMPSON, Chris
  Torchlite:
    Whispers Of Desire

_____

_____

THOMPSON, Julian F.   <YA>
  Facing It

_____

_____

THOMPSON, Kate
  Great House

_____

_____

THOMPSON, Robert
         (see Rebecca Drury)

THOMPSON, Vicki Lewis
  Harlequin Temptation:
    9 Mingled Hearts
  • *Butterflies in the Sun*

_____

THORNE, April
  Silhouette Intimate Moments:
    50 Forgotten Promises
  Silhouette Special Edition:
   111 Make-Believe Magic

_____

_____

THORNE, Avery
  Harlequin Presents:
   677 Splendid Passion, A
   693 No Other Chance

_____

_____

THORNE, Nicola
        [Rosemary Ellerbeck]
  Affairs Of Love
  Cashmere

_____

_____

THORNTON, Carolyn
    [Carolyn Stromeyer Thornton]
  Silhouette Romance:
   229 For Eric's Sake
  Silhouette Special Edition:
    81 Looking Glass Love
   138 Smile And Say Yes
   146 By The Book
   168 Mail Order Bride
   182 Changing Seasons

_____

_____

THORNTON, Helene   <HR>
  Journey To Desire
  Scarlet Ribbons: <HR>
    Passionate Exile

_____

_____

THORPE, Kay
  Harlequin Presents:
    573 Man Of Means, A
    597 Master Of Morley
    646 Land Of The Incas, The
    678 Never Trust A Stranger
    709 Inheritance, The
  Other:
  Man In A Box   <M&B>

THORPE, Sylvia
                [J. S. Thimblethorpe]
  Mistress Of Astington   <RE>
  Strangers On The Moor (Smuggler's
    Moon)   <GOT>

THUM, Marcella   <HR>
  Blazing Star
  Jasmine

THURLO, Aimee
                    (Aimee Duvall)
                    (Aimee Martel)

THURSTON, Anne
  Harlequin American Romance:
    53 Pink Beds, The

TIERNEY, Ariel
  Second Chance At Love:
    129 Conquering Embrace

TITCHENOR, Louise w/ Eileen
  BUCKHOLTZ & Ruth GLICK
                    (Alyssa Howard)

TITCHENOR, Louise w/ Ruth GLICK
                    (Alexis Hill Jordan)

TODD, Elizabeth   <RE>
                [Alicia Todd Rasley]
  Earl's Intrigue, The

TONE, Teona   <RS>
  Lady On The Line

TOOMBS, Jane
                [Jane Jenke Toombs]
                    (Diana Stuart)
                (see Rebecca Drury)
  Arapaho Spirit   <AIS:#13>
  Tule Witch   <GOT>
  Dark Desire Romance:
    Shadowed Hearts
  Harlequin Gothic Romance:
    Restless Obsession

TOOMBS, John
                    (Fortune Kent)
                    (Jocelyn Wilde)
            (see Richard Hale Curtis)
  Silverfire

TOPAZ, Jacqueline
                [Jacqueline Hyman]
  To Have And To Hold:
    39 Deeper Than Desire

TOTH, Emily Jane   <HR>
  Daughters Of New Orleans   *

TOWNSEND, Tom
                    (Tammie Lee)
            (see Leather And Lace <L&L>)

149

TRAINA, Danielle Steel
                (Danielle Steel)

TRANBARGER, Charlotte
  Avalon:
    Destiny's Love
    Love Beyond Yesterday

_____

_____

TRAVIS, Neal   <CO>
  Mansions
  Palaces

_____

_____

TRAYNOR, Page w/ Anthony TRAYNOR
                (Page Anthony)

TREE, Cornelia
  Child Of The Night

_____

_____

TRENT, Brenda
                [Brenda Himrod]
  Silhouette Desire:
    122 Without Regrets
  Silhouette Romance:
    193 Runaway Wife   *
    245 Steal Love Away
    266 Hunter's Moon

_____

_____

TRENT, Danielle
                [Dan Trent w/
                 Lynda Trent]
  Harlequin SuperRomance:
    121 Winter Roses

_____

_____

TRENT, Lynda
                [Dan Trent w/
                 Lynda Trent]
  Silhouette Intimate Moments:
    36 Designs
        Taking Chances
                        (cont'd)

TRENT, Lynda (continued)
  Tapestry: <HR>
        In sequence:
    14   Embrace The Storm
    17   Embrace The Wind
    28   Willow Wind

_____

_____

TREVOR, June
                [June E. Casey]
  Silhouette Desire:
    88 Winged Victory
  Silhouette Intimate Moments:
    11 Until The End Of Time

_____

_____

TRIEGEL, Linda
                (Elisabeth Kidd)

TROLLOPE, Joanna   <HO>
  Eliza Stanhope
  Leaves From The Valley
  Parson Harding's Daughter

_____

_____

TROY, Katherine   <RS>
                (Anne Buxton)
                (Anne Maybury)
  Roseheath

_____

_____

TUCKER, Elaine
                [Deborah Elaine Camp]
  To Have And To Hold:
    4   They Said It Wouldn't Last
    12 Strange Bedfellows

_____

_____

TUCKER, Helen
  Tapestry: <HR>
    29 Ardent Vows
    38 Bound By Honor

_____

_____

TURNBULL, Agnes Sligh   <RS>
  Two Bishops, The

TURNER, Linda
                      (Linda Raye)
  SuperRomance:
    65 Persistent Flame, A

TURNER, Lynn
                    [Mary Watson]
  Harlequin Temptation:
     8 For Now, For Always

TYLER, Alison
  Candlelight Ecstasy:
    227 Business Before Pleasure
    245 Too Good To Be True
    259 Tender Awakening
    283 Daring Alliance, A
  Candlelight Ecstasy Supreme:
    36 Playing It Safe

TYLER, Anne
                [Anne Modarressi]
  Dinner At The Homesick
    Restaurant

U

UPSHALL, Helen
  Surgeon, RN   <M&B>

V

VAIL, Linda
                  [Steve Hamilton w/
                    Melinda Hobaugh]
  Candlelight Ecstasy:
    160 Fool's Paradise
    243 Best Things In Life, The
    289 Amber Persuasion

VALCOUR, Vanessa
                  [James Conaway]
  Second Chance At Love:
    121 Play It By Heart

VALENTI, Justine
                      (Barbara Max)
                   (Vanessa Victor)
  Twin Connections

VANDERGRIFF, Aola   <HR>
                      (Kit Brown)
  "Daughters" series: (continued)
    Daughters Of The Storm

VAN DER ZEE, Karen
                [Wendella Kilmer]
  Harlequin Presents:
    694 One More Time
  Harlequin Romance:
    2652 Soul Ties

VAN HAZINGA, Cynthia   <HO>
     [Cynthia Van Hazinga Kutz]
  Farewell My South
  Our Hearts Divided

VAN SLYKE, Helen   (deceased)
                         (Sharon Aston)
  In sequence: *
   Heart Listens, The
   Mixed Blessing, The

VAN ZWIENEN, John   <HO>
  China Clipper

VARLINSKY, Deborah M.
                    (Deborah LeVarre)

VAUGHAN, Louise
  Lovequest

VAUGHAN, Robert   <HO>
                    (Paula Fairman)
                    (Paula Moore)
  Savages
  War-Torn Series:
   Brave And The Lonely, The
   Masters And Martyrs
   Fallen And The Free, The
   Divine And The Damned, The

VERNON, Dorothy
  Silhouette Romance:
   233 Edge Of Paradise
   276 Paradise Found
   295 That Tender Feeling
                         (cont'd)

VERNON, Dorothy (continued)
   312 Wild And Wanton

VERNON, Rosemary
  Sweet Dreams: <YA>
   33 Dear Amanda
   64 Love In The Fast Lane

VERRETTE, Joyce   <HR>
                    [Joyce Petratur]
  Rebel's Love, A

VERYAN, Patricia   <RE>
                    [Paticia Bannister]
  Married Past Redemption
  Nanette
  Sanguinet Series: In sequence: *
   Feather Castles
   Noblest Frailty, The

VICTOR, Vanessa
                    [Justine Valenti]
  Silhouette Desire:
   70 Dinner For Two

VIENS, Carol
                    (Carol Daniels)

VIERTEL, Joseph
  Life Lines

VILLARS, Elizabeth
                [Ellen (Bette) Feldman]
  Adam's Daughter

VILLIERS, Margot   <GOT>
  Serpent Of Lilith, The

_____

_____

VINE, Kerry
  Silhouette Romance:
    264 Alpine Idyll

_____

_____

VINES-HAINES, Beverly
                 (Becca Cassidy - YA)
                      (Jamie West)

VITEK, Donna
                 [Donna Kimel Vitek]
  Silhouette Romance:
    217 Blue Mist Of Morning

VITEK, Donna Kimel
                 (Donna Alexander)
  Candlelight Ecstasy:
    136 Dangerous Embrace
    166 No Promise Given
    262 An Unforgetable Caress
  Candlelight Ecstasy Supreme:
     3 Warmed By The Fire
     9 Never Look Back
    21 Breaking The Rules
    42 Asking For Trouble

_____

_____

VIVIAN, Daisy   <RE>
                 [Bruce Kenyon]
  Rose White, Rose Red

_____

_____

W

WADE, Elizabeth Evelyn   <RE>
  Gallant Hearts

_____

_____

WAGER, Walter
  (see Lee Davis Willoughby <MOAS>)

WAGNER, Carol I.
                      (Malissa Carroll)

WAGNER, Carol I. w/ Jo BREMER
                      (Joellyn Carroll)

WAGNER, Kimberli
  Loveswept:
    56 Encore

_____

_____

WAGNER, Sharon
                 [Sharon B. Wagner]
                 (Casey Stephens)
  First Love From Silhouette: <YA>
    68 Change Partners
  Rapture Romance:
    26 Strangers Who Love

_____

_____

WAGONS WEST SERIES
                 (see Dana Fuller Ross)

WAHL, Summit
  Birth Rights

_____

_____

WAHLSTROM, Carolyn
  Silhouette Inspirations:
    12 Sara's Story

_____

_____

WAKELY, Dorothy
  Sweet Revenge

_____

_____

WALDEN, Luanne   <HR>
  Forbidden Flame

_____

_____

```
WALKER, Barbara K.                          WALL, Robert E. (continued)
                 (Barbara Kaye)                Dominion

WALKER, Elizabeth            <RE>            _____
         [Elizaeth Walker Rotter]
   Loving Seasons, The                       _____

   _____           WALLACE, Anne Tolstoi
                                                Women's Work
   _____
                                             _____

WALKER, Elizabeth Neff                       _____
         [Elizabeth Walker Rotter]
   Silhouette Special Edition:               WALLACE, Pamela
      122  Antique Affair                       Silhouette Intimate Moments:
      176  That Other Woman                        24  Fantasies
                                                   48  Cry For The Moon
   _____                 58  Promises In The Dark
                                                Silhouette Special Edition:
   _____              102  Dreams Lost, Dreams Found

WALKER, Irma                                 _____
            [Irma Ruth Walker]
            (Andrea Harris)                  _____
   Lucifer Wine, The           <RS>
   Murdock Legacy, The                       WALLACE, Pat
   Other Passions, Other Loves  <HR>                 [Pat Wallace Strother]
   Harlequin SuperRomance:                      Wand And The Star, The
      104  Sonata For My Love                   Silhouette Intimate Moments:
   Love & Life:                                    4  Sweetheart Contract
      Next Step, The                               53  Objection Overruled
      Surrender                                 Silhouette Special Edition:
                                                   104  My Loving Enemy
   _____                 145  Shining Hour

   _____           _____

WALKER, Lois Arvin           <RE>            _____
                 (Candice Adams)
                 (Rebecca Ashley)            WALLS, Patricia
                 (Sabrina Myles)                            (Patricia Rae)
   An Elusive Love
                                             WALSH, Sheila               <RE>
   _____              Diamond Waterfall, The
                                                Incorrigible Rake, The
   _____              Runaway Bride, The

WALKER, Lucy                                 _____
      34  So Much Love          *
                                             _____
   _____
                                             WALTERS, Jade
   _____              Silhouette Romance:
                                                   211  Greek Idyll
WALL, Robert E.              <HO>
   The Canadians: (continued)                _____
      Inheritors
                          (cont'd)           _____


                               154
```

WARBY, Marjorie
  Bachelor Doctor
  Gregory Girls, The
  Quiet House, The

_____

_____

WARD, Lynda
                    (Julia Jeffries)
  SuperRomance:
    89 Sea Change, A
  Harlequin SuperRomance:
    119 Never Strangers

_____

_____

WARNER, Lucille S.
  Wildfire: <YA>
    Love Comes To Anne

_____

_____

WARREN, Beatrice
  Avalon:
    Hoodriver Nurse
    Nurse In Yosemite
    Nurse Monica's Legacy
    Nurse Onstage
    Nurse Paula's New Look

_____

_____

WARREN, Beverly C.
  Starlight Romance:
    Invitation To A Waltz
    That Gentle Touch

_____

_____

WARTSKI, Maureen Crane
                    (Sharon Francis)
                    (Francine Shore)
                    (Cynthia Sinclair)

WATERS, T. A   <GOT>
  Shrewsbury Horror, The (In The
    Halls Of Evil)   *

_____

_____

WATSON, Julia   <HO>
                    (Jane deVere - Eng)
                    (Julia Fitzgerald)
                    (Julia Hamilton)
  Lovechild, The
  Winter Of The Witch
  Gentian Trilogy:
    Mistress For The Valois, The
    King's Mistress, The
    Wolf And The Unicorn, The
  Other: <ENG>
    Medici Mistress
    Saffron At The Court Of
      Edward III
    Tudor Rose, The

_____

_____

WATSON, Mary
                    (Lynn Turner)

WATT, Ruth McFetridge
  Avalon:
    Love Makes A Difference
    Love Unveiled

_____

_____

WAY, Isabel Stewart   <GOT>
  Fleur Macabre

_____

_____

WAY, Margaret
  Harlequin Romance:
    2537 Spellbound
    2539 Silver Veil, The
    2556 Hunter's Moon
    2591 Girl Of Cobolt Creek
    2609 House Of Memories
                    (cont'd)

WAY, Margaret (continued)
    2632 Almost A Stranger
    2639 No Alternative

_____

_____

WAYNE, Rachel
    Second Chance At Love:
    136 Entwined Destinies

_____

_____

WAYNE, Rochelle   <HR>
    Ecstasy's Dawn
    Surrender To Ecstasy

_____

_____

WEALE, Anne
                        (Andrea Blake)
    Flora
    Harlequin Classic:
    110 Until We Met   (855)
    124 Hope For Tomorrow   (901)
    133 Islands Of Summer   (948)
    Harlequin Presents:
    565 Wedding Of The Year
    613 All That Heaven Allows
    622 Yesterday's Island
    670 Ecstasy
    Summer's Awakening

_____

WEATHERBY, W. J.   <HO>
    Chariots Of Fire
    Moondancers, The

_____

_____

WEBB, Mary
    Precious Bane

_____

_____

WEBBER, Nancy
                        (Jennifer Rose)

WEBSTER, Mary E.
    Avalon:
    Love Storm

_____

_____

WEGER, Jackie
    Harlequin American Romance:
    5   Strong And Tender Thread, A
    48 Count The Roses
    Harlequin Temptation:
    7   Cast A Golden Shadow

_____

_____

WEINER, Margery
                        (see Norah Lofts)

WELLER, Dorothy
                    (Dorothy Ann Bernard)
                    (Jane Beverley)
                    (Dorthea Hale)

WELLES, Alyssa
                        [Nomi Berger]
    Scarlet Ribbons: <HR>
    Dragon Flower

_____

_____

WELLES, Caron
                        [Jan Jones]
    Harlequin American Romance:
    13 Raven's Song

_____

_____

WELLES, Elisabeth
                        [Mary Linn Roby]
    Waterview Manor

_____

_____

WELLINGTON, Kate
                        [Hertha Schulze]
    To Have And To Hold:
    22 Delicate Balance, A

_____

_____

WELLS, Elaine F.   <GOT>
  Avalon:
    Run, Ellen, Run   *
  _____

  _____

WENDT, Joann   <HR>
  Beyond The Dawn

  _____

  _____

WENTWORTH, Sally
  Harlequin Presents:
    581 Flying High
    614 Jilted
    629 Shattered Dreams
    662 Lion Rock, The
    686 Backfire
    733 Dark Awakening
  _____

  _____

WERNER, Herma w/ Joyce GLEIT
                 (Eve Gladstone)

WESLEY, Elizabeth,
              [Adeline McElfresh]
  Doctor Barbara
  Sharon James: Free Lance
    Photographer
  _____

  _____

WEST, Jamie
          [Beverly Vines-Haines]
  Dawnstar Romance:
    Flame In The Mountains, A
  _____

  _____

WEST, Jennifer
             [Jennifer Justin]
  Silhouette Intimate Moments:
    10 Season Of Rainbows, A
    31 Star Spangled Days
  _____

  _____

WEST, Nicola
  Harlequin Presents:
    589 Lucifer's Brand
  Harlequin Romance:
    2526 Devil's Gold
    2592 No Room In His Life
    2610 Wildtrack
    2640 Tyzak Inheritance, The
    2646 Carver's Bride
  _____

  _____

WEST, Sara Ann
  Silhouette Desire:
    44 Heart Over Mind
  _____

  _____

WESTMINSTER, Aynn   <GOT>
  Moon In Shadow

  _____

  _____

WESTWOOD, Gwen
  Harlequin Romance:
    2586 Secondhand Bride
  _____

  _____

WEYRICH, Becky Lee   <HR>
  Rainbow Hammock
  Tainted Lilies
  _____

  _____

WHARTON, Althea   <GOT>
  White Ghost Of Fenwick Hall, The
  _____

  _____

WHITE, Charlotte
  Caprice Romance: <YA>
    42 Change Of Heart
  _____

  _____

WHITE, Charlotte
                    (Marianne Cole)
                    (Jennifer Dale)
  Judy Sullivan Books:
    Impossible Love   <CO>

WHITE, Ethel Lina   <GOT>
  Lady Vanishes, The (The Wheel
    Spins)   *

WHITE, Jude Gilliam
                    (Jude Deveraux)

WHITE, Patricia   <HR>
  To Last A Lifetime

WHITED, Charles   <HO>
  Spirit Of America: (continued)
    3 Power

WHITEHEAD, Barbara   <RE>
  Ramillies

WHITNEY, Phyllis A.   <RS>
  Rainsong

WHITTAL, Yvonne
  Harlequin Presents:
    574 Late Harvest
    582 Web Of Silk
    590 Chains Of Gold
    598 Silver Falcon, The
    630 Dark Heritage
    726 Where Two Ways Meet
                    (cont'd)

WHITTAL, Yvonne (continued)
  Harlequin Romance:
    2538 House Of Mirrors
    2616 Ride The Wind

WHITTENBURG, Karen
  Candlelight Ecstasy:
    216 Winds Of Heaven
    253 Golden Vows

WHITWORTH, Karen
  McFadden Romance: *
    12 Satin Promise, The
    12 Touch Of Velvet, A

WIDDEMER, Margaret   <HO>
  Red Castle Woman, The
  Red Cloak Flying

WILDE, Jennifer   <HR>
                    [Tom E. Huff]
  Once More, Miranda
  In sequence: *
    Love's Tender Fury
    Love Me, Marietta
    When Love Commands

WILDE, Jocelyn
                    [John Toombs]
  Dark Desire Romance:
    Mists Of Passion

WILDER, Joan
            [Catherine Lanigan]
    Romancing The Stone

WILDMAN, Faye
            [Jillian Dagg]
    Silhouette Romance:
      307 Fletcher Legacy, The
    Silhouette Special Edition:
      126 Lovesong

WILHITE, Bettie
            (Betsy Page)

WILLIAMS, Anne
    Circle Of Love:
      31 Rare Gem, The

WILLIAMS, Claudette   <HR>
    Lord Wildfire
    Song Of Silkie

WILLIAMS, Jeanne   <HR>
            (Megan Castell)
            (Jeanne Crecy)
            (Jeanne Foster)
            (Kristin Michaels)
            (Deirdre Rowan)
    So Many Kingdoms

WILLIAMS, Lee
    Second Chance At Love:
      189 Starfire
      216 Pillow Talk

WILLIAMS, Mary
            (Marianne Harvey)
    Stormswept

WILLIAMS, Mona   <GOT>
    Messenger, The

WILLMAN, Marianne
            (Marianne Clark)
            (Sabina Clark)

WILLOUGHBY, Lee Davis   <HO>
    Making Of America Series: (cont'd)
      30 Soldiers Of Fortune
            [George Ryan]
      31 Wranglers, The
            [Karl Meyer]
      32 Baja People, The
            [Charles Beardsley]
      33 Yukon Breed, The
            [Barry Myers]
      34 Smugglers, The
            [Richard Deming]
      35 Voyageurs, The
            [William L. DeAndrea]
      36 Barbary Coasters, The
            [Joanne Metro Rothweiler
             w/ Paul R. Rothweiler]
      37 Whalers, The
            [Michael Jahn]
      38 Canadians, The
            [Tad Richards]
      39 Prophets People, The
            [Leo P. Kelley]
      40 Lawmen, The
            [Richard Laymon]
      41 Copper Kings, The
            [Lou Cameron]
      42 Caribbeans, The
            [Walter Wager]
      43 Trail Blazers, The
            [Daniel Streib]
      44 Gamblers, The
            [Ian McMahan]
      45 Robber Barons, The
            [Barry Myers]
            (cont'd)

WILLOUGHBY, Lee Davis (continued)
  46 Assassins, The
                    [James Scafidel]
  47 Bounty Hunters, The
                    [Richard Deming]
  48 Texas Rangers, The
                    [John Toombs]
  49 Outlaws, The

  50 Fugitives, The
                    (end)

_____

_____

WILLS, Ann Meredith
  SuperRomance:
    62 Tempest And Tenderness

_____

_____

WILSON, Barbara w/ Pamela WILSON
                    (Margaret Summerville)

WILSON, Derek   <HO>
  Her Majesty's Captain

_____

_____

WILSON, Fran
              [Frances Engle Wilson]
  Silhouette Romance:
    237 Winter Promise   *
    251 After Autumn
    263 Souvenirs
    277 Together In Lisbon

_____

_____

WILSON, Joyce   <HR>
                    (Sally James)
  Cressida

_____

_____

WILSON, Pamela w/ Barbara WILSON
                    (Margaret Summerville)

WILSON, Renee
                    (Renee Roszel)

WILSON, Sandra
                    (Sandra Heath)

WIND, David
                    (Monica Barrie)
                    (Jenifer Dalton)
                    (Marilyn Davids)

WINDHAM, Susannah
  Silhouette Romance:
    207 More Precious Than Pearls

_____

WING, Janice
                    (Lenora Barber)

WINSLOW, Ellie
                    [Winslow Eliot]
  Rapture Romance:
    10 Wine-Dark Sea, The
    25 Painted Secrets
    39 Distant Light, A
    54 Red Sky At Night

_____

WINSLOW, Laurel
                    [Maura Seger]
  The Avon Romance:
    Heart Songs
  Velvet Glove:
    Captured Images

_____

WINSOR, Kathleen
  An Unholy Love Story
  Jacintha

_____

WINSPEAR, Violet
  Harlequin Presents:
    566 Man She Married, The
    718 By Love Bewitched
    734 Bride's Lace

_____

160

WINSTON, Daoma
  Fall River Line, The   <Saga>

_____

_____

WISDOM, Linda
              [Linda Randall Wisdom]
  Silhouette Romance:
    241 Snow Queen
  Silhouette Special Edition:
     74 Unspoken Past
    160 Island Rogue
         Business As Usual
         World Of Their Own, A
  Torch:
    Forbidden Love

_____

_____

WISDOM, Linda Randall
              (Linda Wisdom)
  Candlelight Ecstasy:
    196 Guardian Angel
    249 For Better Or For Worse
         Come What May
  Candlelight Ecstasy Supreme:
     31 Caution: Man At Work
         Two Of A Kind

_____

_____

WISELY, Charlotte
              [Charlotte Hastings]
  Rapture Romance:
      4 Welcome Intruder   *
     14 Love Has No Pride
     40 Passionate Enterprise

_____

_____

WISENER, Jean w/ J. J. NETHER
              (Sharon McCaffree)

WITTEBORN, Dirk
  Zoe   <CO>

_____

_____

WOLF, Joan   <RE>
  American Duchess, The
  Double Deception, A
  Fool's Masquerade
  Lord Richard's Daughter
  Rebellious Ward, The
  Rapture Romance:
      8 Summer Storm
     19 Change Of Heart
     58 Beloved Stranger
     73 Affair Of The Heart
     89 Portrait Of A Love

_____

_____

WOLFE, Paige
              [Rhoda Cohen]
  Harlequin Temptation:
         Footlights

_____

_____

WOLMAN, David
  Whispers On The Wind

_____

_____

WOMAN'S DESTINY, A <AWD>   <HO>
  Woman Of San Francisco, A
                  Lynn Erickson
  Woman Of New Orleans, A
                  Rochel DeNorre
  Woman Of Boston, A
                  Alicia Meadows
  Woman Of New York, A
                  Marcia Mager
  Woman Of Chicago, A
                  Kit Prate

_____

_____

WOMEN AT WAR SERIES   <HO>
              (see Rebecca Drury)

WOOD, Barbara
  Domina

_____

_____

WOOD, Deborah   <GOT>
  Mistress Of Soundcliff Manor
  _____

  _____

WOOD, Nuria
                [Josephine Nobisso]
  Second Chance At Love:
    132 With No Regrets
  To Have And To Hold:
    7 Family Plan, The

  _____

  _____

WOODIWISS, Kathleen E.   <HR>
  Come Love A Stranger

  _____

  _____

WOODRUFF, Marian
  Sweet Dreams: <YA>
    35 Forbidden Love
    42 Perfect Match, The
    48 Dial L For Love
    63 Kiss Me, Creep

  _____

  _____

WOODRUM, Lon
  A Hearth Romance:
    20 Trumpets In The Morning

  _____

  _____

WOODS, Eleanor
                [Eleanor Rogers]
  Candlelight Ecstasy:
    128 Gentle Whisper, A
    141 Loving Exile
    174 Tempestuous Challenge
    199 Sensuous Persuasion
    224 Passionate Pursuit
    236 Beguiled By A Stranger
    251 No Love Lost
    270 High Stakes
    297 Forgotten Dreams

  _____

  _____

WOODS, Sherryl Ann
                (Alexandra Kirk)
                (Suzanne Sherrill)

WOODWARD, Jean
  Avalon:
    Brandy's Awakening
    Eyes Of Love
    Flowers Of Love
    Love's Inheritance
    Valley Of Romance   *

  _____

  _____

WOOLRICH, Cornell
                (George Hopley)

WORTHINGTON, Avis   <HR>
  Love, Sacred And Profane

  _____

  _____

WORTHY, Judith   <M&B>
  Nurse With Wings
  Runaway Nurse

  _____

  _____

WRIGHT, Cynthia   <HR>
                [Cynthia Challed Wright]
                (Devon Lindsay)
  You And No Other

  _____

  _____

WRIGHT, Francesca
                [Denise Robins]
  Loves Of Lucrezia, The
  She Devil

  _____

  _____

WRIGHT, Lucretia
                [Alicia Knight]
  Silhouette Desire:
    146 Eternal Flame

  _____

  _____

WRIGHT, Patricia <HR>
  Storms Of Fate

WUNSCH, Josephine
  First Love From Silhouette: <YA>
    77 Free As A Bird

WYNDHAM, Esther
  Harlequin Classic:
    111 Once You Have Found Him
                                (880)
    151 Tiger Hall   (936)

Y

YALE, Diane   <GOT>
  Avalon:
    Deadly Manor
    Veiled Cliffs

YAPP, Kathleen
  Silhouette Inspirations:
    6 Fire In My Heart

YATES, Judith
                    [Judith Yoder]
  Second Chance At Love:
    207 Tempting Magic, A

YERBY, Frank
  Devilseed
  Western   <Saga><HO>

YODER, Judith
                    (Judith Yates)

YORK, Alison   <HO>
                 [Christopher Nicole]
  Scented Sword, The
  Haggard
  Haggard Inheritance (also
    published as "The Inheritors")

YORK, Amanda
                        [Joan Dial]
  Silhouette Intimate Moments:
    56 An Old Fashioned Love

YORK, Georgia   <HR>
  Savage Conquest

YOUNG, Brittany
                     [Sandra Harris]
  Silhouette Romance:
    297 Separate Happiness, A
    308 No Special Consideration

YOUNG, Karen
                      [Karen Stone]
  Silhouette Romance:
    212 Yesterday's Promise
    284 Irrestible Intruder

YOUNG, Mary Jo
                              (Jenny Nolan)

YOUNGBLOOD, Marilyn
  First Love From Silhouette: <YA>
    76 Send In The Clowns
    86 Boy Next Door, The

  _____

  _____

Z

ZACH, Cheryl Byrd
  Harlequin Temptation:
    18 Twice A Fool

  _____

  _____

ZAROULIS, Nancy
  Last Waltz, The

  _____

  _____

ZAYNE, Valerie
                          [Leigh Shaheen]
  Rapture Romance:
    79 Silver Dawn

  _____

  _____

ZEIG, Joan w/ Linda BURAK
                        (Alicia Meadowes)

ZEIGER, Helane
  Caprice Romance: <YA>
    29 Love Byte

  _____

  _____

ZELDIS, Chayym
  Forbidden Love, A

  _____

  _____

ZIOBRO, Marie
  Harlequin American Romance:
    59 Strange Bedfellows

  _____

  _____

ZUMWALT, Eva
  Starlight Romance:
    Elusive Heart, The
    When The Heart Remembers

  _____

  _____

Numbered/Category

Anderson, Ken
Arnold, Francena
Bell, Sallie Lee
Brown, Elizabeth
Crawford, Matsu
Hill, Ruth Livingston
Howard, Guy
Hunter, James H.
Saloff-Astakhoff, N. I.
Woodrum, Lon

1 THE DOCTOR'S RETURN
   Ken Anderson

2 DEEPENING STREAM, THE
   Francena Arnold

3 FRUIT FOR TOMORROW
   Francena Arnold

4 LIGHT IN MY WINDOW
   Francena Arnold

5 THE BARRIER
   Sallie Lee Bell

6 BY STRANGE PATHS
   Sallie Lee Bell

7 THE LAST SURRENDER
   Sallie Lee Bell

8 THE LONG SEARCH
   Sallie Lee Bell

9 ROMANCE ALONG THE BAYOU
   Sallie Lee Bell

10 THE SCAR
   Sallie Lee Bell

11 THE SUBSTITUTE
   Sallie Lee Bell

12 THROUGH GOLDEN MEADOWS
   Sallie Lee Bell

13 UNTIL THE DAYBREAK
   Sallie Lee Bell

14 THE CANDLE OF THE WICKED
   Elizabeth Brown

15 LOVE IS LIKE AN ACORN
   Matsu Crawford

16 THIS SIDE OF TOMORROW
   Ruth Livingston Hill

17 GIVE ME THY VINEYARD
   Guy Howard

18 THE MYSTERY OF MAR SABA
   James H. Hunter

19 JUDITH
   N. I. Saloff-Astakhoff

20 TRUMPETS IN THE MORNING
   Lon Woodrum

21 LIGHT FROM THE HILLS
   Sallie Lee Bell

Adams, Candice
Andrews, Barbara
Bennett, Emma
Bernard, Dorothy Ann
Black, Jackie
Blayne, Diana
Brader, Norma
Brandon, Joanna
Bremer, Joanne
Bryan, Eileen
Calloway, Jo
Cameron, Barbara
Carroll, Joellyn
Carroll, Malissa
Castle, Jayne
Catley, Melanie
Chase, Elaine Raco
Copeland, Lori
Daley, Kit
Dobson, Margaret
Drake, Bonnie
Dunaway, Diane
Elliott, Emily
Fairfax, Gwen
Ferris, Rose Marie
Gamel, Nona
Graham, Heather
Grove, Joan
Hager, Jean
Hale, Antionette
Hamilton, Paula
Hamlin, Dallas
Hart, Shirley
Herter, Lori
Hill, Alexis
Hooper, Kay
Howard, Julia
Hudson, Anna
Hughes, Samantha
Jennings, Sara
Jordan, Alexis Hill
Kincaid, Nell
Lacy, Tira
Lane, Megan
Linz, Cathie
Markham, Patricia
Martin, Prudence
Massey, Jessica
McBride, Harper
McKenna, Tate

Monteith, Hayton
Morgan, Alyssa
Neggers, Carla
Norris, Carol
Patrick, Lynn
Paulos, Sheila
Prince, Margot
Raffel, Elizabeth
Randolph, Elise
Rasmussen, Alysse
Ryan, Rachel
Scott, Samantha
Sherrill, Suzanne
Silverlock, Anne
Small, Lass
Sommers, Beverly
Stone, Natalie
Stuart, Jan
Tyler, Alison
Vail, Linda
Vitek, Donna Kimel
Whittenburg, Karen
Widsom, Linda Randall
Woods, Eleanor

186	GEMSTONE Bonnie Drake	204	AFTER THE LOVING Samantha Scott
187	A TIME FOR LOVE Jackie Black	205	DANCE FOR TWO Kit Daley
188	WINDSONG Jo Calloway	206	THE MAN WHO CAME TO STAY Margot Prince
189	LOVE'S MADNESS Sheila Paulos	207	BRISTOL'S LAW Rose Marie Ferris
190	DESTINY'S TOUCH Dorothy Ann Bernard	208	PLAY TO WIN Shirley Hart
191	NO OTHER LOVE Alyssa Morgan	209	DESIRABLE COMPROMISE Suzanne Sherrill
192	THE DEDICATED MAN Lass Small	210	LOVER'S KNOT Hayton Monteith
193	MEMORY AND DESIRE Eileen Bryan	211	TENDER JOURNEY Margaret Dobson
194	A LASTING IMAGE Julia Howard	212	ALL OUR TOMORROWS Lori Herter
195	RELUCTANT MERGER Alexis Hill Jordan	213	LOVER IN DISGUISE Gwen Fairfax
196	GUARDIAN ANGEL Linda Randall Wisdom	214	TENDER DECEPTION Heather Graham
197	DESIGN FOR DESIRE Anna Hudson	215	MIDNIGHT MAGIC Barbara Andrews
198	DOUBLE PLAY Natalie Stone	216	WINDS OF HEAVEN Karen Whittenburg
199	SENSUOUS PERSUASION Eleanor Woods	217	ALL OR NOTHING Lori Copeland
200	MIDNIGHT MEMORIES Emily Elliott	218	STORMY SURRENDER Jessica Massey
201	DARING PROPOSAL Tate McKenna	219	MOMENT TO MOMENT Bonnie Drake
202	REACH FOR THE STARS Sara Jennings	220	A CLASSIC LOVE Jo Calloway
203	A CHARMING STRATEGY Cathie Linz	221	A NIGHT IN THE FORREST Alysse Rasmussen

Adams, Candice
Andrews, Barbara
Black, Jackie
Bryan, Eileen
Calloway, Jo
Chambers, Ginger
Copeland, Lori
Dobson, Margaret
Elliott, Emily
Graham, Heather
Hart, Shirley
Henrichs, Betty
Herter, Lori
Hudson, Anna
Hughes, Samantha
Jackson, Betty
Kincaid, Nell
Lane, Megan
Lorin, Amii
Martin, Prudence
Monteith, Hayton
Morgan, Alice
Nunn, Rebecca
Raine, Nicole
Randolph, Elise
Scott, Samantha
Tyler, Alison
Vitek, Donna Kimel
Wisdom, Linda Randall

1   TEMPESTUOUS EDEN
    Heather Graham

2   EMERALD FIRE
    Barbara Andrews

3   WARMED BY THE FIRE
    Donna Kimel Vitek

4   LOVERS AND PRETENDERS
    Prudence Martin

5   TENDERNESS AT TWILIGHT
    Megan Lane

6   TIME OF THE WINTER LOVE
    Jo Calloway

7   WHISPER ON THE WIND
    Nell Kincaid

8   HANDLE WITH CARE
    Betty Jackson

9   NEVER LOOK BACK
    Donna Kimel Vitek

10 NIGHT, SEA AND STARS
    Heather Graham

11 POLITICS OF PASSION
    Samantha Hughes

12 NO STRINGS ATTACHED
    Prudence Martin

13 BODY AND SOUL
    Anna Hudson

14 CROSSFIRE
    Eileen Bryan

15 WHERE THERE'S SMOKE
    Nell Kincaid

16 PAYMENT IN FULL
    Jackie Black

17 RED MIDNIGHT
    Heather Graham

175

168   The Duke Comes Home   CAMFIELD ROMANCE
                                   Berkley/Jove Publishing Group
169   A King In Love

170   Journey To A Star   7   Bride To A Brigand

171   Love And Lucia   8   Love Comes West

172   The Unwanted Wedding   9   A Witch's Spell

173   Gypsy Magic   10   Secrets

174   Help From The Heart   11

175   A Duke In Danger   12

176   Tempted To Love   13

177   Lights, Laughter And A Lady 14

178   Riding To The Moon   15

179   The Unbreakable Spell   16

180   Diona And A Dalmation   17

181   Fire In The Blood   18

182   The Scots Never Forget   19

183   A Rebel Princess   20

184   21

185   22

186   23

187   24

188   25

189   26

190   27

191   28

192   29

193

Algermissen, JoAnn	TWICE IN A LIFETIME `<PROM>`
Alsobrook, Rosalyn	Rebecca Flanders
Ashley, Jacqueline	
Bierce, Jane	1 TOMORROW'S PROMISE
Blair, Rebecca	Sandra Brown
Bretton, Barbara	
Brown, Sandra	2 THE SAME LAST NAME
Carnell, Lois	Kathleen Gilles Seidel
Chambers, Ginger	
Coffaro, Katherine	3 LOVE CHANGES
Craig, Rianna	Barbara Bretton
Davidson, Andrea	
De Leon, Ana Lisa	4 NOW AND FOREVER
Diamond, Jacqueline	Sharon McCaffree
Flanders, Rebecca	
Francis, Robin	5 A STRONG AND TENDER THREAD
Glenn, Elizabeth	Jackie Weger
Hale, Dorothea	
Harvey, Judy	6 A MATTER OF TRUST
Henry, Anne	Rebecca Flanders
Hills, Ida	
Hudson, Meg	7 MIRACLES TAKE LONGER
James, Sarah	Zelma Orr
Jeffries, Jessica	
Jensen, Muriel	8 THIN WHITE LINE
Kaye, Barbara	Rayanne Moore
Kitt, Sandra	
Lane, Kami	9 CANVAS OF PASSION
Lang, Heather	Deirdre Mardon
Lemery, Alysse	
London, Hilary	10 HOSTAGE HEART
Mardon, Deirdre	Renee Roszel
McCaffree, Sharon	
Minger, Elda	11 CITY LIFE, CITY LOVE
Moon, Modean	Beverly Sommers
Moore, Rayanne	
Morgan, Alice	12 UNTAMED HEART
Munn, Vella	Elda Minger
Orr, Zelma	
Parris, Laura	13 RAVEN'S SONG
Roszel, Renee	Caron Welles
Saunders, Bree	
Seidel, Kathleen Gilles	14 DARK STAR OF LOVE
Sommers, Beverly	Elizabeth Glenn
Starr, Martha	
Stuart, Anne	15 BUILDING PASSION
Taylor, Janelle	Jane Bierce
Thacker, Cathy Gillen	
Thurston, Anne	16 MUSIC IN THE NIGHT
Weger, Jackie	Andrea Davidson
Welles, Caron	
Ziobro, Marie	

179

Arbor, Jane
Barrie, Susan
Blair, Kathryn
Blake, Andrea
Brett, Rosalind
Burchell, Mary
Burghley, Rose
Chase, Isosbel
Conway, Celine
Dingwell, Joyce
Farnes, Eleanor
Fraser, Jane
Hilliard, Nerina
Hoy, Elizabeth
Ives, Averil
Kent, Pamela
Lindsay, Rachel
MacLeod, Jean S.
Rowan, Barbara
Seale, Sara
Starr, Kate
Summers, Essie
Weale, Anne
Wyndham, Esther

100 THE TIME AND THE PLACE
    Essie Summers

101 ALL I ASK
    Anne Weale

102 ABOVE THE CLOUDS
    Esther Wyndham

103 TENDER CONQUEST
    Joyce Dingwell

104 THE BLUE CARIBBEAN
    Celine Conway

105 THE DARK STRANGER
    Sara Seale

106 AWAY WENT LOVE
    Mary Burchell

107 THE HOUSE OF ADRIANO
    Nerina Hilliard

108 NOW AND ALWAYS
    Andrea Blake

109 MOON OVER THE ALPS
    Essie Summers

110 UNTIL WE MET
    Anne Weale

111 ONCE YOU HAVE FOUND HIM
    Esther Wyndham

112 THE THIRD IN THE HOUSE
    Joyce Dingwell

113 AT THE VILLA MASSINA
    Celine Conway

114 CHILD FRIDAY
    Sara Seale

115 NO SILVER SPOON
    Jane Arbor

116 SUGAR ISLAND
    Jean S. MacLeod

Arbor, Jane	
Ashton, Elizabeth	
Asquith, Nan	1 MORE THAN YESTERDAY
Bianchin, Helen	Jeneth Murrey
Britt, Katrina	
Carter, Rosemary	2 LION'S DEN, THE
Cooper, Ann	Ann Cooper
Cork, Dorothy	
Dalzell, Helen	3 RUAIG INHERITANCE, THE
Dingwell, Joyce	Jean S. MacLeod
Donnelly, Jane	
Douglas, Sheila	4 WILLING HEART, THE
Elver, Rose	Helen Bianchin
Gilbert, Jacqueline	
Gillen, Lucy	5 STORM EAGLE
Jameson, Claudia	Lucy Gillen
Jeffrey, Elizabeth	
Lane, Roumelia	6 KURRANULLA ROUND, THE
Lewty, Marjorie	Dorothy Cork
MacLeod, Jean S.	
Mayo, Margaret	7 BELOVED SURGEON
Moore, Mary	Sheila Douglas
Murrey, Jeneth	
Neels, Betty	8 FLASH OF EMERALD
Smith, Doris E.	Jane Arbor
Strutt, Sheila	
Vinton, Anne	9 AT THE VILLA ROMANA
	Anne Vinton

Alexander, Susan
Armstrong, Lindsay
Bauling, Jayne
Bianchin, Helen
Carpenter, Amanda
Carter, Rosemary
Clair, Daphne
Craven, Sara
Darcy, Emma
Donald, Robyn
Field, Sandra
Firth, Susanna
Flanders, Rebecca
Frazer, Alison
George, Catherine
Gilbert, Jacqueline
Graham, Elizabeth
Goldrick, Emma
Gordon, Victoria
Harrison, Claire
Holland, Sarah
Jameson, Claudia
Jordan, Penny
Ker, Madeleine
Kidd, Flora
Lake, Patricia
Lamb, Charlotte
Lyons, Mary
Mather, Anne
McGiveny, Maura
Michaels, Leigh
Mortimer, Carole
Nicholson, Peggy E.
Oldfield, Elizabeth
Pargeter, Margaret
Peake, Lilian
Pope, Pamela
Steele, Jessica
Stevens, Lynsey
Thorne, Avery
Thorpe, Kay
Van Der Zee, Karen
Weale, Anne
Wentworth, Sally
West, Nicola
Whittal, Yvonne
Winspear, Violet

559 MELT A FROZEN HEART
     Lindsay Armstrong

560 DAREDEVIL
     Rosemary Carter

561 COUNTERFEIT BRIDE
     Sara Craven

562 BOUGHT WITH HIS NAME
     Penny Jordan

563 A PASSIONATE AFFAIR
     Anne Mather

564 PASSION FROM THE PAST
     Carole Mortimer

565 WEDDING OF THE YEAR
     Anne Weale

566 THE MAN SHE MARRIED
     Violet Winspear

567 MANSION FOR MY LOVE
     Robyn Donald

568 WALK BY MY SIDE
     Sandra Field

569 ESCAPE FROM DESIRE
     Penny Jordan

570 A STEP BACKWARD
     Patricia Lake

571 PERFECT PARTNER
     Carole Mortimer

572 PRELUDE TO A SONG
     Margaret Pargeter

573 A MAN OF MEANS
     Kay Thorpe

574 LATE HARVEST
     Yvonne Whittal

575 MASTER OF TINARUA
     Rosemary Carter

576	DEADLY ANGEL Sarah Holland	594	LOVE'S ONLY DECEPTION Carole Mortimer
577	TEMPTED TO LOVE Flora Kidd	595	MAN FROM THE KIMBERLEYS Margaret Pargeter
578	THE SILVER CASKET Patricia Lake	596	PRICE TO BE MET Jessica Steele
579	GOLDEN FEVER Carole Mortimer	597	MASTER OF MORLEY Kay Thorpe
580	SUBSTITUTE BRIDE Margaret Pargeter	598	THE SILVER FALCON Yvonne Whittal
581	FLYING HIGH Sally Wentworth	599	SUP WITH THE DEVIL Sara Craven
582	WEB OF SILK Yvonne Whittal	600	A HOUSE CALLED BELLEVIGNE Jacqueline Gilbert
583	VISION OF LOVE Elizabeth Graham	601	FEVER PITCH Sarah Holland
584	THE FLAWED MARRIAGE Penny Jordan	602	RESCUE OPERATION Penny Jordan
585	BETRAYED Charlotte Lamb	603	CAPTIVE LOVING Carole Mortimer
586	AN ELUSIVE DESIRE Anne Mather	604	DREAM HERO Elizabeth Oldfield
587	HIDDEN LOVE Carole Mortimer	605	INTIMATE ENEMIES Jessica Steele
588	CLOUDED RAPTURE Margaret Pargeter	606	MAN OF VENGEANCE Lynsey Stevens
589	LUCIFER'S BRAND Nicola West	607	ENTER MY JUNGLE Lindsay Armstrong
590	CHAINS OF GOLD Yvonne Whittal	608	SECOND TIME AROUND Elizabeth Oldfield
591	PHANTOM MARRIAGE Penny Jordan	609	DESIRE'S CAPTIVE Penny Jordan
592	DARK SEDUCTION Flora Kidd	610	CAGE OF SHADOWS Anne Mather
593	MOMENT OF MADNESS Patricia Lake	611	FANTASY GIRL Carole Mortimer

648	TWISTING SHADOWS Emma Darcy	666	FALKONE'S PROMISE Rebecca Flanders
649	AN OLD PASSION Robyn Donald	667	FORGOTTEN PASSION Penny Jordan
650	SAVAGE ATONEMENT Penny Jordan	668	DARKNESS OF THE HEART Charlotte Lamb
651	SUBTLE REVENGE Carole Mortimer	669	TRUST IN SUMMER MADNESS Carole Mortimer
652	BELOVED STRANGER Elizabeth Oldfield	670	ECSTASY Anne Weale
653	CHAINS OF REGRET Margaret Pargeter	671	PROPHECY OF DESIRE Claire Harrison
654	FORBIDDEN WINE Lynsey Stevens	672	PACIFIC APHRODITE Madeleine Ker
655	MAN-HATER Penny Jordan	673	CARIBBEAN CONFUSION Mary Lyons
656	VIRTUOUS LADY Madeleine Ker	674	A GRAND ILLUSION Maura McGiveny
657	DANGEROUS ENCOUNTER Flora Kidd	675	THE FAILED MARRIAGE Carole Mortimer
658	A SECRET INTIMACY Charlotte Lamb	676	TAKE IT OR LEAVE IT Elizabeth Oldfield
659	PAGAN ENCHANTMENT Carole Mortimer	677	A SPLENDID PASSION Avery Thorne
660	STORM IN THE NIGHT Margaret Pargeter	678	NEVER TRUST A STRANGER Kay Thorpe
661	RELUCTANT RELATIVE Jessica Steele	679	A RULING PASSION Daphne Clair
662	THE LION ROCK Sally Wentworth	680	TANGLE OF TORMENT Emma Darcy
663	VALENTINE'S DAY Jayne Bauling	681	A MISTAKE IN IDENTITY Sandra Field
664	SERPENT IN PARADISE Rosemary Carter	682	PASSIONATE PURSUIT Flora Kidd
665	THE GATES OF RANGITATAU Robyn Donald	683	SIROCCO Anne Mather

Absalom, Stacy
Allyne, Kerry
Arbor, Jane
Armstrong, Lindsay
Ayre, Jessica
Badger, Rosemary
Bevan, Gloria
Burchell, Mary
Byfield, Sue
Carpenter, Amanda
Carson, Angela
Clark, Sandra
Clifford, Kay
Cooper, Ann
Corrie, Jane
Cranmer, Kathryn
Dalzell, Helen
Daveson, Mons
Dingwell, Joyce
Donnelly, Jane
Field, Sandra
Firth, Susanna
Flanders, Rebecca
Francis, Sara
Gair, Diana
George, Catherine
Gilbert, Jacqueline
Gordon, Victoria
Griffin, Jocelyn
Hammond, Rosemary
Harvey, Samantha
Henaghan, Rosalie
James, Dana
Jameson, Claudia
Ker, Madeleine
Lane, Roumelia
Lewty, Marjorie
May, Wynne
Mayo, Margaret
MacLean, Jan
McGrath, Laura
McMahon, Barbara
Moore, Mary
Murray, Annabel
Murrey, Jeneth
O'Hara, Kate
Page, Betsy
Pargeter, Margaret
Peake, Lilian
Parv, Valerie
Peters, Sue

Pope, Pamela
Reid, Henrietta
Rome, Margaret
Scott, Alexandra
Scott, Celia
Smith, Marion
Spark, Natalie
Steele, Jessica
Stevens, Lynsey
Stratton, Rebecca
Strutt, Sheila
Sullivan, Jo
Summers, Essie
Van Der Zee, Karen
Way, Margaret
West, Nicola
Westwood, Gwen
Whittal, Yvonne

2521	ROSS'S GIRL Jane Corrie	2539	THE SILVER VEIL Margaret Way
2522	THE DISTANT MAN Samantha Harvey	2540	BATTLE OF WILLS Victoria Gordon
2523	LESSON IN LOVE Claudia Jameson	2541	BOY WITH KITE Samantha Harvey
2524	NEW BOSS AT BIRCHFIELDS Henrietta Reid	2542	ALL ELSE CONFUSION Betty Neels
2525	DAUGHTER OF THE MISTY GORGES Essie Summers	2543	THE MAN FROM NOWHERE Rebecca Stratton
2526	DEVIL'S GOLD Nicola West	2543	THE WHITE WAVE <PROM> Jocelyn Griffin
2527	SPRING FEVER Kerry Allyne	2544	SUSPICION Jo Sullivan
2528	MASQUERADE WITH MUSIC Mary Burchell	2545	HANDMAID TO MIDAS Jane Arbor
2529	TO BE OR NOT TO BE Sue Byfield	2546	MAKESHIFT MARRIAGE Marjorie Lewty
2530	JUNGLE ANTATONIST Diana Gair	2547	ALL OUR TOMORROWS Jan MacLean
2531	DINNER AT WYATT'S Victoria Gordon	2548	WAYSIDE FLOWER Wynne May
2532	PEACOCK IN THE JUNGLE Wynne May	2549	ROOTS OF HEAVEN Annabel Murray
2533	MOONLIGHT ENOUGH Sandra Clark	2550	A DREAM COME TRUE Betty Neels
2534	MY LORD KASSEEM Mons Daveson	2551	MAN WITH TWO FACES Jane Corrie
2535	RELUCTANT PARAGON Catherine George	2552	CALL UP THE STORM Jane Donnelly
2536	LUPIN VALLEY Roumelia Lane	2553	RAPTURE OF THE DEEP Margaret Rome
2537	SPELLBOUND Margaret Way	2554	CATCH A STAR Alexandra Scott
2538	HOUSE OF MIRRORS Yvonne Whittal	2555	DISTRUST HER SHADOW Jessica Steele

2556 HUNTER'S MOON Margaret Way	2574 CLOSEST PLACE TO HEAVEN Lynsey Stevens
2557 DANGEROUS JOURNEY Margaret Mayo	2575 MACKENZIE COUNTRY Mons Daveson
2558 KEEGAN'S KINGDOM Annabel Murray	2576 FACE THE TIGER Jane Donnelly
2559 TAME A PROUD HEART Jeneth Murrey	2577 THE TIDE OF SUMMER Sandra Field
2560 SUMMERHAZE Kate O'Hara	2578 NEVER SAY NEVER Claudia Jameson
2561 LORD OF THE LAND Margaret Rome	2579 ONE WHO KISSES Marjorie Lewty
2562 THE FLIGHT OF THE GOLDON HAWK Sheila Strutt	2580 TETHERED LIBERTY Jessica Steele
2563 THE ROUSEABOUT GIRL Gloria Bevan	2581 KNAVE OF HEARTS Stacy Absalom
2564 LION'S WALK ALONE Susanna Firth	2582 PERHAPS LOVE Lindsay Armstrong
2565 THE MELTING HEART Claudia Jameson	2583 LIGHTNING STRIKES TWICE Sue Peters
2566 MIDSUMMER STAR Betty Neels	2584 BAY OF ANGELS Margaret Rome
2567 FORSAKING ALL OTHERS Jeneth Murrey	2585 LOVE COMES STEALING Alexandra Scott
2568 SEEDS OF APRIL Celia Scott	2586 SECONDHAND BRIDE Gwen Westwood
2569 STORMY WEATHER Sandra Clark	2587 DANGEROUS MALE Marjorie Lewty
2570 NOT THE MARRYING KIND Helen Dalzell	2588 MAYAN MAGIC Laura McGrath
2571 DREAM OF MIDSUMMER Catherine George	2589 THE TALL DARK STRANGER Valerie Parv
2572 THE MAN FROM TI KOUKA Rosalie Henaghan	2590 A MOUNTAIN FOR LUENDA Essie Summers
2573 THE CANDLEBERRY TREE Pamela Pope	2591 THE GIRL OF COBOLT CREEK Margaret Way

2592	NO ROOM IN HIS LIFE Nicole West	2610	WILDTRACK Nicola West
2593	SOMEWHERE TO CALL HOME Kerry Allyne	2611	MAN OF GOLD Kay Clifford
2594	YOURS... FAITHFULLY Claudia Jameson	2612	VILLA OF VENGEANCE Annabel Murray
2595	VOYAGE OF THE MISTRAL Madeleine Ker	2613	THE SILVER FLAME Margaret Pargeter
2596	THE CHRYSANTHEMUM AND THE SWORD Annabel Murray	2614	COME LOVE ME Lilian Peake
2597	ROSES AND CHAMPAGNE Betty Neels	2615	CASTLE OF THE LINE Margaret Rome
2598	THE BEACHCOMBER Marion Smith	2616	RIDE THE WIND Yvonne Whittal
2599	HARD TO HANDLE Jessica Ayre	2617	CORPORATE LADY Rosemary Badger
2600	BROTHER WOLF Joyce Dingwell	2618	GREEK ISLAND MAGIC Gloria Bevan
2601	FULL CIRCLE Rosemary Hammond	2619	FACE OF THE STRANGER Angela Carson
2602	RETURN A STRANGER Margaret Mayo	2620	PAS DE DEUX Kathryn Cranmer
2603	NIGHT OF POSSESSION Lilian Peake	2621	FOR EVER AND A DAY Rosalie Henaghan
2604	BORROWED GIRL Alexandra Scott	2622	A LAMP FOR JONATHAN Essie Summers
2605	A DEEPER DIMENSION Amanda Carpenter	2623	A MODERN GIRL Rebecca Flanders
2606	SPRINGS OF LOVE Mary Moore	2624	KATE'S WAY Sara Francis
2607	TOMORROW - COME SOON Jessica Steele	2625	DEAR GREEN ISLE Annabel Murray
2608	THE ASHBY AFFAIR Lynsey Stevens	2626	NEVER TOO LATE Betty Neels
2609	HOUSE OF MEMORIES Margaret Way	2627	THE BONDED HEART Betsy Page

2664	2682
2665	2683
2666	2684
2667	2685
2668	2686
2669	2687
2670	2688
2671	2689
2672	2690
2673	2691
2674	2692
2675	2693
2676	2694
2677	2695
2678	2696
2679	2697
2680	2698
2681	2699

Bockoven, Georgia
Collins, Marion Smith
Conrad, Helen
Delinsky, Barbara
Dominque, Meg
King, Dianne
Krentz, Jayne Ann
MacDonald, Elizabeth
Mardon, Deirdre
McNaught, Judith
Michaels, Margie
Paul, Danielle
Sellers, Alexandra
Soule, Maris
Spencer, LaVyrle
Thompson, Vickie Lewis
Turner, Lynn
Weger, Jackie
Zach, Cheryl Byrd

FIRST IMPRESSIONS <PROM>
Maris Soule

1 SPRING FANCY
LaVyrle Spencer

2 WHEN STARS FALL DOWN
Meg Dominque

3 EVERLASTING
Helen Conrad

4 A SPECIAL SOMETHING
Barbara Delinsky

5 BY MUTUAL CONSENT
Marion Smith Collins

6 THE FOREVER KIND
Alexandra Sellers

7 CAST A GOLDEN SHADOW
Jackie Weger

8 FOR NOW, FOR ALWAYS
Lynn Turner

9 MINGLED HEARTS
Vicki Lewis Thompson

10 FRIEND OF THE HEART
Dianne King

11 UNEASY ALLIANCE
Jayne Ann Krentz

12 UNTAMED DESIRE
Margie Michaels

13 CHAMELEON
Danielle Paul

14 TRACINGS ON A WINDOW
Georgia Bockoven

15 A JEALOUS MISTRESS
Deirdre Mardon

16 DOUBLE STANDARDS
Judith McNaught

Alexander, Megan
Anzelon, Robyn
Bechko, Peggy
Bockoven, Georgia
Bowe, Kate
Carson, Rosalind
Clare, Shannon
Collins, Kathryn
Connolly, Vivian
Cott, Christine Hella
Crane, Leah
Crockett, Christina
Crowe, Evelyn A.
Douglas, Casey
Duncan, Judith
Fabian, Erika
Garrett, Sally
Gayle, Margaret
Glenn, Margaret
Griffin, Jocelyn
Haley, Jocelyn
Hamilton, Daphne
Healy, Catherine
Howard, Joy
Hudson, Meg
Jeffries, Jessica
Jones, Marian
Jordon, Joanna
Joyce, Deborah
Kaye, Barbara
King, Dianne
Lambert, Willa
Lee, Lucy
Livingston, Georgette
Logan, Jessica
Loring, Jenny
Louis, Jacqueline
MacKenzie, Maura
McCaffree, Sharon
McNaught, Judith
Mesta, Emily
Myers, Virginia
Nelson, Louella
Nielsen, Virginia
Orwig, Sara
Palmer, Rachel
Parker, Cynthia
Roberts, Leigh
Saucier, Donna
Sellers, Alexandra

Snow, Lucy
Trent, Danielle
Turner, Linda
Walker, Irma
Ward, Lynda
Wills, Ann Meredith

46 A HEART DIVIDED
    Barbara Kaye

47 DARK SIDE OF LOVE
    Peggy Bechko

48 PREDUDE TO PARADISE
    Daphne Hamilton

49 THE FOREVER SPELL
    Robyn Anzelon

50 DANGEROUS DELIGHT
    Christine Hella Cott

51 TENDER RHAPSODY
    Judith Duncan

52 PRECIOUS INTERLUDE
    Margaret Gayle

53 RETURN TO RAPTURE
    Meg Hudson

54 SERENADE FOR A LOST LOVE
    Jocelyn Haley

55 TO TOUCH A DREAM
    Christina Crockett

56 PROUD SURRENDER
    Casey Douglas

57 MAGIC OBSESSION
    Sara Orwig

58 NO SWEETER SONG
    Rachel Palmer

59 LOVE'S GOLDEN SPELL
    Willa Lambert

Boswell, Barbara	1 HEAVEN'S PRICE
Bramsch, Joan	Sandra Brown
Brown, Sandra	
Carlson, Nancy	2 SURRENDER
Combs, Becky	Helen Mittermeyer
Conrad, Helen	
Curtis, Sharon And Tom	3 THE JOINING STONE
Domning, Joan J.	Noelle Berry McCue
Downes, Kathleen	
Garlock, Dorothy	4 SILVER MIRACLES
Green, Billie	Fayrene Preston
Harper, Liv and Ken	
Holder, Nancy	5 MATCHING WITS
Hooper, Kay	Carla Neggers
James, B. J.	
Johansen, Iris	6 A LOVE FOR ALL TIME
McCue, Noelle Berry	Dorothy Garlock
McDonnell, Margie	
Michael, Marie	7 A TRYST WITH MR LINCOLN?
Mittermeyer, Helen	Billie Green
Neggers, Carla	
Orwig, Sara	8 TEMPTATION'S STING
Pickart, Joan Elliott	Helen Conrad
Preston, Fayrene	
Reisser, Anne N.	9 DECEMBER 32nd...AND ALWAYS
Shock, Marianne	Marie Michael
Wagner, Kimberli	

10 HARD DRIVIN' MAN
   Nancy Carlson

11 BELOVED INTRUDER
   Noelle Berry McCue

12 HUNTER'S PAYNE
   Joan J. Domning

13 TIGER LADY
   Joan J. Domning

14 STORMY VOWS
   Iris Johansen

15 BRIEF DELIGHT
   Helen Mittermeyer

16 A VERY RELUCTANT KNIGHT
   Billie Green

17 TEMPEST AT SEA
   Iris Johansen

Adams, Kasey	1	LOVE SO FEARFUL
Allison, Elizabeth		Nina Coombs
Ashe, Megan		
Benet, Deborah	2	RIVER OF LOVE
Carroll, Rosalynn		Lisa McConnell
Chandler, Laurel		
Clark, Marianne	3	LOVER'S LAIR
Coombs, Nina		Jeanette Ernest
Dale, Jennifer		
Darwin, Jeanette	4	WELCOME INTRUDER
Davids, Marilyn		Charlotte Wisely
Edwards, Estelle		
Ernest, Jeanette	5	CHESAPEAKE AUTUMN
Erskine, Andra		Stephanie Richards
Essex, Marianna		
Frost, Eleanor	6	PASSION'S DOMAIN
Graves, Tricia		Nina Coombs
Kent, Kathryn		
McClure, Anna	7	TENDER RHAPSODY
McConnell, Lisa		Jennifer Dale
McKenzie, Melinda		
Moore, Lisa	8	SUMMER STORM
Morgan, Diana		Joan Wolf
Morgan, Leslie		
Neggers, Carla	9	CRYSTAL DREAMS
Osborne, Maggie		Diana Morgan
Ransom, Katherine		
Richards, Stephanie	10	THE WINE - DARK SEA
Robb, JoAnn		Ellie Winslow
Roth, Jillian		
St. John, Lisa	11	FLOWERS OF DESIRE
Shore, Francine		Francine Shore
Stone, Elisa		
Thomas, Bree	12	DEAR DOUBTER
Wagner, Sharon		Jeanette Ernest
Winslow, Ellie		
Wisely, Charlotte	13	SWEET PASSION'S SONG
Wolf, Joan		Deborah Benet
Zayne, Valerie		
	14	LOVE HAS NO PRIDE
		Charlotte Wisely
	15	TREASURE OF LOVE
		Laurel Chandler
	16	GOSSAMER MAGIC
		Lisa St. John
	17	REMEMBER MY LOVE
		Jennifer Dale

Adams, Candice
Alexander, Marsha
Alexie, Angela
Arkham, Candace
Barrie, Monica
Belmont, Kate
Bode, Margo
Bradley, Muriel
Brewster, Martha
Bright, Elizabeth
Butler, Rae
Campbell, Drusilla
Carr, Madeleine
Carsley, Anne
Dalton, Jenifer
Damon, Lee
Daniels, Jordana
Dare, Jessica
Deveraux, Jude
Erickson, Lynn
Faith, Barbara
Fleming, Victoria
Garlock, Dorothy
Good, Susanna
Gray, Angela
James, Anna
James, Kristin
Johnson, Maud B.
Jordan, Laura
Joyce, Janet
Karron, Kris
Kelrich, Victoria
Kent, Katherine
Leigh, Petra
LeMon, Lynn
Lindsay, Devon
Lyons, Leila
Makepeace, Joanna
Marten, Jacqueline
Moore, Paula
Moray, Helga
Morgan, Diana
Morris, Kathleen
Morse, Nancy
Norman, Nicole
Norris, Carol
O'Brien, Sofi
Pemberton, Margaret
Pryor, Vanessa
Ross, Clarissa

Shaw, Linda
Shelley, Elizabeth
Shepherd, Perdita
Sommers, Jeanne
Spencer, LaVyrle
Standage, Virginia
Stevens, Serita
Stuart, Dee
Stuart, Diana
Suson, Marlene
Thiels, Kathryn Gorsha
Trent, Lynda
Wherlock, Julia
Wilde, Jocelyn
Yorke, Katherine

10/79	ENCHANTRESS, THE Katherine Yorke	\<HO>	8/80	PILLARS OF HEAVEN Leila Lyons	\<HO>
10/79	ROSEWOOD Petra Leigh	\<HO>	8/80	THIS PERILOUS ECSTASY Jeanne Sommers	\<HO>
11/79	BURNING SECRETS Susanna Good	\<HO>	9/80	THIS RAVISHED ROSE Anne Carsley	\<HO>
11/79	REAP THE WILD HARVEST Elizabeth Bright	\<HO>	9/80	WINGS OF MORNING Dee Stuart	\<HO>
1/80	FEAST OF PASSIONS, A Carol Norris	\<HO>	10/80	FIRE BRIDE, THE Julia Wherlock	\<HO>
1/80	MOON KISSED, THE Barbara Faith	\<HO>	10/80	THIS GOLDEN RAPTURE Paula Moore	\<HO>
2/80	FAN THE WANTON FLAME Clarissa Ross	\<HO>	11/80	HEATHER SONG Nicole Norman	\<HO>
2/80	THIS RAGING FLOWER Lynn Erickson	\<HO>	11/80	LOVE OF THE LION, THE Angela Gray	\<HO>
3/80	SILVER LADY Nancy Morse	\<HO>	12/80	MASQUERADE Clarissa Ross	\<HO>
3/80	SWEET NEMESIS Lynn Erickson	\<HO>	12/80	TEMPEST LILY, THE Helga Moray	\<HO>
4/80	SAVAGE FANCY Kathryn Gorsha Thiels	\<HO>	1/81	DESIRE'S COMMAND Marlene Suson	\<HO>
4/80	THIS REBEL HUNGER Lynn LeMon	\<HO>	1/81	JASMINE SPLENDOR Margo Bode	\<HO>
5/80	FROST AND THE FLAME, THE Drucilla Campbell	\<HO>	4/81	GOLDEN SKY, THE Kristin James	\<CO>
5/80	THIS TENDER PRIZE Nancy Morse	\<HO>	4/81	SOME DISTANT SHORE Margaret Pemberton	\<HO>
6/80	TANYA Muriel Bradley	\<HO>	4/81	SUN DANCERS, THE Barbara Faith	\<CO>
6/80	TOMORROW AND FOREVER Maud B. Johnson	\<HO>	4/81	VELVET PROMISE, THE Jude Deveraux	\<HO>
7/80	BRIDE OF THE BAJA Jocelyn Wilde	\<HO>	5/81	CRY FOR PARADISE Diana Stuart	\<HO>
7/80	CARAVAN OF DESIRE Elizabeth Shelley	\<HO>	5/81	DREAM TIDE Katherine Kent	\<CO>

5/81	HIGH FASHION Victoria Kelrich	\<CO\>		10/81	FIREBIRD, THE Nicole Norman	\<HO\>
5/81	THIS BITTER ECSTASY Serita Stevens	\<HO\>		10/81	PROMISE ME FOREVER Jacqueline Marten	\<CO\>
6/81	PASSION'S HEIRS Elizabeth Bright	\<HO\>		10/81	STAR QUALITY Leila Lyons	\<CO\>
6/81	RAINBOW CHASE Kris Karron	\<CO\>		10/81	SWEET ENEMY Martha Brewster	\<HO\>
6/81	RHAPSODY Jessica Dare	\<CO\>		11/81	ARABESQUE Rae Butler	\<HO\>
6/81	SATIN VIXEN, THE Linda Shaw	\<HO\>		11/81	DESIRE'S LEGACY Elizabeth Bright	\<HO\>
7/81	FORTUNE'S CHOICE Eleanor Howard	\<HO\>		11/81	SAPHIRE SKY, THE Kristin James	\<CO\>
7/81	PERFECT COUPLE, THE Paula Moore	\<CO\>		11/81	TRADE SECRETS Diana Morgan	\<CO\>
7/81	SILVER KISS Lynn Erickson	\<HO\>		12/81	AN INNOCENT DECEPTION Linda Shaw	\<CO\>
7/81	SUDDEN SUMMER, THE Muriel Bradley	\<CO\>		12/81	CRIMSON INTRIGUE Devon Lindsay	\<HO\>
8/81	AN ELEGANT AFFAIR Kathleen Morris	\<CO\>		12/81	GOLDEN REBEL Virginia Standage	\<HO\>
8/81	DREAM OF FIRE, A Drucilla Campbell	\<HO\>		12/81	HARVEST OF DREAMS Jessica Dare	\<CO\>
8/81	ROMAN CANDLES Sofi O'Brien	\<CO\>		1/82	BRIDGE OF TOMORROW Leila Lyons	\<HO\>
8/81	WATERS OF EDEN Katherine Kent	\<HO\>		1/82	FOR LOVE ALONE Candice Adams	\<CO\>
9/81	ALL MINE TO GIVE Marsha Alexander	\<CO\>		1/82	TASTE OF WINE, A Vanessa Pryor	\<CO\>
9/81	LASTING SPLENDOR, A Elizabeth Bright	\<HO\>		1/82	SUNRISE TEMPTATION Lynn LeMon	\<HO\>
9/81	SOMETIMES A STRANGER Angela Alexie	\<CO\>		2/82	ISLAND OF PROMISE Madeleine Carr	\<HO\>
9/81	THIS LOVING LAND Dorothy Garlock	\<HO\>		2/82	OPAL FIRES Lynda Trent	\<CO\>

2/82	SCARLET LILY Dee Stuart	<HO>	7/82	GENTLE BETRAYER Lynn Erickson	<CO>

2/82   SCARLET LILY   <HO>   7/82   GENTLE BETRAYER   <CO>
        Dee Stuart   Lynn Erickson

2/82   WITH EYES OF LOVE   <CO>   7/82   HERITAGE OF PASSION, A   <HO>
        Victoria Fleming   Elizabeth Bright

3/82   BY INVITATION ONLY   <CO>   7/82   HIDDEN FIRES   <HO>
        Monica Barrie   Laura Jordan

3/82   DESTINY'S STAR   <HO>   7/82   THAT CERTAIN SMILE   <CO>
        Muriel Bradley   Kate Belmont

3/82   ENDEARMENT, THE   <HO>   8/82   AGAIN THE MAGIC   <CO>
        LaVyrle Spencer   Lee Damon

3/82   MORNINGS IN HEAVEN   <CO>   8/82   FLOWERS IN WINTER   <CO>
        Perdita Shepherd   Muriel Bradley

4/82   NOTHING BUT ROSES   <CO>   8/82   ON WINGS OF SONG   <HO>
        Paula Moore   Martha Brewster

4/82   SEARCHING HEARTS, THE   <HO>   8/82   WAYWARD ANGEL   <HO>
        Dorothy Garlock   Candace Arkham

4/82   TEMPTATION'S TRIUMPH   <HO>   9/82   PROMISE IN THE WIND, A   <HO>
        Joanna Makepeace   Perdita Sheperd

4/82   WORLD OF HER OWN, A   <CO>   9/82   ROYAL SUITE   <CO>
        Anna James   Marsha Alexander

5/82   ENCHANTED DAWN   <HO>   9/82   SHINING NIGHTS   <HO>
        Barbara Faith   Lynda Trent

5/82   MIDNIGHT TANGO   <CO>   9/82   SILKEN WEB, THE   <CO>
        Katherine Kent   Laura Jordan

5/82   MOMENTS TO SHARE   <CO>
        Diana Morgan

5/82   WHISPERS OF DESTINY   <HO>
        Jenifer Dalton

6/82   AFTERGLOW   <CO>
        Jordana Daniels

6/82   BREATH OF PARADISE, A   <HO>
        Carol Norris

6/82   CONQUER THE MEMORIES   <HO>
        Janet Joyce

6/82   SUMMER SKY, THE   <CO>
        Kristin James

Adams, Kelly
Andrews, Nicole
Ashley, Sarah
Barlow, Linda
Bates, Jenny
Bishop, Claudia
Blake, Laurel
Brookes, Beth
Brown, Sandra
Buck, Carole
Carr, Sherry
Carter, Helen
Charles, Marie
Cole, Marianne
Collins, Susanna
Craig, Jasmine
Crawford, Diane
Crewe, Sarah
Cristy, Ann
Curry, Elissa
Curzon, Lucia
Dair, Christina
Damon, Lee
Davies, Frances
Day, Jocelyn
Devon, Anne
Duvall, Aimee
Eaton, Laura
Evans, Claire
Fairfax, Lynn
Fox, Lauren
Francis, Sharon
Frederick, Thea
Grady, Liz
Granger, Katherine
Grant, Jeanne
Hadary, Simone
Harris, Melinda
Haskell, Mary
Hines, Charlotte
Hughes, Cally
Hunt, Jena
Ireland, Jane
Janes, Josephine
Joyce, Deborah
Keast, Karen
Kent, Amanda
Kingston, Meredith
LaRue, Brandy

Lawrence, Lynn
LeGrand, Sybil
Leslie, Margot
Logan, Daisy
Lynn, Robin
Mars, Diana
Marsh, Lillian
Matthews, Jan
Merlin, Christa
Morgan, Faye
Nevins, Kate
Norris, Maureen
Peck, Maggie
Phillips, Johanna
Raye, Linda
Rivers, Francine
Robbins, Kay
Roland, Michelle
Sinclaire, Francesca
Spencer, LaVyrle
Stone, Sharon
Thacker, Cathy
Tierney, Ariel
Trent, Jena
Valcour, Vanessa
Wayne, Rachel
Williams, Lee
Wood, Nuria
Yates, Judith

Adams, Candice	1 THE TESTIMONY
Adams, Tricia	Robin James
Bates, Jenny	
Bishop, Claudia	2 A TASTE OF HEAVEN
Brian, Marilyn	Jennifer Rose
Cole, Hilary	
Connolly, Vivian	3 TREAD SOFTLY
Craig, Jasmine	Ann Cristy
Cristy, Ann	
Curry, Elissa	4 THEY SAID IT WOULDN'T LAST
Damon, Lee	Elaine Tucker
Diamond, Petra	
Edwards, Adrienne	5 GILDED SPRING
Granger, Katherine	Jenny Bates
Grant, Jeanne	
Haskell, Mary	6 LEGAL AND TENDER
Hines, Charlotte	Candice Adams
Hughes, Cally	
James, Robin	7 THE FAMILY PLAN
Miles, Cassie	Nuria Wood
Randolph, Melanie	
Rose, Jennifer	8 HOLD FAST 'TIL DAWN
Topaz, Jacqueline	Mary Haskell
Tucker, Elaine	
Wellington, Kate	9 HEART FULL OF RAINBOWS
Wood, Nuria	Melanie Randolph

10 I KNOW MY LOVE
   Vivian Connolly

11 KEYS TO THE HEART
   Jennifer Rose

12 STRANGE BEDFELLOWS
   Elaine Tucker

13 MOMENTS TO SHARE
   Katherine Granger

14 SUNBURST
   Jeanne Grant

15 WHATEVER IT TAKES
   Cally Hughes

16 LADY LAUGHING EYES
   Lee Damon

17 ALL THAT GLITTERS
   Mary Haskell

Allison, Penny
Barber, Lenora
Berk, Ariel
Bishop, Cassandra
Blair, Laurien
Browning, Dixie
Caimi, Gina
Carey, Suzanne
Chance, Sara
Charlton, Josephine
Chase, Elaine Raco
Clay, Rita
Corbett, Paula
Cresswell, Jasmine
Dee, Sherry
Dennis, Roberta
Douglass, Billie
Evans, Laurel
Fulford, Paula
Galt, Serena
Gladstone, Eve
Hart, Susannah
Howard, Alyssa
James, Stephanie
John, Nancy
Joyce, Janet
Kennedy, Marilyn
Langtry, Ellen
Larson, Shirley
Lind, Pamela
Lowell, Elizabeth
Major, Ann
Malek, Doreen Owens
Mallory, Kathryn
Martel, Aimee
McCoy, Cathlyn
McKenna, Lindsey
Michelle, Suzanne
Milan, Angel
Monet, Nicole
Morgan, Raye
Nicolel, Marie
Paige, Laurie
Palmer, Diana
Powers, Nora
Robbins, JoAnn

Ross, Erin
Roszel, Renee
St. Claire, Erin
St. George, Edith
Scott, Melissa
Simms, Suzanne
Stewart, Ruth
Summers, Ashley
Trent, Brenda
Trevor, June
Victor, Vanessa
West, Sara Ann
Wright, Lucretia

67	GAMEMASTER Stephanie James	85	THE SILVER SNARE Stephanie James
68	SHADOW OF YESTERDAY Dixie Browning	86	NATIVE SEASON Doreen Owens Malek
69	PASSION'S PORTRAIT Suzanne Carey	87	RECIPE FOR LOVE Suzanne Michelle
70	DINNER FOR TWO Vanessa Victor	88	WINGED VICTORY June Trevor
71	MAN OF THE HOUSE Janet Joyce	89	TIME FOR TOMORROW Erin Ross
72	NOBODY'S BABY Susannah Hart	90	WILD FLIGHT Renee Roszel
73	A KISS REMEMBERED Erin St. Claire	91	IMAGE OF LOVE Dixie Browning
74	BEYOND FANTASY Billie Douglass	92	MOUNTAIN MEMORY Suzanne Carey
75	CHASE THE CLOUDS Lindsay McKenna	93	SILENT BEGINNINGS Ariel Berk
76	STORMY SERENADE Suzanne Michelle	94	WINNING SEASON JoAnn Robbins
77	SUMMER THUNDER Elizabeth Lowell	95	THE MARRYING KIND Ashley Summers
78	BLUEPRINT FOR RAPTURE Lenora Barber	96	SUMMERSON Angel Milan
79	SO SWEET A MADNESS Suzanne Simms	97	BATTLE PRIZE Stephanie James
80	FIRE AND ICE Diana Palmer	98	MAN OF GLORY Janet Joyce
81	OPENING BID Marilyn Kennedy	99	LOVE ME AGAIN Ann Major
82	SUMMER SONG Rita Clay	100	SOUTHERN PERSUASION Alyssa Howard
83	HOME AT LAST Sara Chance	101	SUMMER WIND Raye Morgan
84	IN A MOMENTS TIME Nora Powers	102	SNOW KISSES Diana Palmer

Allison, Moeth	1 DREAMS OF EVENING
Barrie, Monica	Kristin James
Baxter, Mary Lynn	
Belmont, Kathryn	2 ONCE MORE WITH FEELING
Bird, Beverly	Nora Roberts
Blake, Jillian	
Bonds, Parris Afton	3 EMERALDS IN THE DARK
Bradley, Muriel	Beverly Bird
Clare, Jane	
Cole, Sue Ellen	4 SWEETHEART CONTRACT
Faith, Barbara	Pat Wallace
Gladstone, Eve	
Hastings, Brooke	5 WIND SONG
Hohl, Joan	Parris Afton Bonds
Howard, Linda	
Jackson, Lisa	6 ISLAND HERITAGE
James, Anna	Monica Barrie
James, Kristin	
James, Stephanie	7 A DISTANT CASTLE
Kenyon, Joanna	Sue Ellen Cole
Lowell, Elizabeth	
Major, Ann	8 LOVE EVERLASTING
Martin, Nancy	Moeth Allison
McKenna, Lindsay	
Miller, Linda Lael	9 SERPENT IN PARADISE
Roberts, Nora	Stephanie James
St. Claire, Erin	
Seger, Maura	10 A SEASON OF RAINBOWS
Sellers, Lorraine	Jennifer West
Stephens, Jeanne	
Thiels, Kathryn	11 UNTIL THE END OF TIME
Thorne, April	June Trevor
Trent, Lynda	
Trevor, June	12 TONIGHT AND ALWAYS
Wallace, Pamela	Nora Roberts
Wallace, Pat	
West,Jennifer	13 EDGE OF LOVE
York, Amanda	Anna James

14 RECKLESS SURRENDER
Jeanne Stephens

15 SHADOW DANCE
Lorraine Sellers

16 THE PROMISE OF SUMMER
Barbara Faith

17 THE AMBER SKY
Kristin James

Adams, Melodie
Allison, Penny
Ashby, Juliet
Barry, Andrea
Beckman, Patti
Brooke, Alice
Browning, Dixie
Camp, Elaine
Carroll, Mary
Chase, Marian
Cockcroft, Ann
Cork, Dorothy
Dailey, Janet
Eden, Laura
English, Genevieve
Forrest, Chelsey
Gordon, Lucy
Gray, Ginna
Halldorson, Phyllis
Halston, Carole
Hampson, Anne
Hardy, Laura
Hunter, Elizabeth
James, Arlene
John, Nancy
Joyce, Janet
King, Josie
Ladame, Cathryn
Langan, Ruth
Lloyd, Frances
Lovan, Thea
Manning, Marilyn
Martin, Ione
Maxam, Mia
McKay, Rena
Morgan, Diana
Paige, Laurie
Palmer, Diana
Payne, Tiffany
Rainville, Rita
Roberts, Nora
St. George, Edith
Saunders, Jean
Scofield, Carin
Sinclair, Tracy
Smith, Joan

Starr, Cynthia
Stephens, Kay
Stevens, Susan
Summers, Ashley
Thornton, Carolyn
Trent, Brenda
Vernon, Dorothy
Vine, Kerry
Vitek, Donna
Walters, Jade
Wildman, Faye
Wilson, Fran
Windham, Suzannah
Wisdom, Linda
Young, Brittany
Young, Karen

226	SWEET SECOND LOVE Anne Hampson	244	STARS IN HER EYES Tracy Sinclair
227	FORBIDDEN AFFAIR Patti Beckman	245	STEAL LOVE AWAY Brenda Trent
228	DANCE AT YOUR WEDDING Josie King	246	WHERE TOMORROW WAITS Mary Carroll
229	FOR ERIC'S SAKE Carolyn Thornton	247	MOUNTAIN MELODY Phyllis Halldorson
230	IVORY INNOCENCE Susan Stevens	248	ROSE-COLORED GLASS Edith St. George
231	WESTERN MAN Janet Dailey	249	SILVERWOOD Carin Scofield
232	SPELL OF THE ISLAND Anne Hampson	250	THERE MUST BE SHOWERS Anne Hampson
233	EDGE OF PARADISE Dorothy Vernon	251	AFTER AUTUMN Fran Wilson
234	NEXT YEAR'S BLONDE Joan Smith	252	UNTAMED Nora Roberts
235	NO EASY CONQUEST Arlene James	253	TWO OF A KIND Arlene James
236	LOST IN LOVE Mia Maxam	254	DARLING ENEMY Diana Palmer
237	WINTER PROMISE Fran Wilson	255	CAPRICE Joan Smith
238	OUTBACK DREAMING Dorothy Cork	256	SOFT VELVET NIGHT Anne Hampson
239	VALLEY OF BROKEN HEARTS Rena McKay	257	A TOWER OF STRENGTH Elizabeth Hunter
240	SHARED DESTINY Elizabeth Hunter	258	MIDNIGHT LOVER Juliet Ashby
241	SNOW QUEEN Linda Wisdom	259	THE FRENCH CONFECTION Genevieve English
242	NO GUARANTEES Alice Brooke	260	THE GOLDENRAIN TREE Ione Martin
243	THE LANQUAGE OF LOVE Jean Saunders	261	TASTE THE WINE Jean Saunders

Adams, Melodie
Barrie, Monica
Baxter, Mary Lynn
Beckman, Patti
Belmont, Kathryn
Bergen, Fran
Bishop, Natalie
Bright, Laurey
Browning, Dixie
Camp, Elaine
Carr, Eleni
Cates, Tory
Charles, Maggi
Claire, Eva
Converse, Jane
Dailey, Janet
Dalton, Gena
Daniels, Rhett
Dixon, Diana
Douglass, Billie
Doyle, Emily
Gladstone, Eve
Gordon, Lucy
Gray, Ginna
Halston, Carole
Hamilton, Lucy
Hastings, Brooke
Howard, Linden
Hurley, Ann
Jackson, Lisa
John, Nancy
Justin, Jennifer
Lacey, Anne
Langan, Ruth
Lee, Amanda
Lee, Doris
Major, Ann
Macomber, Debbie
Malek, Doreen Owens
McKenna, Lindsay
Meriwether, Kate
Mikels, Jennifer
Paige, Laurie
Parker, Laura
Ripy, Margaret
Roberts, Nora
Ross, Erin
Rowe, Melanie
Saxon, Antonio
Scott, Joanna

Seger, Maura
Shaw, Linda
Sinclair, Tracy
Stanford, Sondra
Stephens, Jeanne
Taylor, Abra
Thorne, April
Thornton, Carolyn
Walker, Elizabeth Neff
Wallace, Pamela
Wallace, Pat
Wisdom, Linda
Wildman, Faye

Aks, Patricia	33	YOU & ME
Alexander, Bea		Maude Johnson
Arthur, Elaine		
Bayner, Rose	34	PERFECT FIGURE
Brady, Brett		Josie March
Bush, Nancy		
Caldwell, Claire	35	PEOPLE LIKE US
Cassiday, Becka		Barbara Haynes
Chatterton, Louise		
Cole, Brenda	36	ONE ON ONE
Coy, Barbara		Pam Ketter
Davis, Wendi		
Dellin, Genell	37	LOVE NOTE
Dunne, Mary Jo		Jessica Howell
Enfield, Carrie		
Francis, Dorothy	38	SECRET ADMIRER
Fisher, Fran		Carrie Enfield
Graham, Leslie		
Grimes, Frances Hurley	39	BE MY VALENTINE
Harper, Elaine		Elaine Harper
Harrell, Janice		
Hart, Nicole	40	LUCKY STAR
Hawkins, Laura		Becka Cassiday
Haynes, Barbara		
Howell, Jessica	41	JUST FRIENDS
Johnson, Maude		Dorothy Francis
Ketter, Pam		
Kingsbury, Dawn	42	PROMISES TO COME
Ladd, Veronica		Genell Dellin
Leroe, Ellen		
Lewis, Carrie	43	KNIGHT TO REMEMBER
Madison, Winifred		Pam Martin
Makris, Kathryn		
Malek, Doreen Owens	44	SOMEONE LIKE JEREMY VAUGHN
Manning Marilyn		Bea Alexander
March, Josie		
Marshall, Andrea	45	TOUCH OF LOVE
Martin, Pam		Winifred Madison
Mathews, Michelle		
McKenna, RoseAnne	46	SEALED WITH A KISS
Phillips, Erin		Wendi Davis
Robertson, Carol		
Ryan, Oneta	47	THREE WEEKS OF LOVE
Sommers, Beverly		Patricia Aks
Stuart, Becky		
Wagner, Sharon	48	SUMMER ILLUSION
Wunsch, Josephine		Marilyn Manning
Youngblood, Marilyn		
	49	ONE OF A KIND
		Brett Brady

Argers, Helen	08/80	CALABRIAN SUMMER
Ashton, Ann		Marjorie McEvoy
Ball, Donna		
Berencsi, Susan	09/80	THE MACORVAN CURSE
Bowes, Florence		Florence Bowes
Claire, Evelyn		
Comfort, Iris	10/80	SHADOW MASQUE
DeWeese, Jean		Iris Comfort
Fitzgerald, Amber		
French, Janine	11/80	THE HOYDEN BRIDE
Hager, Jean		Margaret Rau
Hanson, Mary Catherine		
Hinchman, Jane	12/80	THE JADE PAGODA
Husted, Darrell		Betty Hale Hyatt
Hyatt, Betty Hale		
Kitt, Sandra	1/81	THE BACKHOE GOTHIC
Lynn, Karen		Jean DeWeese
MacWilliams, Margaret		
McEvoy, Marjorie	2/81	LOVER'S KNOT
Miller, Cissie		Janet Templeton
Ragosta, Millie J.		
Rau, Margaret	3/81	CONCESSION
Reed, Miriam		Ann Ashton
Robins, Eleanor		
Scott-Drennan, Lynne	4/81	INTERLUDE IN VENICE
Seely, Norma		Florence Bowes
Shelley, Lillian		
Stephens, Barbara	5/81	GERAIT'S DAUGHTER
Templeton, Janet		Millie J. Ragosta
Warren, Beverly C.		
Zumwalt, Eva	6/81	MISTRAL
		Margaret MacWilliams
	7/81	DOUBLE MASQUERADE
		Karen Lynn
	8/81	YELLOW-FLOWER MOON
		Jean Hager
	9/81	WILDWOODS AND WISHES
		Susan Berencsi
	10/81	THE BELLE OF BATH
		Lillian Shelley
	11/81	THE SUSPICIOUS HEART
		Amber Fitzgerald
	12/81	TISH
		Cissie Miller

Aaron, Anna
Blake, Susan
Burman, Margaret
Campbell, Joanna
Conklin, Barbara
Cowan, Dale
Crawford, Alice Owen
Dukore, Jesse
Fisher, Lois I.
Foster, Stephanie
Johns, Janetta
Kent, Deborah
Maravel, Gailanne
Nobile, Jeanette
Park, Anne
Pines, Nancy
Pollowitz, Melinda
Quin-Harkin, Janet
Rand, Suzanne
Saal, Jocelyn
Spector, Debra
Vernon, Rosemary
Woodruff, Marian

29 NEVER LOVE A COWBOY
    Jesse Dukore

30 LITTLE WHITE LIES
    Lois I. Fisher

31 TOO CLOSE FOR COMFORT
    Debra Spector

32 DAYDREAMER
    Janet Quin-Harkin

33 DEAR AMANDA
    Rosemary Vernon

34 COUNTRY GIRL
    Melinda Pollowitz

35 FORBIDDEN LOVE
    Marian Woodruff

36 SUMMER DREAMS
    Barbara Conklin

37 POTRAIT OF LOVE
    Jeanette Nobile

38 RUNNING MATES
    Jocelyn Saal

39 FIRST LOVE
    Debra Spector

40 SECRETS
    Anna Aaron

41 THE TRUTH ABOUT ME AND
    BOBBY V.   Janetta Johns

42 THE PERFECT MATCH
    Marian Woodruff

43 TENDER LOVING CARE
    Anne Park

44 LONG DISTANCE LOVE
    Jesse Dukore

45 DREAM PROM
    Margaret Burman

Barrie, Monica
Conway, Theresa
Dureau, Lorena
Deveraux, Jude
Erickson, Lynn
Flournoy, Sheryl
Foote, Victoria
Gardner, Joy
Halliday, Ena
Hammond, Mary Ann
Hill, Johanna
Howard, Eleanor
Jerina, Carol
Joyce, Janet
Lyndell, Catherine
Marten, Jacqueline
Miller, Linda Lael
Mitchell, Erica
O'Hallion, Sheila
Parker, Laura
Patrick, DeAnn
Pellicane, Patricia
Seger, Maura
Sinclair, Cynthia
Stephens, Sharon
Stevens, Serita
Trent, Lynda
Tucker, Helen

MARIELLE
Ena Halliday

DEFIANT LOVE
Maura Seger

THE BLACK EARL
Sharon Stephens

FLAMES OF PASSION
Sheryl Flournoy

KINDRED SPIRITS
DeAnn Patrick

HIGH COUNTRY PRIDE
Lynn Erickson

CLOAK OF FATE
Eleanor Howard

FORTUNE'S BRIDE
Joy Gardner

9   IRON LACE
Lorena Dureau

10   LYSETTE
Ena Halliday

11   LIBERTINE LADY
Janet Joyce

12   LOVE CHASE
Theresa Conway

13   REBELLIOUS LOVE
Maura Seger

14   EMBRACE THE STORM
Lynda Trent

15   SWEETBRIAR
Jude Deveraux

16   EMERALD AND SAPPHIRE
Laura Parker

17   EMBRACE THE WIND
Lynda Trent

CAPRICE ROMANCE
Berkley/Jove Publishing Group
Tempo Books

Ball, Barbara
Boyle, Ann
Carson, Nola
Dionne, Leah
Enderle, Judith
Hunter, Terry
Kent, Deborah
Ketter, Pam
Lantz, Francess Lin
Lenz, Jeanne R.
Quin-Harkin, Janet
Rae, Judie
Scariano, Margaret M.
Selden, Neil
Shaw, Susan
White, Charlotte
Zeiger, Helane

CHERISH ROMANCE
Thomas Nelson Publishers

Brand, Irene
Dunaway, Patricia
Peart, Jean
Staton, Anna Lloyd

DARK DESIRE ROMANCE
Blue Heron Press

Moore, Paula
Sommers, Jeanne
Toombs, Jane
Wilde, Jocelyn

DAWNSTAR ROMANCE
Bantam Books, Inc.

Ash, Melissa
Christopher, Mary
Conrad, Helen
Gadsden, Angela
Gray, Alison
Innes, Jean
James, Amalia
Lang, Eve

(cont'd)

DAWNSTAR ROMANCE (continued)
Moore, Jill
Parrish, Patt
Smith, Joan
West, Jamie

FINDING MR. RIGHT
Avon Books

Calloway, Jo
Chase, Elaine Raco
Christopher, Beth
Henrichs, Betty
Meadows, Alicia
Neggers, Carla
Parker, Laura
Satran, Pamela
Walker, Elizabeth Neff

FOLLOW YOUR HEART
Avon Books

Cooney, Caroline
Gelman, Jan

JUDY SULLIVAN BOOKS
Walker And Company

de St. Jeor, Owannad
Dixon Rhonda
Johnson, Norma
Kent, Katherine
Meacham, Leila
White, Charlotte

LOVE & LIFE
Ballantine Books

Adams, Candice
Allyn, Jennifer
Austin, Stephanie
Bacon, Nancy
Blair, Cynthia
Chandler, Bryn
Douglas, Carole Nelson
Harrowe, Fiona
Haymond, Ginny

(cont'd)

LOVE & LIFE (continued)
Michaels, Fern
Myers, Mary Ruth
Parenteau, Shirley
Smith, Carol Sturm
Walker, Irma

MAGIC MOMENTS & TURNING POINTS
NAL-Signet Vista

Kennedy, M. L
Norby, Lisa
Stewart, Jo

MAKE YOUR DREAMS COME TRUE <YA>
Warner Books

Bradford, Mary Ellen
Carr, Nicole
McNicol, Amanda

SCARLET RIBBONS
The New American Library

Cameron, Kay
Coulter, Catherine
Grice, Julia
Maxwell, Kathleen
Osborne, Maggie
Thornton, Helene
Welles, Alyssa

SENIORS
Dell

Goudge, Eileen

SERENADE/SAGA
Zondervan

Dengler, Sandy
Feldhake, Susan C.
Gilge, Jeannette
Graham, Brenda Knight
Kletzing, Karen
Peart, Jane
Watson, Elaine

SERENADE/SERENATA
Zondervan

Baer, Judy
Daniels, Velma S w/ Peggy E. King
Darty, Peggy
Feldhake, Susan C.
Heerman, Lydia
Herring, Linda
Hoover, Mab Graff
Schulte, Elaine L.

SPECIAL CATEGORY ROMANCE
Harlequin Books

Anzelon, Robyn
Ashton, Mollie
Holliday, Delores
Martin, Marian
Orwig, Sara
Quinn, Alison
Toombs, Jane

THE AVON BANNER ROMANCE

Ascani, Sparky
Canham, Marsha
Douglas, Kate
Edwards, Andrea
Henley, Virginia
Lanigan, Catherine
Lehr, Helene
McCarty, Betsy
Moulton, Nancy
Myers, Katherine
Nash, Jean
Pade, Victoria
Thomas, Rosie
Winslow, Laurel

TORCH/TORCHLITE

Aid, Frances
Casey, June
Chatfield, Susan
Coburn, Jean Ann
Dore, Christy

(cont'd)

<u>TORCH/TORCHLITE</u> (continued)

Edwards, Kathryn
Himrod, Brenda
Lloyd, Marta
Malone, Bev
Moore, Diana
Rosemoor, Patricia
Thompson, Chris
Wisdom, Linda

<u>TWO BY TWO ROMANCE</u>
<u>Warner Books</u>

Aks, Patricia
Carroll, Abby
Casey, Sara
Filichia, Peter
Harrell, Janice
Kennedy, Kim
Makris, Kathryn
Malone, Lucy

<u>VELVET GLOVE</u>
<u>Avon Books</u>

Neggers, Carla
Seger, Maura

Index

A

AARON, Anna 1
ABBOTT, Mary Jeanne 1
  (Elizabeth Hewitt)
ABSALOM, Stacy 1
ADAIR, Dennis and Janet
  ROSENSTOCK 1
ADAMS, Candice 1
  [Lois A. Walker]
ADAMS, Daniel 1
  [Christopher Nicole]
ADAMS, Kasey 1
  [Valerie Whisenand]
ADAMS, Kelly 1
ADAMS, Melodie 1
ADAMS, Patricia K 1
  (Julia Howard)
ADAMS, Tricia 1
ADLER, Warren 1
AEBY, Jacquelyn 2
  (Jocelyn Carew)
  (Vanessa Gray)
AFRICANO, Lillian 2
AGHADJIAN, Mollie 2
  (Moeth Allison)
  (Mollie Ashton)
AHERN, Patricia 2
  (Kate Meriwether)
AID, Francis 2
AIKEN, Joan 2
AKS, Patricia 2
ALEXANDER, Bea 2
ALEXANDER, Megan 2
  [Mildred Fisch]
ALEXANDER, Susan 2
ALEXIE, Angela 2
  [Angela Talias]
ALGERMISSEN, Jo Ann 2
  (Anna Hudson)
ALLEN, Anita 2
ALLEN, Catherine R w/
  Dorothea JENSEN 2
  (Catherine Moorhouse)
ALLEN, Charlotte Vale 2
ALLEN, Sheila R. 3
  (Sheila O'Hallion)
ALLISON, Elizabeth 3
  [Alice Harron Orr]
ALLISON, Moeth 3
  [Mollie Aghadjian]

ALLISON, Penny 3
  [Carol Katz]
ALLISTER, Barbara 3
  [Barbara Teer]
ALLYN, Jennifer 3
ALLYNE, Kerry 3
ALLYSON, Kym 3
  [John M. Kimbro]
ALSOBROOK, Rosalyn 3
ALSOBROOK, Rosalyn w/
  Jean HAUGHT 3
  (Jalynn Friends)
AMERICAN EXPLORERS SERIES <AES> 3
AMERICAN INDIAN SERIES <AIS> 4
ANDERSON, Ken 4
ANDERSON, Lee 4
ANDERSON, Roberta w/
  Mary KUCZKIR 4
  (Fern Michaels)
ANDERSON, Virginia 4
  (Megan Ashe)
ANDERSSON, C. Dean w/
  Nina Romberg ANDERSSON 4
  (Asa Drake)
ANDERSSON, Nina Romberg 4
  (Jane Archer)
ANDREWS, Barbara 4
ANDREWS, Felicia 4
  [Charles L. Grant]
ANDREWS, Nicola 4
  [Orania Papazoglou]
ANNE-MARIEL 4
ANTHONY, Diana 4
  [Diane Antonio]
ANTHONY, Evelyn 4
  [Evelyn Bridget Patricia
  Stephens Ward-Thomas]
ANTHONY, Page 5
  [Page & Anthony Traynor]
ANTONIO, Diane 5
  (Diana Anthony)
  (Diana Lyndon)
ANZELON, Robyn 5
ARBOR, Jane 5
ARCHER, Jane 5
  [Nina Romberg Andersson]
ARGERS, Helen 5
ARMSTRONG, Carolyn T. 5
ARMSTRONG, Charlotte 5
  [Charlotte Armstrong Lewi]
ARMSTRONG, Lindsay 5
ARNOLD, Francena 6
ARNOLD, Margot 6
ARNOUT, Susan 6
ARTHUR, Elaine 6

ASCANI, Sparky 6
ASH, Melissa 6
[June E. Casey]
ASHBY, Juliet 6
[Louise Lee Outlaw]
ASHE, Megan 6
[Virginia Anderson]
ASHER, Inez 6
ASHFIELD, Helen 6
[Pamela Bennetts]
ASHFORD, Jane 6
[Jane LeCompte]
ASHLEY, Faye 6
(Ashley Summers)
ASHLEY, Jacqueline 6
[Jacqueline Casto]
ASHLEY, Sarah 7
ASHTON, Ann 7
[John M. Kimbro]
ASHTON, Mollie 7
[Mollie Aghadjian]
ASTLEY, Juliet 7
[Nora Lofts]
AUBERT, Rosemary 7
(Lucy Snow)
AUEL, Jean M. 7
AUFDEM-BRINKE, Eleanor 7
(Nora Roberts)
AUMENTE, Joy 7
(Joy Darlington)
(Joy Gardner)
AUSTIN, Stephanie 7
AYRE, Jessica 7

B

BACON, Nancy 7
BADGER, Rosemary 7
BADGLEY, Anne 7
BAKER, Darlene 8
(Heather Lang)
BAKER, Fran 8
(Cathlyn McCoy)
BAKER, Marceil 8
(Marica Miller)
BALDWIN, Cathryn Jo 8
(Cathryn Ladame)
(Cathryn Ladd)
BALDWIN, Faith 8
[Faith Baldwin Cuthrell]

BALDWIN, Rebecca 8
[Helen Chappel]
BALE, Karen A. 8
BALIN, Beverly 8
BALL, Barbara 8
BALL, Donna 8
(Rebecca Flanders)
BALL, Margaret 8
(Kathleen Frasher)
(Catherine Lyndell)
BANCROFT, Iris 8
(Iris Brent)
(Andrea Layton)
BANGERT, Ethel 8
BANNISTER, Patricia 8
(Patricia Veryan)
BARBER, Lenora 8
[Janet Wing]
BARBER, Noel 8
BARBIERI, Elaine A. 8
BARKER, Berta LaVan 8
BARLOW, Linda 9
BARNARD, Judith w/ Michael FAIN 9
(Judith Michael)
BARRETT, Jr., Neal 9
BARRETT, William E. 9
BARRIE, Monica 9
[David Wind]
BARRIE, Susan 9
(Anita Charles)
(Pamela Kent)
BARRY, Andrea 9
[Hania 'Annette' Bartle]
BARRY, Jane 9
BARRY, Lucy 9
BARTHOLOMEW, Barbara 9
BARTLE, Hania 'Annette' 9
(Andrea Barry)
BARTLETT, Kathleen 9
BASILE, Gloria Vitanza 9
BASTIEN, Dorothy 9
BATES, Jenny 9
[Maura Seger]
BATTLE, Lois 10
BAUGHMAN, Dorothy 10
BAULING, Jayne 10
BAUMGARDNER, Cathie 10
(Cathie Linz)
BAUMGARTEN, Sylvia 10
(Ena Halliday)
BAWDEN, Nina 10
BAXTER, Mary Lynn 10
BAYNER, Rose 10
BEARDSLEY, Charles 10
BEATY, Betty w/ David BEATY 10

BEAUMONT, Helen 10
  (Jill Anderson)
  (Jill Eckersley)
  (Anna Stanton)
BECHKO, Peggy 10
BECKMAN, Patti 10
  [Charles and/or Patti
   Boechman]
BEEBE, Elswyth 10
  (Elswyth Thane)
BELL, Anthea 11
BELL, Betsy 11
BELL, Josephine 11
BELL, Sallie Lee 11
BELMONT, Kathryn 11
  [Mary Jo Territo]
BENEDICT, Barbara 11
BENET, Deborah 11
  [Deborah Elaine Camp]
BENJAMIN, Linda 11
BENNETT, Christine 11
  [William Arthur Neubauer]
BENNETT, Emma 11
  [Emma Merritt]
BENNETTS, Pamela 11
  (Helen Ashfield)
  (Margaret James)
BERCKMAN, Evelyn 11
BERENCSI, Susan 12
BERENSON, Laurie 12
  (Laurien Blair)
BERGEN, Fran 12
  [Frances deTalavera Berger]
BERGER, Frances deTalavera 12
  (Fran Bergen)
  (Frances Flores)
BERGER, Nomi 12
  (Alyssa Welles)
BERGSTROM, Kay 12
  (Cassie Miles)
BERGSTROM, Louise 12
BERK, Ariel 12
  [Barbara Keiler]
BERNADETTE, Ann 12
  [Karen Ray w/ D. H. Gadzak]
BERNARD, Dorothy Ann 12
  [Dorothy Weller]
BERNARD, Thelma Rene 12
BEVAN, Gloria 12
BEVERLEY, Jane 12
  [Dorothy Weller]
BIANCHIN, Helen 12
BIEBER, Janet w/ Joyce THIES 12
  (Janet Joyce)

BIERCE, Jane 13
BINCHY, Maeve 13
BIRD, Beverly 13
BIRD, Patricia 13
BIRD, Sarah 13
  (Tory Cates)
BISHOP, Cassandra 13
BISHOP, Claudia 13
BISHOP, Lee 13
BISHOP, Natalie 13
BISSELL, Elaine 13
  (Whitney Faulkner)
BITTNER, F. Rosanne 13
BJORN, Thyra Ferre' 13
BLACK, Hermina 13
BLACK, Jackie 13
  [Jacqueline Casto]
BLACK, Laura 14
BLAIR, Christina 14
BLAIR, Cynthia 14
BLAIR, Kathryn 14
  (Rosalind Brett)
  (Celine Conway)
BLAIR, Laurien 14
  [Laurie Berenson]
BLAIR, Leona 14
BLAIR, Rebecca 14
BLAIRSON, Peter T. 14
BLAKE, Andrea 14
  (Anne Weale)
BLAKE, Jennifer 14
  [Patricia Maxwell]
BLAKE, Jillian 14
BLAKE, Laurel 14
  [Elaine Fowler Palencia]
BLAKE, Stephanie 15
  [Jack Pearl]
BLAKE, Susan 15
BLAKE, Vanessa 15
BLANFORD, Virginia 15
  (Sarah Crewe)
BLAYNE, Diana 15
  [Susan Spaeth Kyle]
BLICKLE, Katrinka 15
BLOCKLINGER, Betty 15
  [Peggy O'More]
BLOOM, Usrula 15
  (Sheila Burns)
  (Mary Essex)
BLOOM, Ursula w/ Charles EADE 15
  (Lozania Prole)
BOCKOVEN, Georgia 15
BOECHMAN, Patti and/or Charles
  BOECHMAN 15
  (Patti Beckman)

CLAIR, Daphne   30   COLETTE   32
  (Laurey Bright)   COLLETT, Dorothy   32
  (Claire Lorel)   COLLINS, Kathryn   32
CLAIRE, Eve   30   COLLINS, Marion Smith   33
  [Claire Delong]   (Marion Smith)
CLAIRE, Evelyn   30   COLLINS, Susanna   33
CLAPP, Patricia   30   [Sue Ellen Gross]
CLARE, Jane   30   COLLINS, Wilkie   33
  [Dinah Shields]   COMBS, Becky   33
CLARE, Shannon   30   COMFORT, Iris   33
  (Linda Harrel)   COMPTON, Anne   33
CLARK, Eleanor   30   CONARAIN, Alice 'Nina'   33
CLARK, Marianne   31   (Elizabeth Hoy)
  [Marianne Williams]   CONAWAY, James   33
CLARK, Norma Lee   31   (Leila Lyons)
CLARK, Roberta   31   (Vanessa Valcour)
CLARK, Sandra   31   CONKLIN, Barbara   33
CLARKE, Janet K.   31   CONLEY, Karen   33
  (Jane Christopher)   CONN, Phoebe   33
  (Joanna Kenyon)   CONNOLLY, Vivian   33
  (Nell Kincaid)   (Susanna Rosse)
CLARY, Sydney Ann   31   CONRAD, Helen   33
  (Sara Chance)   [Helen Manak Conrad]
CLAY, Rita   31   (Jena Hunt)
  [Rita Clay Estrada]   (Raye Morgan)
CLIFFORD, Kay   31   CONROY, Janet   34
CLUMPNER, Mick   31   [Joseph Chadwick]
COBURN, Jean Ann   31   CONVERSE, Jane   34
COCKCROFT, Ann   31   [Adela Maritano]
COFFARO, Katherine   31   CONWAY, Celine   34
COFFMAN, Virginia   31   [Kathryn Blair]
  (Kay Cameron)   CONWAY, Theresa   34
  (Victor Cross)   COOK, Ida   34
  (Virginia C. Deuvaul)   (Mary Burchell)
  (Jeanne Duval)   COOKSON, Catherine   34
  (Ann Stanfield)   (Catherine Marchant)
COHEN, Rhoda   32   (Katie McMullen)
  (Eleanora Brownleigh)   COOMBS, Nina   34
  (Paige Wolfe)   [Nina Pykare]
COHEN, Sharleen Cooper   32   COONEY, Caroline B.   34
COHEN, Susan   32   COOPER, Ann   34
  (Elizabeth St. Clair)   COPELAND, Frances   34
COLE, Brenda   32   (Fran Fisher)
COLE, Dorothy   32   COPELAND, Lori   34
COLE, Hilary   32   CORBETT, Paula   34
  [Valerie Miller]   CORBY, Jane   35
COLE, Hubert   32   CORCORAN, Dotti w/
COLE, Justine   32   Mary Ann SLOJKOWSKI   35
  [Susan Phillips w/   (DeAnn Patrick)
   Claire Kiehl]   CORK, Dorothy   35
COLE, Marianne   32   CORRIE, Jane   35
  [Charlotte White]   CORSON, Martha   35
COLE, Sue Ellen   32   (Anne Lacey)
  [Sue Ellen Gross]   (Kristin Michaels)

FOX, Gardner 54
(Lynna Cooper)
FOX, Lauren 54
[Penny Fowler w/
Dennis Fowler]
FOXX, Rosalind 54
[June Haydon w/
Judy Simpson]
FRANCIS, Clare 54
FRANCIS, Dorothy 54
[Dorothy Brenner Francis]
(Ellen Goforth)
(Pat Louis)
FRANCIS, Robin 54
[Rose Marie Ferris]
FRANCIS, Sara 54
FRANCIS, Sharon 54
[Maureen Wartski]
FRANKEL, Ruby 54
(Rebecca Bennett)
(Constance Conrad)
(Lillian Marsh)
FRASER, Alison 55
FRASER, Jane 55
(Rosamunde Pilcher)
FRASER, Kathleen 55
[Margaret Ball]
FREDERICK, Thea 55
[Barbara Keiler]
FREED, Lynn 55
FREEMAN, Joy 55
(Beverly Sommers)
FREMANTLE, Anne, 55
(Lady Caroline Lamb)
FRENCH, Janie 55
FRIENDS, Jalynn 55
[Rosalyn Alsobrook w/
Jean Haught]
FRITCH, Elizabeth 55
FRITZGERALD, Nancy 55
FROST, Eleanor 55
[Elsa Frohman]
FROST, Joan 55
FULFORD, Paula 55
FURSTENBERG-FORBES, Lyn 55

G

GADDIS, Peggy 56
[Peggy Gaddis Dern]
GADSDEN, Angela 56

GADZAK, D. H. w/ Karen RAY 56
(Ann Bernadette)
GAIR, Diana 56
GALIARDI, Spring 56
(Spring Hermann)
GALT, Serena 56
GAMEL, Nona 56
GANN, Ernest K. 56
GARDNER, Joy 56
[Joy Aumente]
GARDNER, Marjorie H. 56
GARLAND, Nicholas 56
GARLAND, Sherry 56
(Lynn Lawrence)
GARLOCK, Dorothy 56
(Dorothy Phillips)
(Johnna Phillips)
GARRETT, George 56
GARRETT, Sally 57
GARRISON, Joan 57
[William Arthur Neubauer]
GARTNER, Chloe 57
GARVICE, Charles 57
(Caroline Hart)
(Carolyn G. Hart)
GAYLE, Margaret 57
GAYNOR, Anne 57
GELLIS, Roberta 57
(Max Daniels) <SF>)
(Priscilla Hamilton)
GELMAN, Jan 57
GEORGE, Catherine 57
GIBBONS, Marian Chesney 57
(Marion Chesney)
(Helen Crampton)
(Ann Fairfax)
(Jennie Tremaine)
GIBERSON, Dorothy 57
(Penelope Field)
GILBERT, Anna 57
[Marguerite Lazarus]
GILBERT, Jacqueline 57
GILES, Raymond 57
GILLESPIE, Jane 58
GILMER, Ann 58
[W. E. D. Ross]
GILZEN, Elizabeth 58
(Elizabeth Houghton)
(Mary Hunton)
GISCARD, Valerie 58
[Emily Mesta]
GLADSTONE, EVE 58
[Herma Werner w/
Joyce Gleit]

GLADSTONE, Maggie 58
  [Arthur M. Gladstone]
GLASCO, Gordon 58
GLAZE, Eleanor 58
GLEIT, Joyce w/ Herma WERNER 58
  (Eve Gladstone)
GLENN, Elizabeth 58
  [Martha Gregory]
GLENN, Victoria 58
GLICK, Ruth w/
  Eileen BUCKHOLTZ 58
  (Amanda Lee)
GLICK, Ruth w/ Eileen BUCKHOLTZ
  and Louise TITCHENOR 58
  (Alyssa Howard)
GLICK, Ruth w/
  Louise TITCHENOR 58
  (Alexis Hill Jordan)
GLUYAS, Constance 58
GODDEN, Rumer 59
GODWIN, Gail 59
GOLDENBAUM, Sally w/
  Adrienne STAFF 59
  (Natalie Stone)
GOLDREICH, Gloria 59
GOLDRICK, Emma 59
GOODMAN, Irene w/
  Alex KAMAROFF 59
  (Diana Morgan)
GOODWIN, Hope 59
GORDON, Barbara 59
GORDON, Deborah 59
  (Brooke Hastings)
GORDON, Lucy 59
  [Christine Sparks]
GORDON, Ruth 59
GORDON, Susan 59
GORDON, Victoria 59
GOUDGE, Eileen 59
GOWAR, Antonia 59
GOWER, Iris 59
GRADY, Liz 59
  [Pat Coughlin]
GRAHAM, Elizabeth 60
  [E. Schattner]
GRAHAM, Heather 60
  [Heather Graham Pozzessere]
GRAHAM, Leslie 60
GRAHAM, Marteen 60
GRAHAM, Olivia 60
GRANGE, Peter 60
  [Christopher Nicole]
GRANGER, Katherine 60
  [Mary Sederquest]

GRANT, Charles L. 60
  (Felicia Andrews)
  (Deborah Lewis)
GRANT, Jeanne 60
  [Alison Hart]
GRANT, Kathryn 60
  (Kathleen Maxwell)
GRANTLEY, Samantha 60
GRAVES, Tricia 60
GRAY, Alicia 61
GRAY, Alison 61
  {Alma Moser]
GRAY, Brenna 61
GRAY, Ginna 61
  [Virginia Gray]
GRAY, Vanessa 61
  [Jacqueline Aeby]
GRAY, Virginia 61
  (Ginna Gray)
GREEN, Billie 61
GREENBERG, Jan 61
  (Jill Gregory)
GREENFIELD, Irving A. 61
  (Riva Charles)
  (Alicia Grace)
  (Anita Grace)
  (Gail St. John)
GREENLEA, Denice 61
GREER, Francesca 61
  [Frankie-Lee Janas]
GREGG, Jess 61
GREGORY, Jill 61
  [Jan Greenberg]
GREGORY, Lisa 61
  [Candace Camp]
GREGORY, Martha 61
  (Elizabeth Glenn)
GREGORY, Mollie 61
  (Estelle Edwards)
GRICE, Julia 62
  [Julia Haughey]
GRIFFIN, Jocelyn 62
  [Laura Sparrow]
GRIMES, Frances Hurley 62
GROSECLOSE, Elgin 62
GROSS, Joel 62
GROSS, Susan Ellen 62
  (Sue Ellen Cole)
  (Susanna Collins)
  (Susan deLyonne)
GROVE, Joan 62
GRUNDMAN, Donna 62
GUNTRUM, Suzanne 62
  (Suzanne Simmons)
  (Suzanne Simms)

H

HAASE, John 62
HADARY, Simone 62
HAGAN, Patricia 62
HAGER, Jean 62
  (Leah Crane)
  (Marlaine Kyle)
  (Jeanne Stephens)
HAHN, Lynn Lowery 63
  (Lynn Lowery)
HAILEY, Elizabeth Forsythe 63
HAINES, Pamela 63
HALE, Antoinette 63
  [Antoinette Stockenberg]
HALE, Arlene 63
  [Mary Arlene Hale]
  (Tracy Adams)
  (Gail Everette)
  (Mary Tate)
  (Lynn Williams)
HALE, Dorthea 63
  [Dorothy Weller]
HALE, Katherine 63
HALEY, Jocelyn 63
  [Sandra Field]
HALL, Bennie C. 63
HALL, Carolyn 63
  (Carol Halston)
HALL, Gillian 63
HALL, Gimone 63
HALL, Olivia M. 63
  (Laurie Paige)
HALLDORSON, Phyllis 63
HALLIDAY, Ena 63
  [Sylvia Baumgarten]
HALLIN, Emily W. 64
  (Elaine Harper)
HALL OF FAME SERIES <HofFS> 64
HALSTON, Carole 64
  [Carolyn Hall]
HAMILTON, Daphne 64
HAMILTON, Julia 64
  [Julia Watson]
HAMILTON, Lucy 64
  [Julia A. Rhyne]
HAMILTON, Paula 64
HAMILTON, Priscilla 64
  [Roberta Gellis]

HAMILTON, Steve w/
  Melinda HOBAUGH 64
  (Linda Vail)
HAMLIN, Dallas 64
HAMMETT, Lafayette 64
HAMMILL, Grandin 64
HAMMOND, Mary Ann 64
  [Mary Ann Slojkowski]
HAMMOND, Rosemary 64
HAMPSON, Anne 65
HANCOCK, Lucy Agnes 65
HANNA, Evelyn 65
  [Michael Dyne w/
  Ethel Frank]
HANSON, Mary Catherine 65
HARDING, Christina 65
HARDWICK, Mollie 65
HARDY, Antoinette 65
HARDY, Laura 65
  [Sheila Holland]
HARPER, Elaine 65
  [Emily W. Hallin]
HARPER, Karen 65
  [Karen Harris]
HARPER, Madeline 65
  [Shannon Harper w/
  Madeline Porter]
HARPER, Olivia 66
  (Jolene Adams)
HARPER, Olivia w/ Ken HARPER 66
  (JoAnna Brandon)
HARPER, Shannon w/
  Madeline PORTER 66
  (Melinda Harper)
  (Anna James)
HARRELL, Janice 66
HARRINGTON, Sharron w/ Rick
  HARRINGTON 66
  (Rianna Craig)
HARRIS, Karen 66
  (Karen Harper)
HARRIS, Melinda 66
  [Melinda Snodgrass]
HARRIS, Norma 66
HARRIS, Sandra 66
  (Abigail Wilson)
  (Brittany Young)
HARRISON, Barbara 66
HARRISON, Claire 66
  (Laura Eden)
  (Ellen Harris)
  (Claire St. John)
HARROD-EAGLES, Cynthia 66
HARROWE, Fiona 66
  [Florence Hurd]

HOBAUGH, Melinda w/
  Steve HAMILTON   71
  (Linda Vail)
HODGE, Jane Aiken   71
HODGSON, Eleanor   71
  (Eleanor Howard)
  (Norah Parker)
HOHL, Joan   71
  (Amii Lorin)
  (Paula Roberts)
HOLDEN, Joanne   71
HOLDER, Nancy   71
  [Nancy L. Jones Holder]
  (Laurel Chandler)
  (Wendi Davis)
  (Nancy L. Jones)
HOLDING, Vera w/ John CHRISTY   71
HOLLAND, Cecelia   71
HOLLAND, Isabelle   71
HOLLAND, Sarah   71
HOLLAND, Sheila   71
  (Sheila Coates)
  (Laura Hardy)
  (Charlotte Lamb)
  (Sheila Lancaster)
  (Victoria Woolf)
HOLLIDAY, Dolores   72
HOLLINS, Mary   72
HOLMES, Deborah Aydt   72
HOLMES, Mary Mayer   72
HOLT, Victoria   72
  [Eleanor Burford Hibbert]
HOLT, Will   72
HOOPER, Kay   72
  (Kay Robbins)
HOOVER, Mab Graff   72
HOPLEY, George   72
  [Cornell Woolrich]
HORSMAN, Jennifer   72
HORTON, Marian   72
  (Marian Lorraine)
HORTON, Naomi   72
  [Susan Horton]
HOTCHKISS, Bill   72
HOTCHKISS, Bill w/
  Judith SHEARS   72
HOWARD, Alyssa   72
  [Eileen Buckholtz w/ Ruth
    Glick & Louise Titchenor]
HOWARD, Eleanor   73
  [Eleanor Hodgson]
HOWARD, Guy   73
HOWARD, Jessica   73
  [Monroe Schere]

HOWARD, Joy   73
HOWARD, Julia   73
  [Patricia K. Adams-Manson]
HOWARD, Linda   73
  [Linda Howington]
HOWARD, Linden   73
  [Audrie Manley-Tucker]
HOWARD, Lyn   73
  (Lynde Howard)
  (Lynsey Stevens)
HOWARD, Lynde   73
  [Lyn Howard]
HOWARD, Mary   73
  [Mary Mussi]
HOWATCH, Susan   73
HOWE, Margaret   73
HOWE, Susanna   74
  (Bree Thomas)
HOWELL, Jessica   74
HOWINGTON, Linda   74
  [Linda Howard]
HOY, Elizabeth   74
  [Alice 'Nina' Conarain]
HUDSON, Anna   74
  [JoAnn Algermissen]
HUDSON, Meg   74
  [Margaret Hudson Koehler]
HUFF, Tom E.   74
  (Edwina Marlow)
  (Beatrice Parker)
  (Katherine St. Clair)
  (Jennifer Wilde)
HUFFORD, Susan   74
  (Samantha Hughes)
HUGHES, Cally   74
  [Lass Small]
HUGHES, Rose   74
HUGHES, Samantha   74
  [Susan Hufford]
HUNT, Greg   75
HUNT, Jena   75
  [Helen Manak Conrad]
HUNTER, Damion   75
HUNTER, Elizabeth   75
  (Isobel Chace)
  (Elizabeth deGuise)
HUNTER, Margaret   75
  [Ronald Singer]
HUNTER, Terry   75
HURD, Florence   75
  (Fiona Harrowe)
  (Flora Hiller)
HURLEY, Ann   75

JUSKEVICE, Mildred Havill 80
   (Antonio Blake)
   (Sarah James)
JUSTIN, Jennifer 80
   (Jennifer West)

K

KACHELMEIER, Glenda 80
KAHN, Mary 80
   (Miranda Cameron)
   (Amanda Troy)
KAIL, Robert 81
KAKU, Louzana 81
   (Christina Dair)
KALMAN, Yvonne 81
KAMAROFF, Alex w/
  Irene GORDON 81
   (Diana Morgan)
KANIN, Garson 81
KAPLAN, Barry Jay 81
KATZ, Carol 81
   (Penny Allison)
   (Rosalynn Carroll)
KAUFMAN, Pamela 81
KAVANAUGH, Cynthia 81
   [Dorothy Daniels]
KAVANAUGH, Ian 81
   [Morris Hershman]
KAY, Catherine 81
   [Catherine Dees w/
   Kay Croissant]
KAYE, Barbara 81
   [Barbara K. Walker]
KAYE, Joanne 81
KAYE, M. M. 81
KAZAN, Elia 81
KEAST, Karen 81
KEILER, Barbara 82
   (Ariel Berk)
   (Thea Frederick)
KELLEY, Leo P. 82
KELLS, Susannah 82
KENNEDY, Adam 82
KENNEDY, Jr. Cody 82
   [John Reese]
KENNEDY, Kim 82
KENNEDY, Lena 82
KENNEDY, M. L. 82
KENNEDY, Marilyn 82
KENNEDY, Nancy M. 82
   [Nancy MacDougall Kennedy]

KENT, Amanda 82
   [Betty L. Henrichs]
KENT, Deborah 82
KENT, Jean Salter 82
   (Kathryn Kent)
KENT, Katherine 82
   [Joan Dial]
KENT, Kathryn 82
   [Jean Salter Kent]
KENT, Pamela 83
   [Susan Barrie]
KENYON, Bruce 83
   (Daisy Vivian)
KENYON, F. W. 83
KENYON, Joanna 83
   [Janet K. Clarke]
KER, Madeleine 83
KETTER, Pam 83
   [Pamela Browning]
KIDD, Elizabeth 83
   [Linda Triegel]
KIDD, Flora 83
KIEHL, Claire w/
  Susan PHILLIPS 83
   (Justine Cole)
KIHLSTROM, April 83
KILMER, Wendella 83
   (Karen Van der Zee)
KIMBRO, John M. 83
   (Kym Allyson)
   (Ann Ashton)
   (Charlotte Bramwell)
   (Jean Kimbro)
   (Katheryn Kimbrough)
KIMBROUGH, Coleen 83
   [Kay Porterfield]
KINCAID, Katherine 84
   [Pamela Daoust]
KINCAID, Nell 84
   [Janet K. Clarke]
KING, Christine 84
   (Thea Lovan)
KING, Dianne 84
KING, Josie 84
KING, Peggy E. 84
   (see Velma S. Daniels)
KINGSBURY, Dawn 84
KINGSTON, Meredith 84
   [Meredith Babeaux Brucker]
KIRBY, Susan E. 84
KITT, Sandra 84
   (Bree Saunders)
KLEVIN, Jill Ross 84
KNIGHT, Alanna 84
   (Margaret Hope)

KNIGHT, Alicia 84
  (Lucretia Wright)
KNIGHT, Doris 84
KNIGHT, Sali 85
  [Tina Serafini]
KNOWLES, Mabel Winnifred 85
  (Wynne May)
KOEHLER, Margaret Hudson 85
  (Maggie Charles)
  (Meg Hudson)
KOHAKE, Rosanne 85
KOLACZYK, Anne w/ Ed KOLACZYK 85
  (Adrienne Edwards)
  (Andrea Edwards)
KOVACS, Katherine 85
  (Katherine Coffaro)
KRAFT-MACOY, Lia 85
KRAHN, Betina M. 85
KRAMER, Kathryn 85
KRASNER, William 85
KRAUZER, Steve 85
KRENTZ, Jayne Ann 85
  (Jayne Bentley)
  (Jayne Castle)
  (Stephanie James)
  (Jayne Taylor)
KUCZKIR, Mary w/
  Roberta ANDERSON 85
  (Fern Michaels)
KUHLIN, Suzanne J. 85
  (Jennifer Mikels)
KWOCK, Laureen 85
  (Clarice Peters)
KYLE, Susan Spaeth 85
  (Diana Blayne)
  (Diana Palmer)

L

LACEY, Anne 85
  [Martha Corson]
LACHLAN, Edythe 85
  (Julia Alcott)
  (Bettina Montgomery)
  (Nicole Norman)
  (Maureen Norris)
  (Rinalda Roberts)
LACY, Tira 86
  [Rita Clay Estrada]
LADAME, Cathryn 86
  [Cathryn J. L. Baldwin]
LADD, Linda (King) 86
  (Jillian Roth)

LADD, Veronica 86
LA FARGE, Oliver 86
LAING, Alexander 86
LAKE, Patricia 86
LAKER, Rosalind 86
  [Barbara Ovstedal]
LAMB, Charlotte 86
  [Sheila Holland]
LAMB, Lady Caroline 86
  [Anne Fremantle]
LAMBERT, Bill 86
  (Willa Lambert)
LAMBERT, Derek 86
LAMBERT, Willa 86
  [Bill Lambert]
LANCASTER, Bruce 87
LANCASTER, Lydia 87
  [Eloise Meaker]
LANE, Allison 87
LANE, Elizabeth 87
LANE, Kami 87
  [Elaine C. Smith]
LANE, Marina 87
LANE, Megan 87
  [Brenda Himrod]
LANE, Roumelia 87
LANG, Eve 87
  [Ruth Ryan Langan]
LANG, Heather 87
  [Darlene Baker]
LANG, Miriam 87
  (Margot Leslie)
LANGAN, Ruth 87
  [Ruth Ryan Langan]
  (Eve Lang)
LANG-CARLIN, Alexandra 88
LANGFORD, Sandra 88
  (Olivia Sinclair)
LANGTRY, Ellen 88
  [Nancy Elliott]
LANIGAN, Catherine 88
  (Joan Wilder)
LANTZ, Francess Lin 88
LARKIN, Rochelle 88
LARSON, Shirley 88
  (Shirley Hart)
LARSON, Susan w/
  Barbara MICHELS 88
  (Suzanne Michelle)
LARUE, Brandy 88
LATHAM, Robin 88
  (Robin Lynn)
LA TOURETTE, Jacqueline 88

LATOW, Roberta 88
LAVARRE, Deborah 88
LAVENDER, William 88
LAWRENCE, Amy 88
  [Joyce Schenk]
LAWRENCE, Fred 88
  [Fred Feldman]
LAWRENCE, Lynn 89
  [Sherry Garland]
LAYMON, Richard 89
LAYTON, Edith 89
LAZARUS, Marguerite 89
  (Anna Gilbert)
LEA, Constance 89
LEATHER AND LACE <L&L> 89
LECOMPTE, Jane 89
  (Jane Ashford)
LEDERER, Paul Joseph 89
LEE, Amanda 89
  [Eileen Buckholtz w/
  Ruth Glick]
LEE, C. Y. 89
LEE, Doris 89
LEE, Elsie 89
  (Elsie Cromwell)
  (Jane Gordon)
LEE, Lucy 90
  [Charlene Talbot]
LEE, Maureen 90
LEE, Tammie 90
  [Tom Townsend]
LE GRAND, Sybil 90
  [Kaa Byington]
LEHR, Helene 90
LEIGH, Susannah 90
LEMERY, Alysse 90
  [Alysse S. Rasmussen]
L'ENGLE, Madeleine 90
  [Madeleine L'engle Franklin]
LENZ, Jeanne R. 90
LEONARD, Phyllis 90
  [Isabel Ortega]
LEROE, Ellen 90
LESLIE, Alice 90
LESLIE, Margot 90
  [Miriam Lang]
LESTER, Teri 91
LE VARRE, Deborah 91
  [Deborah Varlinsky]
LEVINSON, Len 91
LEWENSOHN, Leone 91
  (Frances Davies)
LEWI, Charlotte Armstrong 91
  (Charlotte Armstrong)

LEWIS, Canella 91
  [Jonathan Richards]
LEWIS, Carrie 91
LEWIS, Deborah 91
  [Charles L. Grant]
LEWTY, Marjorie 91
LEY, Alice Chetwynd 91
LIDE, Mary 91
LIND, Pamela 91
LINDSAY, Rachel 91
  (Roberta Leigh)
LINDSEY, Joanna 91
LINZ, Cathie 91
  [Cathie Baumgardner]
LISTON, Robert 92
  (ELizabeth Bright)
LITTLE, Paul 92
  (Marie de Jourlet)
  (Leigh Franklin James)
  (Paula Minton)
LIVINGSTON, Georgette 92
  (Diane Crawford)
LLEWELLYN, Richard 92
LLOYD, Adrien 92
LLOYD, Frances 92
LLOYD, Marta 92
  [Marta Buckholder]
LOCKWOOD, Ethel 92
LOFTS, Norah 92
  (Juliet Astley)
  (Peter Curtis)
LOGAN, Daisy 92
  [Sara Orwig]
LOGAN, Jessica 92
  [Lawrence Foster w/
  Pauline Foster]
LOGAN, Mark 92
  [Christopher Nicole]
LONDON, Hilary 92
  [John Sawyer w/
  Nancy Sawyer]
LONDON, Laura 93
  [Sharon Curtis w/
  Thomas Dale Curtis]
LONG, Gabrielle Margaret 93
  (Marjorie Bowen)
  (Margaret Campbell)
  (Joseph Shearing)
LONG, William Stuart 93
  [Vivian Stuart Mann]
LONGSTREET, Stephen 93
LOOK, Jane H. 93
  (Lee Damon)
LORD, Bette Bao 93

LORD, Graham   93
LORD, Vivian   93
    [Pat Wallace Strother]
LORIN, Amii   93
    [John M. Hohl]
LORING, Jenny   93
    [Marty Sans]
LORING, Lynn   93
LORRAINE, Marian   93
    [Marian L. Horton]
LORRIMER, Claire   93
    [Patricia Denise Robins]
LOTTMAN, Eileen   93
LOUIS, Jacqueline   94
    [Jacqueline Hacsi]
LOVAN, Thea   94
    [Christine King]
LOVELESS, Jane   94
LOWE, Susan L.   94
    (Andrea Davidson)
    (Elise Randolph)
LOWELL, Elizabeth   94
    [A. E. 'Ann' Maxwell]
LOWERY, Lynn   94
    [Lynn Lowery Hahn]
LUEDTKE, Julie   94
LUKE, Mary   94
LUPTON, Mary   94
LUTYENS, Mary   94
    (Esther Wyndham)
LYLE, Elizabeth   94
LYNCH, Frances   94
LYNDELL, Catherine   94
    [Margaret Ball]
LYNN, Karen   94
    [Lynn Taylor w/
     Karen Maxfield]
LYNN, Robin   95
    [Robin Latham]
LYONS, Maggie   95
LYONS, Mary   95
LYONS, Ruth   95

M

MacDONALD, Elizabeth   95
MACDONALD, Malcolm   95
MacDONALD, Megan   95
    [Serita Stevens]
MACE, Gertrude   95
MACK, Dorothy   95
    [Dorothy McKittrick]

MacKENZIE, Maura   95
MacKINNON, C. R.   95
MacLEAN, Jan   95
    [Sandra Field w/
     Anne MacLean]
MacLEOD, Jean S.   96
    (Catherine Airlie)
MacLEOD, Robert   96
MacNEILL, Anne   96
    [Maura Seger]
MACOMBER, Debbie   96
MacPHERSON, A. D. L.   96
    (Sara Seale)
MacWILLIAMS, Margaret   96
MADISON, Winifred   96
MAGER, Marcia   96
MAGNER, Laura   96
    (Laura Paige)
MAJOR, Ann   96
    [Margaret Major Cleaves]
MAKING OF AMERICA SERIES <MOAS>   96
MAKRIS, Kathryn   96
MALCOLM, Aleen   96
MALEK, Doreen Owens   96
    (Faye Morgan)
MALLORY, Kathryn   97
MALONE, Bev   97
MALONE, Lucy   97
MALONE, Vicki   97
MANESS, Faye w/
    Charlotte WOODARD   97
    (April Blair)
MANLEY, Edna Maye   97
MANLEY-TUCKER, Audrie   97
    (Linden Howard)
MANNING, Marilyn   97
MANSFIELD, Elizabeth   97
    [Paula Schwartz]
MANSFIELD, Helene   97
MARAGAKIS, Helen   97
    (Eleni Carr)
    (Helen Carter)
MARAVEL, Gailanne   97
MARCH, Josie   97
MARCHANT, Catherine   97
    [Catherine Cookson]
MARDON, Deirdre   97
    [A. Mardon]
MARINO, Susan   98
    [Julie M. Ellis]
MARITANO, Adela   98
    (Jane Converse)
    (Adela Gale)
    (Kay Martin)

MARK, Polly 98
MARKHAM, Patricia 98
MARLISS, Deanna 98
  (Diana Mars)
  (Diana Moore)
MARLOWE, Stephen 98
MARS, Diana 98
  [Deanna Marliss]
MARSH, Ellen Tanner 98
  [Renate Johnson]
MARSH, Lillian 98
  [Ruby Frankel]
MARSH, Rebecca 98
  [William Arthur Neubauer]
MARSHALL, Andrea 99
MARTEL, Aimee 99
  [Aimee Thurlo]
MARTEN, Jacqueline 99
  [Jacqueline Stern Marten]
MARTIN, Ethel Bowyer 99
MARTIN, Ione 99
MARTIN, Judy Wells 99
  (Jeanette Ernest)
  (Andra Erskine)
MARTIN, Liz 99
MARTIN, Malachi 99
MARTIN, Marian 99
MARTIN, Nancy 99
  [Elissa Curry]
MARTIN, Pam 99
MARTIN, Prudence 99
  [Prudence Bingham Lichte]
MARTIN, Wendy 99
  [Teri Martini]
MARTINI, Teri 99
  (Alison King)
  (Wendy Martin)
  (Therese Martini)
MARTINI, Therese 100
  [Teri Martini]
  (Alison King)
MASCOTT, Holly Anne 100
MASCOTT, Trina 100
MASSEY, Jessica 100
  [Alison Hart]
MASTIN, Venita 100
MATHER, Anne 100
  [Mildred Grieveson]
MATHEWS, Jan 100
  [Jan Milella]
MATHEWS, Michelle 100
MATTHEWS, Laura 100
  [Elizabeth Walker Rotter]

MATTHEWS, Patricia 100
  (Patty Briscoe)
  (Laura Wiley)
MAXAM, Mia 100
MAXFIELD, Karen w/
  Lynn TAYLOR 100
  (Karen Lynn)
MAXWELL, A. E. 100
  [Ann Maxwell]
  (Elizabeth Lowell)
MAXWELL, Kathleen 101
  [Kathryn Grant]
MAXWELL, Patricia 101
  (Jennifer Blake)
  (Maxine Patrick)
  (Patricia Ponder)
MAY, Wynne 101
  [Mabel Winnifred Knowles]
MAYO, Margaret 101

Mc

McALLISTER, Amanda 101
McBAIN, Laurie 101
McBRIDE, Harper 101
  [Judith Weaver]
McCAFFREE, Sharon 101
  [Jean Wisener w/
   J. J. Nether]
McCALL, Virginia Nielsen 101
  (Virginia Nielsen)
McCARTHY, Gary 101
McCARTNEY, Brenna 101
McCARTY, Betsy 101
MCCLURE, Anna 102
  [Roy Sorrels]
McCONNELL, Lisa 102
  [Lorena McCourtney]
McCOURTNEY, Lorena 102
  (Jocelyn Day)
  (Lisa McConnell)
  (Rena McKay)
McCOY, Cathlyn 102
  [Fran Baker]
McCUE, Noelle Berry 102
  (Nicole Monet)
McDONALD, Kay L. 102
McDONNEL, Marjorie 102
  (Margie Michaels)
McELFRESH, Adeline 102
  (Jennifer Blair)
  (Jane Scott)
  (Elizabeth Wesley)

N

O

P

SCHWARTZ, Paula   134
  (Elizabeth Mansfield)
  (Libby Mansfield)
SCHWARTZ, Shiela   134
SCOFIELD, Carin   134
SCOTT, Alexandra   134
SCOTT, Alison   134
SCOTT, Amanda   134
  [Lynne Scott-Drennan]
SCOTT, Celia   134
SCOTT, Elizabeth A.   134
SCOTT, Joanna   134
SCOTT, Melissa   134
SCOTT, Michael William   134
SCOTT, Rachel   134
  (Ana Lisa de Leon)
  (Marisa de Zavala)
SCOTT, Samantha   135
  [Nancy Herman]
SCOTT-DRENNAN, Lynne   135
  (Amanda Scott)
SCRIMGEOUR, G. J.   135
SEALE, Sara   135
  [A. D. L. MacPhearson]
SEDERQUIST, Mary   135
  (Katherine Granger)
  (Katherine Ransom)
SEGAL, Harriet   135
SEGER, Maura   135
  (Jenny Bates)
  (Maeve Fitzgerald)
  (Sara Jennings)
  (Anne MacNeill)
  (Laurel Winslow)
SEIDEL, Kathleen Gilles   135
SEIDICK, Kathie   135
  (Kasey Michaels)
SEIFERT, Elizabeth   135
  [Elizabeth Gasparotti]
SELDEN, Neil   135
SELLERS, Alexandra   136
SELLERS, Con   136
  [Connie Leslie Sellers, Jr.]
  (Lee Raintree)
SELLERS, Lorraine   136
SERAFINI, Tina   136
  (Sali Knight)
SEYMOUR, Janette   136
SHAHEEN, Leigh   136
  (Valerie Zayne)
SHANDS, Sondra   136
SHARMAT, Marjorie   136
SHAW, Linda   136
SHAW, Susan   136

SHAYNE, Sandi   136
  [Sandra Canfield w/
   Penny Richards]
SHEARING, Joseph   136
  [Gabrielle Margaret Long]
SHEARS, Judith w/
  Bill HOTCHKISS   136
SHELBY, Graham   137
SHELL, Peggy   137
SHELLABARGER, Samuel   137
SHERIDAN, Jane   137
SHERRILL, Suzanne   137
  [Sherryl Ann Woods]
SHERWOOD, Valerie   137
  [Jeanne Hines]
SHEWMAKE, Georgia M.   137
SHIELDS, Dinah   137
  (Jane Clare)
SHIMER, Ruth   137
SHIPLETT, June Lund   137
SHOCK, Marianne   137
SHORE, Francine   137
  [Maureen Crane Wartski]
SHUB, Joyce   137
SHURA, Mary Francis   137
  [Mary Francis Craig]
SILVERLOCK, Anne   137
SIMMONS, Suzanne   138
  [Suzanne Guntrum]
SIMMS, Suzanne   138
  [Suzanne Guntrum]
SIMPSON, Judith w/
  June HAYDON   138
  (Rosalind Foxx)
  (Sara Logan)
SINCLAIR, Cynthia   138
  [Maureen Crane Wartski]
SINCLAIR, Tracy   138
SINCLAIRE, Francesca   138
SINGER, June Flaum   138
SINGER, Ronald   138
  (Margaret Hunter)
  (Delphine Marlowe)
SINGER, Sally M.   138
  (Amelia Jamison)
SIZER, Mona   138
  (Deana James)
SKELTON, C L.   138
SKILLERN, Christine   138
SKINNER, June   138
  (Rohan O'Grady)
SLAUGHTER, Frank G.   138
  (C. V. Terry)
SLAUGHTER, Pamela   138

MJK ENTERPRISES
P. O. Box 5571
San Antonio, TX 78201

Send me a copy of:
  The Romantic Spirit
    (8.95 plus 2.50 for postage/handling _____

  1983-1984 Update Only:
    (5.95 plus 1.50 for postage/handling _____

  A set (both books listed above)
    (14.90 plus 2.50 for postage/handling _____

  Texas residents please send
  appropriate sales tax.   _____

                           TOTAL   _____
PAYMENT:
Check or money order acceptable.

M/C OR VISA # [| | | | | | | | | | | | | | | | |]

              Expiration Date (Mo-Yr) [| |]

    M/C Interbank # [| |]

NAME _____
Address_____
City/State/Zip_____

        ALLOW 4 to 6 WEEKS FOR DELIVERY

NOTES

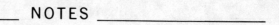

NOTES